BILINGUAL EDUCATION AND BILINGUALISM 3
Series Editor: Colin Baker

Teaching Science to Language Minority Students: Theory and Practice

Judith W. Rosenthal

MULTILINGUAL MATTERS LTD
Clevedon • Philadelphia • Adelaide

This book is dedicated to my daughter Beth

Library of Congress Cataloging in Publication Data

Rosenthal, Judith W., 1945-
Teaching Science to Language Minority Students: Theory and Practice/Judith W.
Rosenthal.
Bilingual Education and Bilingualism: 3
Includes bibliographical references and index.
1. Science–Study and teaching (Higher)–United States. 2. English language–Study and
teaching (Higher)–Foreign speakers. 3. Education, Bilingual–United States. 4. Multicul-
tural education–United States. I. Title. II. Series.
Q183.3.A1R67   1995
507.1'1–dc20   95-6554

British Library Cataloguing in Publication Data

A CIP catalogue record for this book is available from the British Library.

ISBN 1-85359-273-0 (hbk)
ISBN 1-85359-272-2 (pbk)

Multilingual Matters Ltd

UK: Frankfurt Lodge, Clevedon Hall, Victoria Road, Clevedon, Avon BS21 7SJ.
USA: 1900 Frost Road, Suite 101, Bristol, PA 19007, USA.
Australia: P.O. Box 6025, 83 Gilles Street, Adelaide, SA 5000, Australia.

Typeset by Action Typesetting, Gloucester.
Printed and bound in Great Britain by WBC Book Manufacturers Ltd.

Contents

Acknowledgements vii
Glossary ix

Prologue 1

1   Defining the Issues 11

2   Second Language Acquisition Theory and its Application
    to Undergraduate Science Teaching 38

3   The Many Cultures of the Science Classroom 64

4   Learning Styles, Science Instruction, and Ethnicity 80

5   How Instructors Can Help Limited English Proficient Students
    in Traditional Science Courses 92

6   Issues Related to Rhetoric, Writing and Reading 104

7   Case Studies I: Providing Academic Support to Science Students
    Who are Still Learning English 120

8   The Theoretical Basis for Linguistically Modified Science
    Instruction 140

9   Case Studies II: Linguistically Modified Ways of Teaching
    Science to Undergraduates of Limited English Proficiency 150

Epilogue 175

Appendix 180

References 181

Index 193

Acknowledgements

I would not have been able to write this book without the contributions and input of many, many individuals. Therefore, I would like to thank:

- All those faculty members, support staff, and administrators at colleges and universities across the United States who made major contributions to this book. They answered my questionnaires, responded to my phone calls and faxes, graciously giving of their time and energy. Their names are cited throughout the text, in the boxes, and in the case studies.

- The following Kean College personnel: The faculty members who reviewed and constructively critiqued various sections of the book, including Professors Jose Adames, Isali Alsina, Nancy Brilliant, Jessie Reppy, Betsy Rodriguez-Bachiller, and Ana Maria Schuhmann; Dolores Oberlies and Maxine Schlesinger of the Kean College Bookstore, who were particularly helpful in checking bibliographic information, and also Mary Palmiter of the Kean College Library who processed and filled my numerous inter-library loan requests.

- The many individuals who gave me direct 'leads' about case studies, specific references, and who provided data which proved to be especially useful in writing this book. They include Carlos Acevedo, Norman Brandt, Donna Brinton, Lawrence Burton, Effie P. Cochran, Jodi Crandall, Sally Cummings, Yvonne Freeman, W. Vance Grant, Carlos Gutierrez, Susan Hill, Sam Hirsch, Elizabeth Kean, David LaValle, Judith Le Blanc Flores, Bernadette Lyles, Jose Mestre, Terry O'Donnell, Stephen Ritter, Migdalia Romero, Julia Rosen Prais, Ramon Santiago, Javier Totti, and F. Kim Wilcox. There are many others with whom I spoke or corresponded whose ideas helped me focus on and define the themes I most wanted to cover in the book. Since there are too many names to list here, I would like to extend my sincere thanks for the information and input each and every one of you supplied.

- My friends Vic Virkar and Marlene Rosen who read and critiqued a part of my very first draft.

- All those individuals who helped me place notices soliciting information for my book in the following newsletters: *HACU REPORT*, *TESOL Matters*, *ESL in Higher Education Newsletter*, *NABE NEWS*, and the *AAHE Bulletin*. This includes Elizabeth Delgado, Gail Hubbard, Helen

Kornblum, Ted Marchese, Ravi Sheorey, Mark Taylor, Ann Wintergerst, and Nancy Zelasko.

- Orlando Edreira, the Director of Kean College's Spanish-Speaking Program, and my first Spanish teacher. He not only inspired and encouraged me to learn Spanish, but also helped me develop an appreciation for the Hispanic culture.

- Kean College of New Jersey for providing me with released time for research in the 1994–95 academic year and Dean Betty Barber for her support during the 1993–94 academic year.

- Colin Baker, my editor, for his excellent advice and prompt responses to my inquiries.

- All those publishers and authors who kindly granted permission to reproduce copyright material. All sources are cited in the text itself, and I apologize for any that may have been inadvertently overlooked.

- Finally, I would like to thank all the limited English proficient students I have ever taught at Kean College of New Jersey; it is directly from them that I have developed much of my understanding of the challenges they face when studying in a second language.

Judith W. Rosenthal
November 1994

Glossary

Acculturation (*compare* **Assimilation**): Used here to refer to the process by which minority group members acquire the language and culture of the dominant society while retaining their native language and culture.

Adjunct model (*compare* **Sheltered instruction**): Formal pairing of a content-area and an ESL course. The content-area course is taught in English, and both native and non-native speakers of English may enroll in it. However, the non-native speakers also must attend the paired or adjunct course in which a variety of ESL techniques are used to help students not only to learn the subject matter of the content-area course but also to improve their proficiency in English.

Affective filter: As postulated by Krashen, those affective variables such as emotions, motivation, and anxiety which can promote or inhibit language acquisition.

African American (**Black**): A racial category used in the United States Census; self-identification as a person of black African descent.

American: A term often used (and misused) to refer to individuals who reside in the United States; excludes Canadians and Central and South Americans.

American Indian (**Native American**): A racial category used in the United States Census; self-identification as a person who belongs to or is descended from members of one of the native American Indian tribes.

Asian: A racial category used in the United States Census; self-identification as a person of Asian descent such as Cambodian, Chinese, Filipino, Hmong, Japanese, Korean, Laotian, Thai, Vietnamese, Asian Indian, or other Asian.

Assimilation (*compare* **Acculturation**): Used here to refer to the process by which minority group members lose their native culture and language, replacing them with the language and culture of the dominant members of a society; this process may be voluntary or involuntary; the **Melting Pot Theory**.

Basic Interpersonal Communicative Skills (**BICS**): As defined by Cummins, everyday conversational ability that is context embedded.

BEA: *See* **Bilingual Education Act**.

BICS: *See* **Basic Interpersonal Communicative Skills**.

Bilingual: May refer to (1) a person who to varying degrees is proficient in two languages, or (2) a course or educational program that uses two languages when providing instruction, or (3) a country in which more than one language is spoken by its citizens.

Bilingual Education Act (BEA): Title VII of the Elementary and Secondary Education Act; first passed by the United States Congress in 1968 and reauthorized in 1974, 1978, 1984, and 1988; provides funding and guidelines for the education of limited English proficient school children.

Black: *See* **African American**.

Bridge: Often used to refer to a course or program which helps students develop the skills they need to succeed in a more academically challenging setting.

CALP: *See* **Cognitive Academic Language Proficiency**.

Caretaker Speech (Motherese): The simplified way of talking that parents and others use to insure that very young children can understand what is being said; it is both grammatically simple and based in the 'here and now'.

Cognitive Academic Language Proficiency (CALP): A term used by Cummins to refer to the kind of language competency needed to learn cognitively demanding academic subject matter where clues to meaning are often lacking.

College (*compare* **University**): In the United States, a post-secondary institution of higher education that may offer the Associate's, Bachelor's, and/or Master's degree.

Common underlying proficiency (CUP): According to Cummins, knowledge, concepts, and skills which transfer from L1 to L2 (*See* **Linguistic interdependence**).

Comprehensible input: According to Krashen, these are messages in a new language which a learner can for the most part understand.

Content-area: An umbrella term for a specific curriculum area such as biology or history.

Context embedded (*compare* **Context reduced**): Language for which there are physical and social clues as well as shared background and linguistic knowledge that help clarify the meaning of the words.

Context reduced (*compare* **Context embedded**): Abstract language which requires higher levels of content knowledge and language proficiency in order to be understood; language which is lacking in physical and social clues or shared background and linguistic knowledge.

Culture: A learned way of life; the values, beliefs, behavior, and language which are shared by a group of people.

Cummins, J.: Language researcher at the Ontario (Canada) Institute for Studies in Education who has advanced several hypotheses related to second language acquisition including the existence of two kinds of language proficiencies (BICS and CALP) and linguistic interdependence between L1 and L2 (Common underlying proficiency).

CUP: *See* **Common underlying proficiency**

Developmental errors (*compare* **Interference errors**): Errors that reflect the natural order of acquisition of a language; they are the same in children learning their first language and adults who are learning that same language as a second language.

English as a second language (**ESL**): May refer to (1) courses or programs of English instruction offered in English speaking nations for speakers of other languages, or (2) to students who are non-native speakers of English who are enrolled in (or who recently have completed) ESL studies.

English-for-Academic-Purposes (**EAP**): *See* **Learning English-for-Academic-Purposes**.

ESL: *See* **English as a second language**.

Foreign students: *See* **International Students**.

Foreigner talk: The way in which native speakers simplify their speech so that non-native speakers will be more likely to understand what is being said.

High risk courses (*see* **Supplemental instruction**): Mainstream, content-area courses in which many students fail or receive low grades or from which they withdraw.

Hispanic (**Latino**): A category used in the United States Census; self-identification as a person of Mexican, Cuban, Puerto Rican, Dominican, Spanish, or Central or South American descent regardless of skin color; used interchangeably with Latino.

Interference errors (*compare* **Developmental errors**): Errors which occur when L1 structures or pronunciation influence L2 production.

International (**Foreign**) **students:** Used to refer to students who are non-US citizens with temporary visas who are studying in the United States.

Krashen, S.: Language researcher at the University of Southern California (Los Angeles) who has advanced several hypotheses related to second language acquisition including the distinction between language learning and language acquisition; the Monitor Hypothesis; the role of comprehensible input; the Affective Filter, and the Natural Order Hypothesis.

L1: An individual's native language.

L2: An individual's second language.

Language acquisition (*compare* **Language learning**): The unconscious development of language proficiency which does not involve schooling, classes, homework, textbooks, memorization, lessons, or drills; by means of acquisition, children become fluent in their first language and according to Krashen, only by acquisition can individuals become fluent in a second language.

Language learning (*compare* **Language acquisition**): The conscious study of a language, generally involving a teacher, textbook, a series of lessons, homework, memorization, and drills; according to Krashen, does not lead to second language fluency.

Language minority student (Linguistic minority student): Generally used to refer to students who are members of ethnic minority groups and whose native language is not the dominant language of the country; in the United States, this term most often is used to describe native speakers of Spanish, Portuguese, Haitian Creole, and Asian or Native American languages.

Latino: *See* **Hispanic**.

LEAP: *See* **Learning English-for-Academic-Purposes**.

Learning English-for-Academic-Purposes (LEAP): The study of reading, writing, and oral communication by non-native speakers to develop the oral and written literacy skills in English needed to succeed in academically challenging content-area courses.

Learning style(s): The characteristic way(s) in which an individual acquires new knowledge and skills.

LEP: *See* **Limited English Proficient**.

Limited English proficient (LEP): Used to refer to individuals whose native language is not English and who have difficulty with speaking, reading, writing, and/or understanding English.

Linguistic interdependence (*See* **Common underlying proficiency**): According to Cummins, literacy and cognitive skills transfer from one language to another so that much of what an individual already knows in his or her first language does not have to be relearned when acquiring a second language.

Linguistic minority student: *See* **Language minority student**.

Mainstream: Used to refer to (1) the dominant culture of a society and to (2) content-area courses taught in English in the United States.

Mainstreaming: When students are moved out of a program of English as a second language instruction and into content-area courses in which English is the language of instruction.

Melting Pot Theory: *See* **Assimilation**.

Monitor Hypothesis: According to Krashen, the ability of some individuals to self-correct second language usage if they have sufficient time, focus on form, and have knowledge of the rules of the language.

Motherese: *See* **Caretaker speech**.

Native American: *See* **American Indian**.

Natural Order Hypothesis: According to Krashen, people generally acquire the grammar of a given language in a predictable sequence regardless of their age or native language.

Nonverbal communication: Information that is communicated by the use of time, gestures, touch, body movements, interpersonal space, eye contact, and pitch, tone, and voice intonation.

Output: Verbal utterances and written forms of language.

Pacific Islander: A racial category used in the United States Census; self-identification as a person of Hawaiian, Samoan, Guamanian, or other Pacific Islander descent.

Productive skills (*compare* **Receptive skills**): The ability to speak or write a language.

Receptive skills (*compare* **Productive skills**): The ability to understand written and spoken language.

Sheltered instruction (*compare* **Adjunct model**): A content-area course taught in English by a content specialist to a class composed entirely of intermediate and/or advanced ESL students.

SI: *See* **Supplemental Instruction**.

Supplemental instruction (SI): (*see* **High risk courses**) An academic support program for students enrolled in high risk courses; involves regularly scheduled tutorial sessions to help students develop the skills they need to learn the course material and to prepare for exams.

Subject-area: *See* **Content-area**.

Target language: The language the learner is trying to master.

Test of English as a Foreign Languages (TOEFL): A standardized test prepared and administered by the College Entrance Examination Board; in general, it must be taken by students who are non-US citizens, not permanent residents of the US, nor native speakers of English as part of their entrance requirements to colleges and universities in the United States.

TOEFL: *See* **Test of English as a Foreign Language**

Underprepared students: Students who are admitted to college or the university who must take and pass remedial courses to bring their reading, writing, mathematics or study skills up to the levels required by the institution.

University (*compare* **College**): A post-secondary institution of higher education in the United States that in general grants the Bachelor's degree as well Master's and/or the Doctorate.

White: A racial category in the United States Census; self-identification as a person generally of European or Middle Eastern descent.

Prologue

In 1974 I joined the Biology faculty of Kean College of New Jersey. My qualifications for this position were a Bachelor's degree in Human Biology, a Doctorate in Physiological Chemistry, and two years of post-doctoral research. Although my primary work activity would be undergraduate teaching, my only knowledge of instructional practices consisted of what I had experienced as a student and as a graduate teaching assistant. In other words, my formal education did not prepare me for the teaching career upon which I was going to embark.

I had attended an elite 'Ivy League' university so that my first few years at Kean—a public, state college—were quite challenging and full of surprises. As a a new faculty member in an academic environment unlike any I had previously experienced, my real education began.

The majority of Kean College's students were not from the upper and upper-middle classes. Their parents were not college graduates nor white-collar workers. Many students, in order to pay for their education and/or to support their families, held part-time or full-time jobs; besides attending college and working, some were married and had children. All of this was new to me, but at least, back then in the mid-seventies, my Kean College students and I had one thing in common: we could communicate easily with each other because almost all of us were native English speakers.

I do not remember when I began to notice the increasing number of limited English proficient (LEP) students enrolling at Kean. However, in 1980, when I began a four-year stint as a dean, I suddenly discovered that without the assistance of a Colombian, bilingual secretary, I would not have been able to talk to many of the students who came to my office in need of help. About the same time, the chairperson of the Foreign Language Department began offering a Spanish course for faculty and staff members. I signed up and started to go to class twice a week at lunch-time. As I recollect, there were 40 'students' at the beginning of the course and 20 at the end. The next year the number dropped to ten, then to four, and then to one—me.

Quite frankly, I have no unique aptitude for learning languages. I studied four years of French in high school and one year more in college. I remember doing well but disliking it. I certainly could never speak French nor understand a conversation held in French, but I could pass the tests and translate the literature. Nevertheless, at the age of 35, when most people would say

1

they are too old to learn another language, I began studying Spanish. It was still hard work, but I *experienced* Spanish differently. There was always the possibility that one day I could communicate directly with Spanish speaking students and Hispanic colleagues. I started watching television in Spanish and began to take my vacations in Spanish speaking countries.

After something like five years of Spanish classes, I had a mass of knowledge stored in my brain (rules of grammar, vocabulary, verb conjugations, etc.) but still could not speak the language. I could understand some of what was said to me, but responding in Spanish was very difficult. So, I planned a sabbatical leave and went to Mexico for two months, living with a Mexican family and attending a private language school five hours a day, five days a week. I studied and practiced Spanish seven days a week, every waking hour. My English/Spanish dictionary never left my hand. My efforts paid off. After two months, I could speak and communicate relatively effectively in Spanish. Then I headed home to one of the biggest undertakings in my life.

For more than 20 years, Kean College has had a Spanish Speaking Program. The Program was designed to attract Hispanic students to Kean from the neighboring community. By offering undergraduate, credit-bearing general education courses taught in Spanish, students could begin working toward their Bachelor's degree, retain their native language fluency, and develop their proficiency in English by concurrently enrolling in English as a second language (ESL) courses.

In the 1970s, many of the instructors who taught in the Spanish Speaking Program were adjuncts recruited from the surrounding Hispanic community by the Program's director. However, that has changed as the number of Hispanic professors at Kean has increased across the disciplines. Now, most of the content-area courses taught in Spanish are staffed by resident Hispanic faculty members as well as by a small cadre of resident native English speaking faculty members who are proficient in Spanish.

Over the years, the Spanish Speaking Program has grown to involve much more than content-area courses taught in Spanish. With a full-time staff of four, its services now include academic advisement, student counselling, and cultural activities.

As it happened, my first Spanish instructor was the founder and director of the Spanish Speaking Program. About a year after I began studying Spanish, he came to me and said I would soon be teaching the freshman biology course in Spanish as part of the program. I bluntly told him he was 'loco' (crazy), but in the long run, he was right. In the fall of 1986, and every fall and spring semester since, I have taught the Spanish-speaking section of *Principles of Biology* (Bio. 1000). Just like the sections which are taught in English, this is a four credit course—serving both majors and non-majors—which meets twice a week for lectures and once a week for lab. Prior to 1986, the 'Spanish' section of Bio. 1000 was taught by various adjuncts and only offered during the summer session.

Words can hardly describe the effort that went into teaching Biology in Spanish for the first few years. I had to find a text and films in Spanish; I learned to write the exams and handouts in Spanish and ended up translating the laboratory manual. But that was nothing compared to the physical and mental energy that went into teaching a group of 24 native Spanish speaking college students who represented many different Central and South American countries. The sweat would literally pour down my face in my initial efforts to answer their questions and to explain complex concepts in a language that I was and still am trying to master.

When I came to Kean in 1974, I had no idea that there existed college students in the United States who were not as fluent in English as myself. As an undergraduate in the mid-1960s, I knew only two 'international' students, one from Sweden and the other from Nigeria, and both spoke beautiful (though accented) English. I had never heard of bilingual education nor ESL and had never given one moment's thought to how difficult it must be to learn a new subject when the coursework is in one's second language.

Even today, as proficient as I have become in Spanish, I still feel anxiety just trying to imagine going to Spain or Mexico to study economics, history, math, literature, or music, with all the coursework, lectures, exams and reading materials in Spanish. Occasionally, I have that classic dream of having to take exams in courses for which I am not prepared; sometimes the dream manifests itself as a nightmare about having to teach physics in Farsi. However, for me these are only dreams; for the ESL students that we are teaching, this is reality.

Studying Spanish opened up a new world to me. I not only was learning a new language but also a new culture. I became aware of the struggles of our many Hispanic students and started to take notice of the growing number of Asian, Haitian, and other non-native English speaking students enrolling at Kean. I familiarized myself with our ESL program and with the academic support services that were available on campus for LEP students. I began reading the literature on second language (L2) acquisition and multicultural education, and started following the changing demographics of the United States. I was so interested in what I was doing that I once again became a graduate student, enrolling in a Master's program in bilingual/bicultural education.

All of this got me thinking about science instruction. If traditional, native English speaking undergraduates find science 'hard', what must the experience be like for the non-native speaker? Students taking introductory level science courses often note that even if they work and study diligently, they still receive lower grades than in other disciplines. The impersonal and competitive atmosphere of the science classroom, the focus on coverage, and the conceptual complexity and abstract nature of the subject matter are just some of the reasons cited by students as to why science is more difficult than other subjects. In the case of recent immigrant or refugee students, there are even more problems, such as learning the new subject through a new language.

Looking through the literature and reading about efforts to reform science education, I soon discovered that little attention was being paid to LEP undergraduates. Yet, nation-wide, there is enormous concern about diminishing numbers of undergraduate science majors, the nominal results of numerous programs to increase the participation of under-represented minorities and women in the sciences, and the public's general lack of science literacy. In response, the scientific community has become increasingly focused on reforming science education, and various commissions and task forces have produced some widely read reports and books about 'the problem' and possible solutions (AAAS, 1989, 1990; Carnegie Commission on Science, Technology, and Government, 1991; National Science Foundation, 1989; Project Kaleidoscope, 1991).

In reading these documents, I have been continuously amazed by two points. The first is that *how* introductory college science is taught is rarely critiqued. For example, the curriculum as well as the laboratory activities may be deemed in need of revision, or high schools criticized for not preparing students adequately, but what the individual professor does (or does not do) in the classroom in terms of presenting subject matter and interacting with students is rarely referred to. Second, the diverse nature and needs of today's students are mentioned only in passing. There are cultural, linguistic and learning style issues related to science education that are not addressed, and this omission is particularly troublesome considering that the most rapidly growing minority population in the United States are persons who are non-native speakers of English.

The 1990 Census documented that millions of Americans[1] speak a language other than English at home. For example, 13.8% of persons five years and older 'sometimes or always' speak a language other than English at home. In some states this figure is higher: New Mexico 35.5%, California 31.5%, Texas 25.4%, Hawaii 24.8%, New York 23.3%, Arizona 20.8%, New Jersey 19.5%, Florida 17.3%, Rhode Island 17.0%, Massachusetts and Connecticut 15.2%, and Illinois 14.2%. More than 6.3 million children do not speak English at home, which is a 38.4% increase from 1980 (Population Reference Bureau, 1992: 73). Many of these non-native English speaking individuals are recent immigrants and refugees and/or their children, and they are enrolling in large numbers in grades K-12 as well as college.

Clearly, lack of proficiency in English does not imply that individuals are uneducable or incapable of learning. It does mean that we urgently need to reconsider *how* we teach, not only in grades K-12 but also at the college level. Whether or not students have achieved native-like fluency in English should not be a barrier to learning any subject, including science.

Although my particular concern is that science remains accessible to all college students—including those who are still learning English—the obstacles faced by LEP students are not unique to any one discipline. As the number of non-native English speaking students increases at colleges and universities, innovative approaches will be needed to successfully educate this population whatever their majors. ESL programs and their faculty cannot do it all. Professors across the academic disciplines will need training to learn strategies to improve how they provide instruction to LEP students. ESL and content-area faculty will need to work together to implement *adjunct, sheltered,* and *bridge* kinds of courses. Instruction that uses the students' native language may become increasingly important in terms of attracting and retaining non-native English speaking undergraduates while they are still learning English.

Such alternative ways of teaching LEP students must extend into the introductory college science classroom. If they do not, science education reform will bypass many students, thereby closing the doors to scientific and technological careers that will be of increasing importance in the twenty-first century.

Although this book is aimed primarily at those faculty members who teach science to LEP undergraduates, there are many others who may find its content of interest, such as science faculty who teach and supervise 'foreign' graduate students, faculty and staff involved in training programs for the science 'professoriate of tomorrow', those associated with undergraduate academic support systems, the deans and chairpersons of schools of science, faculty involved in science teacher training programs, as well as secondary school science teachers whose classes include language minority students. Actually, all content-area faculty, regardless of discipline and level of instruction, who work with second language students will find relevant and useful information in this book.

How to Use This Book

You can read this book from start to finish or you can use it as a quick reference, picking and choosing among the chapters and information according to your needs. Even though the book was written with recent immigrants and refugees (and their children) in mind, the information it contains applies equally as well to many 'foreign/international' students who are studying in the United States on temporary visas and to many American Indian (Native American) students. All these categories include individuals for whom English is a second language. The recommendations aimed at improving science instruction for students of limited English proficiency will also help native English speaking students who find science to be a particularly difficult subject.

Chapter 1, 'Defining the issues', focuses on the changing demographics of the United States and the growing population of non-native English speaking students. How college students learn English in an ESL program is described as well as what such programs can reasonably be expected to achieve. A brief history of language use in the United States and of educational issues related to immigrants is presented, as well as the unique academic problems faced by today's immigrant students in our higher education system. The myths and misconceptions held by mainstream faculty about ESL students are addressed, and five reasons are given to argue the case for including LEP undergraduates in plans for science education reform.

Chapter 2, 'Second language acquisition theory and its application to undergraduate science teaching', provides an overview of what research tells us about the process of second language acquisition. Considerable emphasis is given to the work of Stephen Krashen (the distinction between language learning and acquisition; the importance of comprehensible input; the affective filter; errors and error correction) and Jim Cummins (the distinction between conversational and academic language proficiency; linguistic interdependence) for their extensive contributions to our present-day understanding of L2 acquisition. Other topics discussed in Chapter 2 include the age factor, the significance of speaking with an accent, the existence of a special 'gift' or 'aptitude' for second language learning/acquisition, and the difficulties encountered by ESL students taking mainstream, content-area courses. As each topic is presented so are its implications as applied to language minority students in mainstream science courses.

Chapter 3, 'The many cultures of the science classroom', examines the various facets of culture that interact in the science classroom, including what information is considered appropriate to teach, the perspective from which it is presented, and how that material is taught; the prior knowledge of science that students bring to the classroom and how it affects the acquisition of new information; the differing expectations held by teachers and students about the processes of teaching and learning; and, how culture influences oral, written and non-verbal forms of communication in the science classroom. While these 'culture-related' topics may seem incongruous in a book about science education, they are of growing importance with an increasingly multilingual and multicultural student population.

Chapter 4, 'Learning styles, science instruction and ethnicity' begins with a general explanation of what is meant by the term 'learning style'. This is followed by a description of several learning styles, including field independence (insensitive)/field dependence (sensitive); global (analytic)/simultaneous (sequential); competitive/cooperative; ability to tolerate ambiguity; need for structure; preferred perceptual modes (visual, auditory, kinesthetic, and tactile), and impulsivity/reflectivity. How each learning style influences student performance in the traditional science classroom is described. Various studies are presented that strongly suggest that learning style preferences are related to culture and ethnicity. What, if anything, this means in terms of undergraduate science instruction is carefully considered.

Lastly, the learning styles of successful science students are contrasted with those of many of today's students who either are not interested in the sciences and/or who choose to switch from science to non-science majors.

Chapter 5, ' How instructors can help limited English proficient students in traditional science courses', includes a list of questions that science faculty can answer in order to discover what techniques they are currently using which are helping students of limited English proficiency. These items deal with the lecture, textbooks, laboratory, written assignments, testing and assessment, interacting with students, and taking advantage of resources available on campus. The instructor who answers 'yes' to many of these questions is well on his or her way to providing appropriate science instruction for language minority students. On the other hand, the instructor who answers 'no' to many of these questions but wants to provide the support needed by many non-native English speaking students will find it possible to implement most of the recommendations without any special training. What is especially useful about the information provided in Chapter 5 is that instructors can select those modifications and strategies that best suit their particular style of teaching as well as the needs of their students.

Chapter 6 is entitled 'Issues related to rhetoric, writing and reading'. In it, several important classroom issues are addressed, keeping in mind those students who are learning science while still mastering the English language. The first deals with the written work of ESL students, which often does not meet teacher expectations. This is because non-native speakers may bring to their written English both the style and pattern of argumentation which are characteristic of their native language. Suggestions are made as to how instructors can address this issue. The second topic in Chapter 6 is writing to learn science. This is a very effective instructional device for both native and non-native speakers of English. Both the purpose and process of writing to learn science are described, and a variety of writing to learn science assignments are presented. The final subject discussed in this chapter is the textbook. While almost every science course has a required textbook, its usefulness to students is quite variable. Some of the issues that are considered here include textbook selection, readability, how students use their texts, and the effects of bilingualism on reading.

Chapter 7, 'Case studies I: providing academic support to science students who are still learning English', includes six case studies illustrating how individual faculty members as well as various types of college-wide programs are addressing the needs of limited English proficient students enrolled in science courses:

- A geology professor at Brooklyn College, The City University of New York (Brooklyn, NY) and a biology professor from National-Louis University (Chicago, IL) describe how they teach ethnically and linguistically diverse students.

- Information is provided about campus-wide efforts at Hostos Community College, The City University of New York (Bronx, NY) to improve instruction for its students, 80% of whom are Hispanic. Content-area courses are being linguistically and methodologically enhanced. Details are provided about the modifications in an environmental science course.
- At California State University, Los Angeles, 67% of the entering freshmen are non-native English speakers. A program in Learning English-for-Academic-Purposes (LEAP) provides faculty training, course enhancements, and the use of supplemental instruction to improve science instruction for language minority students. Two 'enhanced' Project LEAP science courses are described, *Humans and Their Biological Environment* and *Natural History of Animals*.
- At Our Lady of the Lake University (San Antonio, TX), 75% of the undergraduate population is Hispanic. Since numerous studies have shown that Hispanic students learn more in a cooperative (rather than competitive) environment, cooperative learning groups have been incorporated into math and science courses. An overview of how cooperative learning is used in science courses and how faculty members have been persuaded to shift their teaching style from lecturing to a more student-centered pedagogy are presented.
- At Glendale Community College (Glendale, CA) Supplemental Instruction (SI) is being used in science courses and across the curriculum. This college attracts an extraordinarily diverse student population, the largest group (29%) being Armenian immigrants. Three-quarters of Glendale's students are of limited English proficiency. SI provides out-of-class student-led workshops directly related to the content of high risk courses including biology, chemistry and physics. How the SI leaders are selected and trained, the activities carried out in the SI workshops, and the rate of student participation in and the effectiveness of SI are also discussed.

In each case study presented in Chapter 7 (and those in Chapter 9), the characteristics of the college and its ESL program, the demographics of its students, as well as a relatively detailed description of the academic support (individual or institutional) provided to non-native English speakers in science courses is described. The information in the various case studies was provided by faculty, staff and administrators from each of the contributing institutions. At the end of each case study, names and addresses of who to contact are cited should the reader want to obtain additional information.

Chapter 8, 'The theoretical basis for linguistically modified science instruction,' describes two very different linguistically based approaches currently being used to help students learn science while they are still learning English. On the one hand, there is a trend in ESL toward content-based L2 instruction. This involves linking together content-area (e.g. science) and English instruction in what are called the adjunct, sheltered, and sheltered-adjunct models. On the other hand, some colleges that enroll large numbers of Hispanic students offer introductory science courses taught partially or completely in Spanish. However, the students are concurrently registered in ESL. As their proficiency in English increases, the amount of coursework taken in Spanish decreases. The advantages and disadvantages of the various content-based ESL models as well as bilingual modes of instruction are also discussed here.

Chapter 9, 'Case studies II: Linguistically modified ways of teaching science to undergraduates of limited English proficiency', is a showcase of pioneering courses and programs that provide non-traditional science instruction for undergraduates who are still learning English. For each of these case studies, the same kind of information is presented here as in Chapter 7: the general characteristics of the college and its students, the nature of its ESL program, and how and why each course/program evolved. Relatively detailed descriptions of the course/program are provided as well as who to contact for additional information. Most of this material has never before been described in the literature, and readers may be quite surprised by the creative and unconventional ways of teaching science that are documented here.

The case studies of content-based ESL instruction include:

- sheltered science instruction, in which only ESL students can enroll in the course as represented by *General Biology* and *Introductory Chemistry* at the Community College of Philadelphia (Philadelphia, PA);
- the sheltered-adjunct model in which enrollment in the content-area course is restricted to ESL students, and there is an accompanying support course. Three case studies are provided: *Pre-Allied Health Anatomy and Physiology* at Union County College (Elizabeth, NJ), *Introduction to the Sciences* at Cañada College (Redwood City, CA), and *Human Environment*, at Eastern Washington University (Cheney, WA)
- the adjunct model in which a content-area course which enrolls both native and non-native speakers of English is paired with a supporting ESL course (in which only the non-native speakers of English are required to enroll); this is illustrated by *Biology: A Human Perspective* at Saint Michael's College (Colchester, VT).

The case studies involving science instruction using Spanish in the classroom include:

- *Human Biology, Environmental Science*, and *Introductory Chemistry* at Erie Community College (Buffalo, NY), and
- bilingual biology, chemistry, environmental science, and nutrition at Miami-Dade Community College (Miami, FL).

The final case study in Chapter 9—the University of Texas at El Paso (UTEP in El Paso, Texas)—combines features similar to those in some of the case studies already presented in Chapters 7 and 9. UTEP is unique in that it enrolls an exceptionally large number of native Spanish-speaking Mexican and Mexican-American students; many cross the border daily in pursuit of a higher education. Smoothing their transition is coursework offered in Spanish, ESL instruction, and an extensive academic support system including bilingual tutoring.

The case studies in Chapters 7 and 9 demonstrate that each college, depending on its particular mission, resources, faculty, and students will have to find its own best way to address the needs of non-native English speaking undergraduates in the sciences.

The Epilogue ties together the information presented in Chapters 1–9 and provides a summary of the recommendations made throughout this book.

Some chapters contain 'boxes' covering a variety of topics related to the main text but explained in more depth. Like the case studies, much of this information has been contributed by colleagues across the country who are far more expert in these areas than the author, and their names and addresses are provided.

One final note. This book is a beginning. It is designed to get science educators and reformers, faculty members, administrators, and support staff thinking about the changing demographics and what needs to be done to recruit and retain non-native English speaking students in the science 'pipeline'. Possibly, what is written here will influence institutions and faculty to take those first tentative steps toward implementing courses or programs to improve science instruction for students of limited English proficiency. Perhaps the content of this book may help open the eyes of some readers to the immensely difficult task faced by students of limited English proficiency who are learning new subject matter through a new and unfamiliar second language. Maybe this book will stimulate a national 'conversation' about science education and non-native English speaking undergraduates. At the least, a few science instructors who read this book may begin to take into consideration the linguistic needs of some of their students. If any or all of the above comes about, I will feel that the time, energy and effort that went into researching and writing this book will have been more than well spent.

Notes

A version of this prologue first appeared in Rosenthal (1994). Adapted by permission of the Office of Academic Affairs, City University of New York

1. The term 'American' is used here and throughout this book to refer to individuals who reside in the United States and to distinguish them from Canadians and Central and South Americans who also live in the Americas.

1 Defining the Issues

When the new semester begins, take a good look at your class roster. It is quite likely that you will note many names that you can barely say, let alone spell. Listed between Jennifer and Eric are Eleadis, Shephali, Yuberkis, Diores, Liju, Chitra, Bianney, Arismendy and Niurlys. Calling the roll may prove to be an embarrassing experience in mispronunciation. Unlike typically 'American' names, these are not even helpful in determining if students are male or female.

Not so long ago, such unfamiliar names usually indicated international students who were going to study for some time in the United States and then return to their homelands; today, the names are often those of refugees, immigrants, and their children. Indeed, the recent wave of immigration has produced such pronounced diversity—both cultural and linguistic—in the student population that it is affecting not only who we teach but *what* we teach and *how* we teach it (Stewart, 1991, 1993).

The purpose of this chapter is to provide both the rationale for this book as well as background information relevant to the chapters that follow. It begins with a brief history of language usage in what is now the mainland United States. This is a useful starting point since in the midst of recent controversy about making English the 'official' language of the United States, many people have forgotten that from its start, this country has been peopled by speakers of many languages. What this means is that schools in some way have always had to deal with non-native English speaking students, and much of the current debate about the best way to teach English and to educate immigrant students is nothing new.

What is different today is the influx of non-native English speaking students —not 'international' students but immigrants and refugees—into the higher education system. Data is provided in this chapter to document the growth of this population. These students in some ways are similar to but in many ways differ from 'international' students. However, something all these students have in common is the need to learn English, and to do so, many enroll in a program of ESL. Therefore, a typical college-level ESL program is described as well as what it can and cannot realistically accomplish.

Near the end of Chapter 1, the emphasis turns to science: the reasons why the scientific community needs to pay more attention to the special needs of undergraduates of limited English proficiency and how this ties into the science education reform movement.

Chapter 1 addresses a wide range of topics, highlighting the relevant issues in order to orient the reader to what follows in subsequent chapters.

A variety of terms are used throughout this book and there is a glossary on pages ix–xiv. Box 1.1 defines four of these terms in more detail and compares and contrasts them: limited English proficient (LEP), English as a Second Language (ESL), language minority and bilingual.

Box 1.1 Some Definitions: LEP, ESL, Language Minority, and Bilingual

Terms such as limited English proficient (LEP), LEP student, language (or linguistic) minority student, English as a second language (ESL), and ESL student appear frequently in the literature about literacy and language issues, second language acquisition and multicultural education. For those involved in research and teaching in these fields, the meanings of such terms are taken for granted and rarely defined. However, others unfamiliar with this jargon might wonder if there are 'official' or standard definitions and/or if the terms can be used interchangeably.

Only *'limited English proficiency'* and *'limited English proficient'* (LEP) have been 'officially defined' in Section 7003 of the Bilingual Education Act (BEA) of 1968:

> The terms limited English proficiency and limited English proficient when used with reference to individuals means:
>
> (A) individuals who were not born in the United States or whose native language is a language other than English;
> (B) individuals who come from environments where a language other than English is dominant; and
> (C) individuals who are American Indian and Alaska Natives and who come from environments where a language other than English has had a significant impact on their level of English language proficiency;
>
> and who, by reason thereof, have sufficient difficulty speaking, reading, writing, or understanding the English language to deny such individuals the opportunity to learn successfully in classrooms where the language of instruction is English or to participate fully in our society (United States Department of Education 1992, pages 9-10).

Although the BEA's definition was developed to help identify those school children who may encounter difficulties in the all-English classroom, the terms LEP and limited English proficiency are also applied to college students, both undergraduate and graduate, who fit the BEA's descriptions.

'Language minority student(s)' which is often used interchangeably with 'linguistic minority' or 'LEP' student(s) has been defined in a general sense as 'non-native English speaking students who lack full proficiency in English' (Scarcella, 1990: 181), and more specifically as 'Ethnic group members whose first language is other than English. Usually applied to speakers of Spanish, Asian languages, Native American languages, Portuguese, and Haitian Creole (Stein 1986: 207).' The latter definition is important because it emphasizes the fact that the term 'language minority' does not include native speakers of European languages such as German, Italian, Dutch or French.

Although the terms LEP and language minority are used extensively, many professionals are bothered by their intrinsically perjorative connotations. For example, LEP focuses on the lack of fluency in the English language and ignores the intelligence, previous level of education, the knowledge, skills, and proficiency that these students may already possess in their first or native language. 'Language minority' reinforces the ethnic and linguistic minority status of students. Nevertheless, as negative as the terms LEP and language minority may seem, no one to date has come up with more positive terms which have caught on. For example, PEP (potentially English proficient), SLL (Second Language Learners), and ELL (English Language Learners), have been tried out, but they have never come into common usage (Wink, 1992/1993).

An ESL (English as a Second Language) student is one enrolled in an ESL course or program, or a student who has recently completed ESL studies but is still in the process of developing proficiency in English. ESL students, by definition, are also of limited English proficiency, and many are language minority group members. 'ESL' also is used to refer to a course or program of instruction in reading, writing, speaking, and comprehension of English for students who are native speakers of other languages. Since an ESL classroom may include individuals who speak many different languages, English is always the language of ESL instruction.

Another term that is commonly used is 'bilingual'. It may, for example, refer to a bilingual person/student, a bilingual classroom, a bilingual educational program, or a bilingual country. There is a lot of ambiguity built into this word (Baker, 1993). Consider the following: an individual who is bilingual may be equally proficient in two languages or stronger in one than the other. A bilingual educational program may involve the use of one language in the morning and the other language for the afternoon classes; or it might mean the majority of instruction takes place in the students' native language while special classes are held for the teaching of a second language. In a bilingual country, all citizens may speak two languages or individuals may actually be monolingual, speaking one language in one region and another language in another geographic part of the same country. Furthermore, depending on when, where, how, and by whom the word is used, 'bilingual' may have positive or negative connotations.

Out of this profusion of terms, two conclusions can be drawn. One is that *ESL, language minority*, and *LEP students* are also *bilingual*. The other is that there are very subtle differences in the connotations of these terms such that professionals do not just randomly substitute one for another. However, for the purposes of this book, the terms are relatively interchangeable. Used here, they will primarily refer to immigrant, refugee, and foreign students who are non-native speakers of English.

A Nation of Many Languages and the Education of Immigrants

What to do about the growing multilingualism in the United States and the best way to educate today's immigrants are subjects that evoke strong and divided opinions among Americans. Discussion of these topics can cause tempers to flare as patriotism and politics get tied into the language debate. What often gets forgotten in the heat of discussion is that what we now call the United States has never been a land of monolingual speakers of English; there has never existed a time when all 'Americans' solely spoke English.

From its very beginning, this has been a nation of enormous linguistic diversity. For example, more than 500 languages were spoken (by native Americans) in North America prior to the arrival of the Europeans (Castellanos, 1985: 1). As a result of immigration to the Colonies, it is reported that in 1664, 'eighteen different languages were being spoken by people of twenty different nationalities in New Amsterdam [Manhattan Island], (Castellanos, 1985: 1985:5). The Continental Congress (1774–1779) published documents in both English and German, and later with the acquisition of the Louisiana Territory, applicable Federal laws were printed in both English and French (Castellanos, 1985; Crawford, 1989; Heath, 1992). When the United States was founded, no official language was designated in its Constitution although other countries, such as Italy, Spain and France, did have national language academies (Heath, 1992). Clearly, this was not an oversight on the part of the 'founding fathers' but rather a deliberate decision which recognized the pluralistic nature of the new nation and the linguistic diversity of its citizens.

Concerns about educating immigrants, teaching them English, and 'Americanizing' them are neither new nor unique to the 1980s and 1990s (Castellanos, 1985; Crawford, 1989, 1992; Stein, 1986). For example, the concept of bilingual education—in which students receive part of their education in their native language and part in their new language (English)—has a long history in the United States (Castellanos, 1985; Crawford, 1989; Stein, 1986). In the mid-nineteenth century, German–English schools were established in Ohio and across the mid-West, French–English schools in Louisiana, and Spanish–English schools in the Territory of New Mexico.

However, by the turn of the century, many Americans reacted negatively to the newest wave of immigrants, particularly those from eastern and southern Europe: Jews, Slavs and Italians. Monolingual schooling in English was believed necessary in order to produce loyal Americans; immigrant students often were encouraged to 'forget' their native tongues and sometimes were punished for speaking the latter. Bilingual instruction disappeared, and for many immigrant school children it was 'sink or swim'. Xenophobia was so strong that even the study of foreign languages was curtailed.

Then, in the 1960s, bilingual education began to make its comeback in the public school system, and in 1968 The Bilingual Education Act (Title VII of the Elementary and Secondary Education Act) was passed. Castellanos (1985: 71) has attributed this renaissance of bilingual education to the shortcomings of

English as a second language instruction, the Civil Rights Movement, and the 'persuasive powers' of the highly educated Cuban immigrants who settled in Florida when Castro came to power.

What is different today about bilingual programs is that they can be found on college campuses. Here, they serve one of two functions. Some provide access to a college education for non-native English speaking undergraduates who can begin academic coursework in their native language while concurrently studying ESL. Bilingual instruction of this type can be found, for example, at colleges that enroll relatively large numbers of native Spanish speaking students such as Kean College of New Jersey (Union, NJ), Erie Community College (Buffalo, NY), Hostos Community College (Bronx, NY), Lehman College (Bronx, NY), and the University of Texas at El Paso (El Paso, TX). The second type of bilingual program is designed to strengthen foreign language instruction for native English speakers who take related content-area courses taught in the target language. Brown University (Providence, RI) and the University of Minnesota (Minneapolis, MN) offer undergraduate programs of this type.

Bilingual instruction is one way of approaching the educational needs of non-native speakers of English. The other is the teaching of English as a second language. ESL was originally developed in the United States in the 1930s for a target population of educated adults, such as businessmen, government officials and international students. In the 1950s and 60s it spread to the public school system, where it essentially remains a 'pullout program' for non-native speakers (Castellanos, 1985; Crawford, 1989; Stein, 1986). More recently, ESL has firmly taken root on many college campuses, providing intensive courses and programs in English language instruction for both undergraduate and graduate students. The need for ESL instruction at colleges is a reflection of the growing enrollment of non-native speakers of English.

The Higher Education of Today's Immigrants

Between 1981 and 1990, more than 7 million immigrants entered the United States (see Table 1.1). In terms of actual numbers, this is the second largest wave of immigration since the peak years between 1901 and 1910 when the United States admitted 8.8 million immigrants. However, in terms of percent of the total population, the recent wave of immigration is considerably smaller. In 1900, the US population was approximately 76 million; 8.8 million immigrants represented an 11.6% increase in the population. In 1980, the US population was 227 million; 7 million immigrants represents only a 3% population increase.

Table 1.1 Immigration from selected regions and countries of last residence: 1901–1910 and 1981–1990

	1901–1910	1981–1990
All countries	8,795,386	7,338,062
Europe	8,056,040	761,550
Asia	323,543	2,738,157
China	20,605	346,747
Hong Kong	n.a.	98,215
India	4,713	250,786
Iran	n.a.	116,172
Israel	n.a.	44,273
Japan	129,797	47,085
Korea	n.a.	333,746
Phillipines	n.a.	548,764
Turkey	157,369	23,233
Vietnam	n.a.	280,782
Other Asia	11,059	648,354
America	361,888	3,615,225
Mexico	49,642	1,655,843
Caribbean	107,548	872,051
Cuba	n.a.	144,578
Dominican Republic	n.a.	252,035
Haiti	n.a.	138,379
Jamaica	n.a.	208,148
Central America	8,192	468,088
South America	17,280	461,847
Argentina	n.a.	27,327
Colombia	n.a.	122,849
Ecuador	n.a.	56,315
Africa	7,368	176,893
Oceania	13,024	45,205

Data obtained from the US Immigration and Naturalization Service.
n.a. = data not available

There are several other important differences between these two waves of immigration. First, the early twentieth century immigrants were predominantly white Europeans while the majority of immigrants in the 1980s are people of 'color' from Asia, the Caribbean, and Central and South America (see Table 1.1). Second, the European immigrants were much more likely to assimilate and 'melt' into the white majority society while many of today's immigrants cannot because of their skin color and other distinguishing features. Moreover, some of today's immigrants do not want to assimilate. Instead, they are acculturating, adapting to an American way of life and learning English while retaining their native language and cultural traditions.

Third, the level of education needed by recent immigrants in order to be able to find employment and to support their families is often much greater than that required by immigrants in the early twentieth century (Spener, 1988). The strong back and willingness to work that sufficed for many immigrants in the past would lead to a poverty level existence at the minimum wage in today's economy.

The growing enrollment of non-speakers of English in college mirrors the changing nature of higher education in the United States. Although expensive, private institutions with highly competitive admissions standards and five-figure annual tuition rates exist, so do less costly and less competitive colleges and universities. As a result, students—both native and non-native English speakers, majority and minority group members—can gain entry into the higher education system even if they are 'underprepared' and require remediation. Equal opportunity laws and open admissions policies (Simms & Leonard, 1986), as well as the need to maintain enrollments have opened the doors of colleges to many students who would have been excluded in the past.

How faculty members react to the diversity of today's students reflects both their personal level of comfort with people who are different from themselves as well as how much they know about other languages, cultures, customs and styles of learning. This is true for all instructors, not just those who teach ESL. In fact, at the undergraduate level, it is the content-area faculty who, by their attitudes and actions, can strongly influence the educational achievements of LEP students. The ESL faculty can help students to increase their proficiency in English and can get them started on the long and difficult path of second language acquisition. But it is the 'regular' faculty who very much determine if ESL students will graduate one day with degrees in business, education or science.

Some Differences Between International and Immigrant/Refugee Students

In the sciences, faculty must be particularly careful not to confuse two groups of non-native English speaking students who superficially seem quite similar. One group consists of undergraduate students who are immigrants or refugees (or the children of recent immigrants or refugees). The other includes international (foreign) graduate students. While both need to learn 'American' English and to adjust to an American way of life (Cheng, 1993), they differ in many ways from each other.

The international students—particularly those in graduate programs in the sciences—have been described as the "crème de la crème of their countries" (Holden, 1993: 1770). They are hard working, exceptionally well prepared academically, and often bring with them their own financial support. They are already somewhat proficient in English as demonstrated by their scores on the TOEFL (Test of English as a Foreign Language) exam which must be passed at some prescribed level in order to be admitted to graduate school. Most international graduate students also have had the benefit of receiving their undergraduate education in their native language and in familiar surroundings. Upon completion of their graduate work, some choose to return home while others remain in the United States.

In contrast, immigrants and refugees come to the United States for economic, political, and sometimes religious reasons; they are not necessarily the most highly educated individuals from their countries. Obtaining an undergraduate degree while adapting to the mores of a new country and to an unfamiliar educational system while learning and using a second language is more than a bit challenging. This becomes especially difficult when there may be additional problems associated with obtaining work and supporting a family. Unlike international students, many immigrants and refugees cannot return to their homelands. For them, there is no turning back.

How College Students Learn English as a Second Language (ESL)

How do non-native speakers learn English in college? Although there exist private ESL schools, college students most often enroll in college or university ESL courses/programs. These can be an integral part of the institution or offered by the division of continuing education. Although some ESL courses/programs focus on basic communication skills, others are more academically oriented. The latter provide English language instruction including regularly scheduled courses in reading, writing, listening, speaking, pronunciation skills, and vocabulary development. Students are tested to determine where they should be placed initially in the program, and many need two years or more to complete the required course sequence.

Colleges differ considerably in their support of ESL students. Some do not have any ESL classes while others offer only a few. Those with large populations of non-native English speaking students frequently have well-structured programs with beginning, intermediate, and advanced ESL course sequences. Whether or not academic credit is granted for ESL coursework varies from one institution to another.

Although many non-ESL faculty members genuinely believe that an ESL course/program can make non-native speakers ready for mainstream academic coursework in English, this if often not the case. ESL instruction can greatly increase the English proficiency of students. However, even the most comprehensive ESL program cannot guarantee that it will fully prepare its students for the rigors of the academic classroom (Ostler, 1980; Russikoff, 1994; Smoke,

1988; Snow & Kinsella, 1994; Swartley, 1994). This in itself is not surprising since L2 acquisition research has demonstrated that academic language proficiency—especially the kinds of language skills needed for success in the classroom— takes approximately five to seven years to develop (Collier, 1987; Collier & Thomas, 1989; Cummins, 1980, 1981; Cummins & Swain, 1986). Obviously, five to seven years is a considerably longer period of time than that either allotted to any ESL program or to the earning of most college degrees.

At the college level, concerns about mastery of English by non-native speakers usually are relegated to the English department or an ESL program. Faculty members in the other academic disciplines often have no idea how students learn English, nor are they necessarily interested in finding out. However, this separation of the study of English from the study of academic subject matter may no longer be appropriate. At issue is more than the rapid rise in the number of students who are simultaneously learning English and working toward a college degree. Rather, research shows that the acquisition of English as a second language occurs best when students are using the new language purposefully (Benesch, 1988; Brinton, Snow & Wesche, 1989; Cochran, 1992). This would include taking subject matter courses taught in English which can be applied toward a college degree. Nonetheless, many educators still tend to view ESL instruction as remedial such that ESL courses should be completed and the English language 'mastered' before students can enter into the mainstream classroom.

However, proficiency in a second language does not develop just by studying the language in a language course. Most of us know this from our own attempts to learn a foreign language. Several years of study of French or Spanish certainly did not prepare us to speak, read, write and understand those languages. Similarly, students who are non-native speakers will never master English within the confines of the ESL classroom. They must use the new language in meaningful ways, in authentic situations, to make it their own.

Instructors of ESL are well aware of the complexity of the L2 acquisition process and of the limitations as to what they can accomplish with students. In contrast, mainstream faculty members who teach content-area courses often have unrealistic expectations of what ESL students can achieve within the confines of an ESL classroom. For this reason, Chapter 2 is particularly important since it includes a description of the L2 acquisition process and the many variables that affect it.

The New Undergraduate Demographics: The Growing Population of Students of Limited English Proficiency

The change in undergraduate demographics between 1980 and 1990 has been dramatic. While the undergraduate population as a whole increased by

12.3%, the growth of three racial/ethnic groups far exceeded this average: American Indian (+20.3%), Asian (+91.7%), and Hispanic (+60.3%) (*The Chronicle of Higher Education Almanac*, 1992: 11; see also Table 1.2). During the same time period much slower growth was experienced by African-American (+9.3%), white (+7.9%), and foreign (+8.7%) undergraduates (see Table 1.2). Those segments of the undergraduate population that may include students of limited English proficiency (Asian, Hispanic, American Indian, and foreign) increased by 54% between 1980 and 1990 (from 978,000 to 1,508,000), and all types of institutions of higher education have been affected including public, private, 4-year, and 2-year colleges (*The Chronicle of Higher Education Almanac* August 26, 1992: 11; see also Table 1.3).

Table 1.2 Undergraduate enrollment by racial and ethnic group, 1980 and 1990

	1980	1990	% change
American Indian	79,000	95,000	+20.3
Asian	253,000	485,000	+91.7
Black	1,028,000	1,124,000	+9.3
Hispanic	438,000	702,000	+60.3
White	8,556,000	9,231,000	+7.9
Foreign	208,000	226,000	+8.7
All	10,560,000	11,863,000	+12.3

Source: The Chronicle of Higher Education Almanac August 26, 1992: 11.

What is occurring in the undergraduate population reflects a major transformation that is taking place in the United States. The 1990 Census noted that in just one decade the Asian population increased in the United States by 107.8% and the Hispanic by 53%. Although differential fertility rates (Edmonston & Passel, 1992; United States Bureau of the Census 1990: 65–6) are partially responsible, most of this change is a result of recent and massive immigration. Not surprisingly, one significant consequence of the latter is a dramatic rise in the number of individuals in the United States who speak English as a second language.

The 1990 Census reported that 13.8% of persons ages five years and older 'sometimes or always' speak a language other than English at home (*The Chronicle of Higher Education Almanac*, August 26, 1992: 39-112) and 12 states exceed this national average (see Table 1.4).

As for the school-age population, 13.9% of children ages 5–17 do not speak English at home, and this average is exceeded in the same 12 states as mentioned above (Population Reference Bureau, 1992: 73; see also Table 1.4).

Table 1.3 College enrollment by racial and ethnic groups at public, private, 4-year, and 2-year institutions, 1980 and 1990: percentage change

Ethnic group	Year	Public	Private	4-year	2-year
American Indian	1980	74,000	10,000	37,000	47,000
	1990	90,000	12,000	48,000	54,000
	% change	+22 %	+20%	+30%	+15 %
Asian	1980	240,000	47,000	162,000	124,000
	1990	445,000	109,000	343,000	212,000
	% change	+85%	+132%	+112%	+71%
Black	1980	876,000	231,000	634,000	472,000
	1990	952,000	271,000	715,000	509,000
	% change	+9 %	+17 %	+13 %	+8 %
Hispanic	1980	406,000	66,000	217,000	255,000
	1990	648,000	110,000	344,000	414,000
	% change	+60%	+67%	+59%	+62%
White	1980	7,656,000	2,177,000	6,275,000	3,558,000
	1990	8,340,000	2,335,000	6,757,000	3,918,000
	% change	+9 %	+ 7 %	+8 %	+10 %
Foreign	1980	204,000	101,000	241,000	64,000
	1990	265,000	132,000	322,000	75,000
	% change	+30%	+31%	+34%	+17%
American Indian +	1980	924,000	224,000	657,000	490,000
Asian +	1990	1,448,000	363,000	1,057,000	755,000
Hispanic +	% change	+57%	+62%	+61%	+54%
Foreign					

Source: The Chronicle of Higher Education Almanac, August 26, 1992: 11.

There are now 6.3 million children who do not speak English at home, which is a 38.4% increase from 1980. Approximately two-thirds of these children—slightly less than 4.2 million—are native Spanish speakers (Population Reference Bureau, 1992: 73). Nationwide enrollment in public elementary and secondary schools (see Table 1.5) reflects the growing number of Hispanic and Asian school children.

Table 1.4 Use of a language other than English: by State

STATE	% of persons 5 years & older who 'sometimes or always' speak a language other than English at home	% of children ages 5-17 who do not speak English at home
Alabama	2.9	3.0
Alaska	12.1	9.5
Arizona	20.8	22.8
Arkansas	2.8	3.0
California	31.5	35.0
Colorado	10.5	8.4
Connecticut	15.2	14.9
Delaware	6.9	6.5
District of Columbia	12.5	11.8
Florida	17.3	17.8
Georgia	4.8	4.5
Hawaii	24.8	14.9
Idaho	6.4	5.8
Illinois	14.2	14.4
Indiana	4.8	4.9
Iowa	3.9	3.9
Kansas	5.7	5.3
Kentucky	2.5	2.8
Lousiana	10.1	5.5
Maine	9.2	4.4
Maryland	8.9	8.4
Massachusetts	15.2	15.3
Michigan	6.6	5.4
Minnesota	5.6	5.1
Mississippi	2.8	3.0
Missouri	3.8	3.6
Montana	5.0	3.9
Nebraska	4.8	3.6
Nevada	13.2	11.8
New Hampshire	8.7	4.4
New Jersey	19.5	19.4
New Mexico	35.5	29.5
New York	23.3	23.3
North Carolina	3.9	4.7
North Dakota	7.9	2.7
Ohio	5.4	5.0
Oklahoma	5.0	4.6
Oregon	7.3	7.0

Table 1.4 *Continued*

STATE	% of persons 5 years & older who 'sometimes or always' speak a language other than English at home	% of children ages 5-17 who do not speak English at home
Pennsylvania	7.3	6.8
Rhode Island	17.0	16.3
South Carolina	3.5	3.5
South Dakota	6.5	4.1
Tennessee	2.9	3.2
Texas	25.4	28.2
Utah	7.8	5.5
Vermont	5.8	3.1
Virginia	7.3	7.0
Washington	9.0	8.8
West Virginia	2.6	2.7
Wisconsin	5.8	5.5
Wyoming	5.7	3.9
UNITED STATES	**13.8**	**13.9**

Sources: Population Reference Bureau (1992); *The Chronicle of Higher Education Almanac* August 26, 1992: 39-112.

Table 1.5. Enrollment in public elementary and secondary schools, by race or ethnicity (Percent distribution): selected years, Fall 1976–1990

	White[1]	Black[1]	Hispanic	Asian or Pacific Islander	American Indian/ Alaskan Native
Fall 1976	76.0	15.5	6.4	1.2	0.8
Fall 1980	73.3	16.1	8.0	1.9	0.8
Fall 1984	71.2	16.2	9.1	2.5	0.9
Fall 1986	70.4	16.1	9.9	2.8	0.9
Fall 1990	68.0	16.0	12.0	3.0	1.0

[1]Excludes persons of Hispanic origin
Source: Data obtained from U.S. Department of Education, Office of Educational Research and Improvement.

While the Federal government keeps track of the number of ESL or LEP students grades K-12 (United States Department of Education, 1992; United States General Accounting Office, 1994), nothing comparable exists for undergraduates studying at colleges and universities in the United States. Nevertheless, the data in Tables 1.2 and 1.3 plus the trend depicted in Table 1.5 strongly suggest a growing population of non-native English speaking undergraduates. In addition, the Center for the Study of Community Colleges (University of California, Los Angeles) has recently documented that ESL is the 'fastest growing subject area' in the liberal arts credit curriculum taught at community colleges in the United States. As of the spring of 1991, there were an estimated 236,000 students enrolled in ESL courses at community colleges. Most of the growth in the number of ESL section offerings occurred at large community colleges (more than 6,000 students) in urban areas (Ignash, 1992a, 1992b, 1992/1993).

Enrollment in ESL courses is not in itself an accurate measure of the number of LEP college students studying on a given campus. For example, many students who have successfully completed an ESL program still have difficulty with various English language skills. (This is discussed in detail in Chapter 2.) Other students become bored and/or frustrated with being confined to the study of English as a second language. They want to get on with their education. If it is at all possible, they will interrupt their ESL coursework and enroll in mainstream, academic courses, postponing as long as possible any remaining ESL requirements.

The Challenge of Teaching Students of Limited English Proficiency

ESL faculty are generally aware of the wide range of linguistic abilities of the students they are teaching; however, content-area faculty often are not. In fact, the latter may lump all non-native speakers of English in the category of 'foreigners', giving little thought to how different one ESL student may be from another. For example, some ESL students are recent immigrants who do not know a word of English; others have graduated from an American high school after a few years of study in this country but still have problems with English. Another group includes students who are the children of immigrants; they may speak a language other than English with their parents, families, and friends, and only use English in school. Some ESL students may have studied English as a foreign language in their countries but find real life communication in 'American' English to be problematic. There exists another group of students, who for a variety of reasons, are not particularly literate in either their native language or in English.

Faculty members sometimes question how the kinds of students described here get admitted to college; they doubt that an undergraduate who is not proficient in English has the ability to do college coursework. Needless to say, knowledge of English will unquestionably facilitate a student's academic success in the United States. However, English proficiency is not a measure of intelligence, academic ability, or motivation. Moreover, it is not as if these students were *alingual*.

The issue of access to the higher education system of students who are still learning English may be disturbing to some faculty members. These are the professors who want students to 'know' English before enrolling in 'their' classes. Nonetheless, the number of ESL and LEP students is increasing, indicating that the question of should they be admitted to college has already been answered affirmatively.

Concerned faculty members sometimes ask: 'What is the most effective way to provide content-area instruction to students who are still unfamiliar with the language of instruction, English?' In order to answer this, many factors have to be taken into consideration. At the institutional level these would include the total number of LEP students, the educational philosophy and mission of the college, the willingness of content-area and ESL faculty to work together, and the resources and academic support services which are available on campus. At a personal level, faculty members would need to determine just how committed they are to the education of non-native English speaking students and whether or not they are willing to consider the influence of cultural and linguistic factors in the teaching/learning process.

Reasons Why the Scientific Community Needs to Pay More Attention To the Growing Population of LEP Undergraduates

There are many reasons why limited English proficient (LEP) undergraduates should be of special interest to the scientific community:

First, they represent a large pool of talent; they could be tomorrow's university and industry researchers, high school and college science teachers, technicians, and/or technologically and scientifically literate members of the public. If trained in the sciences, they could also be mentors and/or serve as role models for other LEP students moving up through the school system, thereby helping to increase minority participation in the sciences.

Nevertheless, some scientists and educators still view speaking English as a second language or being bilingual as a handicapping condition. For example, *In the National Interest: The Federal Government in the Reform of K-12 Math and Science Education* (Carnegie Commission on Science, Technology, and Government, 1991: 7) states that in the year 2000, 'one child in twelve *will lack the English language proficiency required for learning*' (italics added for emphasis). Similarly, an article on universal literacy that appeared in *Science* (Miller, 1988: 1296) several years ago claims that for many bilingual school age children 'reading is the beginning of school failure. Their lack of familiarity with the syntactic and semantic constraints of English puts them at a disadvantage relative to monolingual children'.

The insistence that only through the use of English can children receive an adequate education ignores compelling arguments to the contrary. According to Reyes (1992: 433): 'The veneration of English leads to two popular but erroneous conclusions. First is the notion that the need to adapt is incumbent on the students, *not* on the teachers. Second is the idea that if students are not performing satisfactorily, it is their fault, and not that of the curriculum, the instruction, or the way these are implemented.' Extra & Verhoeven (1993: 4) point out: 'Many American studies on bilingualism include chapters on effects of bilingualism and few studies pay attention to effects of monolingualism. In Europe, learning more than one language is a common and often highly valued experience of many citizens.'

Clearly, students all over the world learn in many languages, and there is no evidence that being a native speaker of English is the key factor for achievement in science. Many Nobel Prize winners in the sciences speak English as a second language. So do large numbers of the international graduate students studying science in the United States. In other words, there is no reason why the LEP and bilingual students in our educational system cannot do well in science. However, their success may very well depend on eliminating negative attitudes toward non-native English speakers and on a willingness to use innovative ways of teaching science so that the English language does not become an insurmountable barrier.

Second, LEP undergraduates bring to the classroom a wide range of previous educational experiences as well as ethnic, cultural, and linguistic diversity that many science instructors have never before encountered. These students vary considerably in both their proficiency in English and in the extent of their previous schooling. Some are well educated and have graduated from high school and/or university in their homelands; they have knowledge and skills which will help them with their college studies in the United States. Others, because of political or financial problems, have had little prior schooling and thereby are lacking in content knowledge as well as literacy and study skills. Some LEP students enter college speaking English but cannot read or write it; others can do the academic work involving reading and writing but cannot say or correctly pronounce a single word in English. Some come from educational systems that value cooperative and collaborative learning styles; others have been taught not to ask questions or speak up in class. Some LEP students have received the kind of education in which memorization is valued over problem solving and critical thinking. It is for all these reasons that science faculty need to learn more about the kinds of students they may now be teaching. Conventional science instruction in the lecture/lab format may not be particularly effective for today's diverse students, especially those studying new subject matter through a language they are still learning.

Many science professors often are unaware of (and some do not care about) the challenges faced by LEP undergraduates. In fact, most of today's science faculty have not received any training to facilitate the instruction of LEP students. Earning a Master's or Doctorate in the sciences has traditionally involved research, science coursework, and a limited amount of teaching experience (generally in the laboratory or recitation sections). Until recently, as part of the graduate training in the sciences, there were no courses in pedagogy and certainly no special instruction in how to teach science to minority or LEP students. It is often said that most professors teach the same way they were taught. That alone is problematic since today's undergraduates are very different from those a generation ago (Schroeder, 1993).

Fortunately, this situation has begun to change as more and more graduate teaching assistants across the nation receive some kind of preparation for teaching (*Innovative Higher Education*, 1993; Janes & Hauer, 1988; Lambert & Tice, 1993; Nyquist et al., 1991; Smith et al., 1992). Training the 'professoriate of tomorrow' does not, however, mean that the 'professoriate of today' has undergone similar kinds of instruction to learn how to more effectively teach today's diverse undergraduates.

Therefore, the third reason why the scientific community should pay more attention to LEP undergraduates is that science as traditionally taught may no longer be effective with the multilingual and multicultural students now enrolling in college. The standard lecture/lab format may need modification in order to attract more of today's students to the sciences. Actually, this is as true for majority and minority students as it is for native and non-native speakers of English.

During the last twenty-odd years, American undergraduates have been losing interest in science, and the proportion of students majoring in the sciences has been declining (K.C. Green, 1989; National Science Foundation, 1992). The numbers are very clear. According to the National Science Foundation (1992), a total of 76,811 students earned their Bachelor's degree in the biological and physical sciences in 1977; in 1990 that figure had dropped by 29% to 54,243 (see Table 1.6). However, during the same time period (1977 to 1990) the total number of Bachelor's degrees which were granted (in all academic disciplines) increased by 14% (from 928,228 to 1,062,151) (National Science Foundation, 1992: 37). In other words, even though the total number of students receiving the Baccalaureate degree has increased, proportionately fewer are obtaining it in the biological and physical sciences.

White males—who for many years have comprised the overwhelming majority of science majors—are now pursuing other careers, and they have not been replaced by women and other minority group members (K.C. Green, 1989; Higher Education Research Institute, 1992; Hilton & Lee, 1988; National Science Foundation, 1992; see also Tables 1.6, 1.7 and 1.8). Efforts to increase the number of underrepresented minorities (African-Americans, Hispanics, and American Indians) majoring in the sciences have produced some changes, more so for females (Table 1.8) than for males (Table 1.7). However, in 1990, 80.6% of the physical science and and 75.7% of the biological science Bachelor's degrees still were being earned by White, non-Hispanics. Only

Table 1.6 Number of earned bachelor's degrees in the physical and biological sciences (1977 and 1990): by race/ethnicity

	Physical science 1977	Physical science 1990	% change	Biological science 1977	Biological science 1990	% change
Total	22,618	16,203	-28.4	54,193	38,040	-29.8
White, non-Hispanics	20,417	13,055	-36.1	47,695	28,814	-39.6
Asians	377	937	+148.5	1,316	3,245	+146.6
Under-represented minorities, total	1,244	1,245	0	4,131	4,243	+2.7
Black, non-Hispanics	692	650	-6.1	2,415	1,994	-17.4
Hispanics	484	522	+7.9	1,559	2,119	+35.9
American Indians or Alaskan Natives	68	73	+7.4	157	130	-17.2
US citizens & permanent residents	22,038	15,237	-30.9	53,142	36,302	-31.7
Non-resident aliens	571	595	+4.2	1,028	867	-15.7
Unknown race/ ethnicity	9	371	+4022	23	871	+3687
Males: all	18,067	11,109	-38.5	34,474	18,631	-46.0
Females: all	4,551	5,094	+11.9	19,719	19,409	-1.6

Source: National Science Foundation (1992: Tables 1, 2 and 3, pp.45–56)

Asian students, both male and female, have shown large gains in terms of undergraduate degrees in the sciences (see Tables 1.6, 1.7 and 1.8).

The interest, aptitude and persistence of Asians in the sciences, math, and engineering has been widely acclaimed. In 1977 they were awarded 1,693 Bachelor's degrees in the biological and physical sciences and 4,182 in 1990. This is a 147% increase (see Table 1.6). Nonetheless, there are four reasons why Asian students should not and cannot be depended on to counteract the overall decline in science majors. First, Asians and Pacific Islanders comprise only 2.9% of the population of the United States so that the number who actu-

Table 1.7 Number of earned bachelor's degrees in the physical and biological sciences for male recipients by race/ethnicity: 1977 and 1990

	Physical science 1977	1990	% change	Biological science 1977	1990	% change
All males	18,067	11,109	-38.5	34,474	18,631	-46.0
White, non-Hispanics	16,410	9,179	-44.1	30,728	14,488	-52.9
Asians	280	592	+111.4	837	1,573	+87.9
Underrepresented minorities	908	655	-27.9	2,196	1,685	-23.3
Black, non-Hispanics	494	292	-40.9	1,197	658	-45.0
Hispanics	363	311	-14.3	896	955	+6.6
American Indians or Alaskan Natives	51	52	+2.0	103	72	-30.1
U.S. citizens & permanent residents	17,598	10,426	-40.8	33,761	17,746	-47.4
Non-resident aliens	461	415	-10.0	697	431	-38.2
Unknown race/ ethnicity	8	268	+3250	16	454	+2738

Source: National Science Foundation (1992: Table 2, pp. 49–52)

ally earn degrees in science will remain very small. Second, not all Asian students want to study science (Allis, 1991). Third, recent data indicate that the proportion of Asian students majoring in and seeking careers in the sciences is beginning to decline (Higher Education Research Institute, 1992). And fourth, in spite of the 'model minority' image presented in the press, not all Asian subgroups meet with equal success in higher education and in the sciences (Magner, 1993a, 1993b; Shih, 1988; Suzuki, 1989).

A fourth reason why LEP undergraduates should be of special concern is that science faculty sometimes have mistaken notions about how and how rapidly these students can master of the English language. For example, some professors expect such students to learn all the English they need to know in ESL classes; others believe that ESL college students will 'pick up' English by 'osmosis' (somewhat like how babies acquire their first language and how young children learn a second language).

As explained earlier in this chapter, a two year ESL program cannot possibly bring all students up to the level of language proficiency equal to that of their native English speaking peers. And, as for the 'osmosis' argument, it does not apply to LEP undergraduates who are *adult* learners. As adults, they have passed the point when they can 'effortlessly' acquire a second language by simply being immersed in it. For them, the process of L2 acquisition is complex, lengthy, and dependent on many variables including the student's literacy level in his or her first language, the learning environment, and sufficient exposure to comprehensible input (Cummins, 1980, 1981; Cummins & Swain, 1986; Krashen, 1981, 1982; Larsen-Freeman, 1991). These factors are discussed in considerable detail in Chapter 2.

Table 1.8 Number of earned bachelor's degrees in the physical and biological sciences for female recipients by race/ethnicity: 1977 and 1990

| | Physical science | | % | Biological science | | % |
	1977	1990	change	1977	1990	change
All females	4,551	5,094	+11.9	19,719	19,409	-1.6
White, non-Hispanics	4,007	3,876	-3.3	16,967	14,326	-15.6
Asians	97	345	+255.7	479	1,672	+249.1
Underrepresented minorities	336	590	+75.6	1,935	2,558	+32.2
Black, non-Hispanics	198	358	+80.8	1,218	1,336	+9.7
Hispanics	121	211	+74.4	663	1,164	+75.6
American Indians or Alaskan Natives	17	21	+23.5	54	58	+7.4
U.S. citizens & permanent residents	4,440	4,811	+8.4	19,381	18,556	-4.3
Non-resident aliens	110	180	+63.6	331	436	+31.7
Unknown race/ ethnicity	1	103	+10,200	7	417	+5857

Source: National Science Foundation (1992: Table 3, pp. 53–56)

A fifth misconception about science instruction for LEP students is that the technical and scientific words make the discipline particularly difficult. If anything, the vocabulary of science is 'foreign' to both native and non-native speakers of English. However, there are several other aspects of the English language that apparently cause LEP students problems in science classes. One is comprehending typical college science textbooks whose readability levels have been described as being 'beyond those attained by ESL and post-ESL students' (see Chapter 6). Another is understanding what is being said during lectures, which may be problematic if instructors speak rapidly, use unfamiliar vocabulary, and long, complex sentences. For example, a professor might unwittingly say something like: 'Photosynthesis, a process which occurs in green plants and which produces the oxygen that other living organisms need to live, depends on the presence of chlorophyll molecules inside cellular organelles called chloroplasts which are found in abundance in leaves.' So many important ideas and unfamiliar vocabulary words are crammed into this one sentence that any student might have difficulty sorting out the main ideas and their relationships to each other. As for the non-native English speaker, identifying photosynthesis as the subject of the sentence may be easy, but the verb 'depends' does not appear until after 19 other words and several other points of information are given. (For an excellent discussion of troublesome areas related to vocabulary and sentence structure for LEP students, see Sutman, Allan & Shoemaker, 1986: 11–14).

A third language difficulty experienced by both native and non-native English speaking students is that many common, everyday words in English have alternative and very precise scientific meanings. For example, the definition of 'work' in a physics class (Lipson, 1992), has little to do with the jobs we hold to earn a living or the effort we put into accomplishing a particular task. A fluid, to most people, is a liquid that is wet to the touch; however, scientifically, a fluid can also refer to a gas. For many students, especially those who are still learning English, such differences in word meaning can be confusing.

Lastly, there is the problem of being able to adequately 'express' in English what it is that students know and have learned. Many non-native English speakers develop their academic 'receptive' skills in English (listening and reading comprehension) before their 'productive' skills (speaking and writing). For them, it is difficult to find the right words to convey their ideas particularly when pressed for time.

Science Education Reform and LEP Undergraduates

In recent years, the scientific community has increasingly focused attention on both science education reform as well as the need to recruit more minorities into the scientific professions. Numerous commissions and task forces have issued reports about ways to improve both pre-college and college-level science education (AAAS, 1989, 1990; Carnegie Commission on Science, Technology, and Government, 1991; National Science Foundation, 1989; Project Kaleidoscope, 1991).

These documents duly note the changing demographics of American society as well as the importance of making science, math, engineering, and technology education accessible to all students regardless of their 'race, language, sex, or economic circumstances' (AAAS, 1989: 156). Underrepresented minorities—particularly women, African-Americans, Hispanics, and the handicapped—have been targeted for special programs to increase their participation in science. Many of these efforts begin with the middle or high school population and/or assist with the transition into college.

However, careful reading of the reports mentioned above finds that the special needs of a growing population of students for whom English is a second language are not addressed. Perhaps the absence of discussion of this issue is just an oversight or that these proposals are broad in scope and cannot include detailed attention to 'special interest' groups. Whatever the reasons, this situation must be remedied if the goal of reform is to improve science instruction for *all* students and to increase minority participation in the sciences.

The role of language in the instructional process—and related issues such as culture and learning styles—must be taken into consideration with an increasingly multilingual and multicultural student population. And ways to address such matters in the sciences do not have to be invented *de novo*. In other words, considerable information is already available which deals with appropriate science instruction for college students who are still learning English; however, it is not found in places where college science faculty or science education 'reformers' normally look.

There are publications about science instruction for ESL students. Although most are geared toward the elementary and secondary levels, much of this material is applicable at the undergraduate level (for examples see Bilingual Education Office, 1990; Cantoni-Harvey, 1987; Crandall, 1987; Gonzales, 1981; Mason & Barba, 1992; Reilly, 1988; Rendón & Triana, 1989; Secada, 1991; Sutman, Allen & Shoemaker, 1986). A few of these publications do include some information on teaching science to college-level LEP students (Rendón & Triana, 1989; Sutman, Allen & Shoemaker, 1986); however, material that focuses entirely on science instruction for LEP undergraduates is scarce (Case & Lau, 1991; Rosenthal, 1992/1993, 1993a, 1993b).

New and innovative ways to teach content-area courses to non-native English speaking students have been developed on college campuses in the United States and Canada (Benesch, 1988; Brinton, Snow & Wesche, 1989; Snow & Brinton, 1988a, 1988b). They combine subject matter instruction with ESL teaching techniques. Although more likely to be used in the humanities and social and behaviorial sciences, some colleges are applying these models to science. The theory behind content-based ESL instruction is described in Chapter 8, and in Chapter 9 actual case studies in the sciences are presented.

The literature on L2 acquisition also includes a variety of studies whose findings are pertinent to college science instruction. These have to do with topics such as the ways in which ESL students feel they need additional help in their mainstream courses taught in English (Ostler, 1980; Smoke, 1988) and how content-area faculty react to the writing of ESL students (Russikoff, 1994; Santos, 1988; Snow & Kinsella, 1994; Swartley, 1994; Vann, Meyer & Lorenz, 1984; Vann, Lorenz & Mayer, 1991). The findings of many of these studies are reported throughout this book.

Finally, expertise and relevant materials are also available from other sources not usually tapped by scientists. These include organizations such as TESOL (Teachers of English to Speakers of Other Languages), NABE (National Association for Bilingual Education), NCBE (National Clearinghouse for Bilingual Education), CAL (The Center for Applied Linguistics) and the ERIC Clearinghouse on Languages and Linguistics. The addresses and phone numbers of these organizations appear in the Appendix (p. 180) at the end of this book.

The Forgotten LEP Undergraduate

Non-native English speaking students at the two ends of the educational pipeline (K-12 and the graduate level) have received considerably more attention than those in the undergraduate years. This is especially true in the sciences.

In the public school system, the Federal Bilingual Education Act of 1968 ensures that many (but definitely not all) non-native English speaking children have access to bilingual and/or ESL courses (United States Department of Education, 1992; United States General Accounting Office, 1994). The publications cited on page 32 of this Chapter describe useful instructional practices for the science education of LEP students grades K-12. At various national conferences the subject of teaching science to students of limited English proficiency is beginning to receive more attention. For example, at the American Association for the Advancement of Science (AAAS) Annual Meetings, sessions were held entitled 'Applications of Science Instruction R&D for LEP Students to All Students' (1993) and 'Facing the Challenge: Building Scientific Literacy in a Multicultural and Multilinguistic Society' (1994). Both focused on students grades K-12.

At the opposite end of the educational pipeline are the many international students (particularly from the People's Republic of China, Taiwan, South Korea, and India) enrolled in science and engineering graduate programs in the United States. In 1990, non-US citizens with temporary visas earned 22.1% of the doctorates in the life sciences, 31.9% in the physical sciences, and 44.8% in engineering (*The Chronicle of Higher Education*, Oct 16, 1991: A20). The presence of so many foreigners in US graduate schools has provoked considerable public discussion (Bowen, 1988; De Palma, 1990; Holden, 1993; Kotkin, 1993). While international students may be keeping some graduate programs afloat, issues have been raised in reference to the ability of such students to effectively serve as teaching assistants (due to their lack of proficiency with spoken English and their culturally determined attitudes toward women and other minority group members) as well as the possibility of these students eventually returning home and taking with them the scientific expertise gained in the United States.

In contrast to all the attention paid to LEP students grades K-12 and to the international graduate students, we rarely hear or read about the needs of undergraduates of limited English proficiency who are studying science. Does this oversight mean that these students do not exist or that they do not encounter difficulties in their college courses? Obviously, no. Therefore, it is particularly perplexing that appropriate science instruction for college students who are still learning English has received so little consideration. This is especially true since entrance into a graduate science program generally requires an undergraduate science degree.

Conclusions

Both research and real life experience have demonstrated that for college students, learning academic English is a lengthy process which cannot be rushed nor mastered in the isolation of an ESL classroom. The new language must be used and manipulated in purposeful ways in order for proficiency to develop. LEP undergraduates taking mainstream science courses are not just learning biology, chemistry or physics. They are putting to use the kinds of language skills which they began developing in their ESL courses and which are necessary for academic success. These include listening to lectures and simultaneously taking notes, reading and understanding texts, writing reports and papers, participating in discussions, following laboratory instructions, solving problems, and taking timed exams. No amount of practice in any ESL class can fully prepare the student for the implementation of these skills in a rigorous content course.

There are, however, several reasons why science is especially well suited for LEP students. Much of it is mathematically based, which eliminates some of the linguistic barriers. Demonstrations, experiments, hands-on activities, videos and slides can visually, aurally and kinesthetically reinforce the words of the text and the instructor. In addition, as previously mentioned, the language of science is a great equalizer: it is 'foreign' to both native and non-native speakers of English. In other words, majoring in science has certain benefits for students who are still developing their proficiency in English.

Just mentioning the changing demographics of the United States in documents about science education reform will not improve how science is taught nor increase the representation of language minority students. Any plans to reform science education must address the educational and linguistic needs of the rapidly growing population of students of limited English proficiency.

This is not just a 'problem' for science teachers grades K-12. LEP students now make up a significant proportion of the undergraduate population at many colleges and universities. (For some specific examples see Box 1.2.) Much more can be done than has been done to provide non-native English speaking students with appropriate instruction and to interest and possibly persuade them to study science. However, this will require science faculty, educators, and reformers to use research findings and resources from outside those traditionally tapped by the scientific community. The information is there. The question is, are we willing to put it to use?

Box 1.2 Multilingual Undergraduates: From Coast to Coast (to Coast?)

During the 1992–93 academic year, three science faculty members at different colleges participated in an 'unscientific' survey of the language backgrounds of their students. These individuals were Dr Paul Hiemenz (Professor of Chemistry at California State Polytechnic University in Pomona, CA); Dr Roger Persell (Associate Professor of Biological Sciences at Hunter College, The City University of New York); and Dr Ann Lumsden (a Biological Sciences faculty member at Florida State University, Tallahassee, FL).

All three had recently published articles on some aspect of college science instruction. Lumsden's (1992/1993) article, 'The Rewards of Institutional Commitment: Florida State University's Strategy for Large-Course Science Instruction', describes the teaching of a very large lecture course, *General Biology*, which often enrolls more than a thousand freshmen and sophomore students per semester. Hiemenz along with M.C. Hudspeth (1993) wrote about 'Academic Excellence Workshops for Underrepresented Students at Cal Poly, Pomona', describing how group-study workshops offered in conjunction with some of the core math and science courses have significantly benefited minority students. Dr Persell's (1993) article, 'Promoting Active Learning in a Large Introductory Biology Course Through Writing' describes how a large, introductory biology course is being made more student centerd.

Each of these three faculty members carried out a quick, in-class survey to find out the following information about their students: country of birth, native language and language spoken at home. None had ever done this before. Two points need to be mentioned before presenting the results. First, it is assumed that the students answered the questions truthfully. Second, these findings in no way represent a random sample or well controlled study of the number of LEP students enrolled in undergraduate science courses at colleges and universities in the United States! Keeping this in mind, the results are quite interesting.

Dr. Persell teaches *Principles of Biology* at Hunter College in New York City. This is a nine-credit, two-semester course that serves both majors and non-majors. There is a large lecture plus separate laboratory and recitation sections. In the fall 1993 semester, 508 students (of a total enrollment of 675) responded to Dr Persell's questionnaire. The findings are presented below.

Of the respondents, 43% are non-native English speakers; 43% also do not speak English at home. However, there is not complete overlap in these two groups: some native English speakers use a another language at home while some non-native English speakers use English at home. Fifty-five students (11%) speak Spanish at home, 41 (8%) Russian, and 20 (4%) Chinese. The remaining students who do not speak English at home use 35 different languages. Two hundred and thirty (45%) of the respondents were born outside the mainland United States.

Similar results were obtained by Dr Hiemenz and his colleague Dr Ruth Bowen at Cal Poly, Pomona, California. They surveyed three sections of Chemistry 111 during the fall 1993 semester. This is a three-credit, one-quarter lecture course, *General Chemistry I,* which is the first of a three quarter sequence. It is taken by engineering and physical science majors. Of 121 students who responded (of a total enrollment of 134 in the three sections) 63% are non-native English speakers, and 53% speak a language other than English at home. The predominant home languages for the non-native English speakers are Spanish (19 students, 16%) and Vietnamese (10 students, 8%); 12% of the students speak a mixture of English and their native language at home (including Armenian, Cantonese, Chinese, Korean, Mandarin, Punjabi, Russian, Spanish, Tagalog, Vietnamese/English), and for one student, the home language is a mixture of Chinese, Vietnamese and English. Coincidentally, as in the case of the Hunter College biology students, 45% of the 121 Cal Poly chemistry students were born outside the mainland United States.

Quite different results turned up in Florida's pan-handle at Florida State University in Tallahassee. It is here that Dr. Lumsden is the faculty co-ordinator for *General Biology* which is taken by non-science majors. The lecture component of the course is taught by four different professors from the Department of Biological Science; the students are divided among 36 laboratory sections which are taught by graduate assistants.

In the spring 1993 semester, on the day 'the questions' were asked, there were 369 students present in class (of a total enrollment of 800). Of these, only three were born outside the United States and were non-native English speakers. One was born in Mexico and was a native speaker of Spanish; another was born in Germany and was a native speaker of German, and the third was born in Singapore and was a native speaker of Cantonese. We will never know how different the results might have been if more students had been present in class that day!

In spite of the limitations of the unscientific nature of this survey, the findings at Florida State University provide quite a contrast to those from Hunter College and Cal Poly. All three institutions are located in states that have large populations of non-native English speakers. (As already reported in this Chapter, the 1990 Census revealed that the percentage of persons five years and older who 'sometimes or always' speak a language other than English at home is 31.5% in CA, 23.3% in NY, and 17.3% in FL. The US average is 13.8% (see Table 1.4). How LEP students select a college to attend may depend on a variety of factors including admissions policies, availability of ESL instruction, geographical location, and cost.

Some colleges have already begun preparing their content-area faculty to adjust their teaching to the needs of ESL students. Within the CUNY system (of which Hunter College is a part), a recent survey found that approximately one-third of the students speak languages other than English at home, and 15–20% of the entering freshmen need ESL coursework (Cochran, 1992). To improve the instruction of language minority students in all disciplines, a handbook for CUNY faculty members has been prepared (Cochran, 1992), and a variety of faculty training sessions have been held.

At Cal Poly, a questionnaire was distributed in the fall of 1993 to all faculty to find out 'by what means ESL student writing is currently assessed in academic coursework'. The changing demographics in the state of California have increased the enrollment of ESL students at Cal Poly, and there is concern about the writing and reading skills of students. As reported by Russikoff (1994), the respondents attributed the problems encountered by ESL students in their courses to language difficulties (76% of the respondents), inadequate prior academic preparation (37%), and cultural differences (25%). The most significant language problem (according to 68% of the respondents) was weak writing skills, followed by understanding written questions (41%), responding orally to questions (37%), understanding lectures (36%) and spoken questions (36%), and slow/inefficient reading (35%).

Perhaps the cultural and linguistic diversity on your campus is not quite so pronounced as at Hunter College or Cal Poly. However, if you lecture and do not have to directly interact with students in the laboratory or recitation sections, it is possible to remain unaware of startling changes in undergraduate demograhics. By surveying the students you teach about country of birth as well as native and home languages, you may be very surprised by the findings.

2 Second Language Acquisition Theory and its Application to Undergraduate Science Teaching

'Moreover language is much too complex to permit of its being taught explicitly (Macnamara, 1973: 38).'

Growing up the United States, many native English speaking students have had the opportunity to begin studying a foreign language (such as Latin, French, Spanish, or German) in middle or high school. Attempting to master their 'new' language, they may exert considerable effort—diligently memorizing vocabulary, conjugating verbs, translating assignments, and responding to various written exercises. What is the outcome? While these students may earn passing grades, they often cannot understand the spoken language nor converse in it. In college, to meet some kind of foreign language distribution or general education requirement, another semester or year of language study may be mandatory. Yet, unless they are majoring or minoring in a foreign language, many students are visibly relieved when this requirement has been met. Soon, the foreign language is forgotten. Not only have some of us endured this unsuccessful experience of foreign language learning, but also we have seen it repeated by our children.

Developing L2 proficiency involves something much more complex than memorization and repetition, and it certainly seems to bear no connection to how we learned to speak our first (L1 = native) language. Of the latter process, we have no recollection. Developing L1 proficiency—acquiring the sounds, vocabulary and grammatical structures—is unconscious and seemingly effortless. By age three, youngsters without any formal study or schooling chatter away and communicate in an age appropriate manner. This is true for children all over the world, whatever language they speak.

Yet, our experiences as adults and professionals reinforce the belief that learning a foreign language is a difficult, almost impossible task. As visitors to foreign countries we quickly discover that we do not return home speaking Spanish, French or Japanese. In fact, many of us are pretty pleased if we have mastered the essentials such as saying 'thank you', 'yes', 'no', 'Where is the bathroom?', 'How much does this cost?', and 'A glass of water, please'. In other words, even if an individual is surrounded by a new language and hearing it all the time, the language remains essentially incomprehensible. Similarly, we do not learn new languages from watching foreign films or listening to radio programs broadcast in other languages. As these examples point out, the ordinary adult does not absorb a second language the same way that young children seem to 'pick up' their first (and/or perhaps second) language. For most adults, developing L2 proficiency is a daunting task.

Nevertheless, some adults do manage to become quite fluent in a second language. They might be American business executives or government officials who will be sent overseas to work in a foreign country. Others are international students who currently are studying at an American college or university. Some are immigrants to the United States who must learn English in order to work, obtain an education and to function in society. Such individuals are living proof that under the right set of circumstances, with enough motivation and hard work, adults can master new languages. They may speak with an accent and their degree of proficiency may not be that of a native speaker, but they can communicate effectively, thinking, reading, writing, listening and speaking in a second language. To what do we attribute their success? Do they have a special aptitude for learning languages? Superior intelligence? Exceptional motivation? Why do they succeed when so many others fail?

It is interesting to note that the lack of success experienced by many Americans when attempting to learn a foreign language does not necessarily increase their empathy toward those individuals who are trying to make English their second language. Yet, in terms of difficulty or complexity, the study of a foreign language is much more straightforward and considerably less demanding than what is required of a typical ESL student.

First, when studying a foreign language, students have the option to end those studies as soon as some requirement is met. Second, foreign language study is essentially just that, the study of the language, and perhaps a bit of the culture and literature. Learning the foreign language is an end in itself. In contrast, ESL students are learning English so that they can study other subjects, such as history or chemistry, for which English is the language of instruction. Even if they choose to drop out of school or college, they do not have the luxury of 'dropping' English since it is the shared language of most Americans. ESL students need not bother to question if they possess any particular 'gift' for L2 learning, or if they are 'too old' to ever master English. For non-native English speaking students, such questions are irrelevant if they want to pass their courses, earn a college degree, and achieve their career goals in the United States.

Many Americans who are native speakers of English demonstrate considerable ambivalence when it comes to 'foreign' languages. Consider these examples:

1. As a nation, we think language study is in some way worthwhile, or it would not be included in school curricula. Nevertheless, language instruction focuses more on 'intellectual' activities like learning the rules of grammar and/or translation of literature than on developing an effective means of communication. Year after year, students pass their foreign language courses but cannot speak a word of the new language

2. We claim that studying a foreign language is a wonderful thing to do, but make excuses for our own failure to learn another language, saying it is too hard, that we do not have any 'gift' or special 'aptitude' for language learning, or perhaps that we are just 'too old'.

3. Europeans are admired because many are relatively fluent in several languages. Yet, US public schools have done little to promote bilingualism or multilingualism.

4. In the United States when a native English speaker learns French, or Spanish, or Japanese, the study of that foreign language is viewed as enrichment; high school and college students earn academic credit for such efforts. In contrast, the study of English as a second language by 'foreigners' is considered remediation, and few ESL programs grant students any kind of academic credit.

5. We shower praise on our native English speaking, third and fourth generation American friends who do succeed in becoming relatively proficient in a foreign language although most of us cannot determine if they speak grammatically or how strong is their accent. At the same time, immigrants who achieve at least the same level of proficiency in English (which is a foreign language to them) often are deemed uneducated and/or lacking in intelligence because native speakers can hear and judge their accents and grammatical errors (Ford, 1984; Gallois & Callan, 1981; Giles, 1979; Penfield, 1987).

People all over the world use language differences to attribute qualities to speakers including social status, class, personality, level of education, and intelligence (Gallois & Callan, 1981; Giles, 1977; Ryan & Giles, 1982; Scherer and Giles, 1979). In the United States, in which English is the dominant language, those who speak English with a foreign accent or dialects of English are often viewed as somehow being inferior. This is especially true in the case of Spanish accented English (Carranza, 1982; Edwards, 1982; Ford, 1984). Unfortunately, such linguistic prejudice can extend into the mainstream classroom. For example, content-area instructors may not want students enrolled in their courses until they have 'learned' English, and many colleges do not award academic credit for the study of ESL because it is considered a form o remediation.

As this introduction has tried to show, language issues are rarely straight-forward. In fact, discussion of language policies, language instruction, and language learning often elicit very strong opinions. The same person who would beg the question if asked about quarks or prions—saying they know nothing about them—would wax eloquently on how best to educate immi-grant children (without ever reading the literature or studying the research in this field). By virtue of having mastered their native language, people think they automatically qualify as language experts. Fortunately, many researchers are using a much more scientific approach to enhance our under-standing of language acquisition, and some of their findings are discussed below.

Some Fundamentals of Second Language Acquisition Theory and Their Implications in the Science Classroom

Since the 1970s, considerable research has been carried out in the areas of first and second language acquisition. As a result, various factors involved in language learning—such as the impact of the learning environment, the effects of individual learner differences, and the relationship between native language literacy and second language acquisition—are being investigated and identified.

Although many researchers have made significant contributions to the understanding of how languages are learned, the work of two individuals stands out, that of Jim Cummins of the Ontario Institute for Studies in Education, and of Stephen Krashen, Professor of Linguistics at the University of Southern California. Krashen has developed a theoretical framework for understanding the process of L2 acquisition while Cummins has focused on the interdependence of first and second language literacies, the different kinds of language proficiencies, and their implications for bilingual educa-tion. The conclusions drawn by Krashen and Cummins not only have 'intuitive appeal' but also many practical classroom implications. Therefore, in what follows, not only their theories but also what each means in terms of teaching science to college students of limited English proficiency will be discussed.

It is important to note, however, that the findings of Cummins and Krashen are not unconditionally nor universally accepted, and that there are many other investigators who have made significant contributions to the under-standing of second language acquisition and bilingualism. Nonetheless, Cummins and Krashen have been extraordinarily influential, and it is with their work that other studies are usually compared.

In this chapter, five of Krashen's hypotheses will be examined: language learning versus language acquisition; comprehensible input; error correction; the affective filter, and the role of the monitor. Cummins' distinction between conversational and academic language proficiency and the interdependence of first and second language literacies will be described. In addition, special linguistic aptitudes as well as the age factor in the L2 acquisition process will be considered. After presentation of each of these topics, the implications for ESL students in traditional science courses will be addressed.

Language learning versus language acquisition and the role of the monitor

As previously mentioned, babies all over the world appear to absorb their first language in a seemingly effortless process, while adults attempt but often fail to learn a second or foreign language. To better understand this observation, we can turn to the work of Krashen who makes the distinction between unconscious language *acquisition* and conscious language *learning* (Krashen, 1976, 1981, 1982; Krashen, Long & Scarcella, 1979).

According to Krashen, the native language proficiency which all young children develop is an example of unconscious language acquisition. There is no schooling, no lectures, no homework, no vocabulary lists, nor any rules of grammar that must be memorized. Yet, between the ages of two and three— without any lessons—toddlers invariably start speaking.

The struggle embodied in studying a foreign language in high school, college, and later in life represents conscious language learning. This involves the presentation of a new language in a particular sequence by means of a textbook, teacher, classes and homework. Language instruction of this type is based on the belief that if all the rules, vocabulary, verb conjugations, grammar and common idioms can be memorized and remembered, then the learner one day should be able to read, write, speak and understand the new language. As many of us know from personal experience, there is some kind of fallacy to this belief, and as a result, second language learning often is short term and unsuccessful. It might be said that when it comes to first language acquisition, everyone gets a passing grade; however, with second language learning, there are a lot of drop-outs and failures.

Clearly, the processes of language learning and acquisition are not the same. Although Krashen believes that both play a part in the development of second language proficiency by adults, he emphasizes that functioning comfortably in a second language depends primarily on acquisition. In fact, he claims that language learning is useful in a very limited way. According to Krashen, memorizing the 'rules' (e.g. of grammar, verb tenses, or where to place adjectives) helps the language learner to correct or 'monitor' his or her 'output' in the new language. However, 'monitoring'—putting into practice what has been learned about a new language—is only possible *if* there is plenty of time available, *if* correctness of language use is considered important, and *if* the individual can remember the 'rules' (Krashen, 1982: 16).

The monitor can more readily be applied to written language than to oral conversation. Usually there is more time available when preparing written materials, and the writer may have access to various sources of information including books of grammar, dictionaries, textbooks, notebooks, friends and teachers. These resources allow the individual to monitor the text that is being produced, to correct spelling, grammar, word choices, syntax, punctuation, etc. In contrast, conversations take place quickly, and the second language speaker usually does not have time to access learned language. *What* is being said may be much more important than *how* it is being said. In oral exchanges, the speakers do not have time to ponder the 'rules' of a language and may not even be able to remember them. Therefore, a person who has been studying and learning a language for quite some time still may be unable to verbalize his or her thoughts or ask or answer a simple question. This is why Krashen concludes that acquisition is a much more important process in gaining proficiency in L2 than language learning.

Krashen postulates that for acquisition to occur, the human mind needs both sufficient exposure to 'comprehensible input' and time to unconsciously and involuntarily 'appropriate' the new language. When these conditions are met, the learner will develop an intuitive sense that the language sounds right or looks right even if he or she cannot remember the formal rules that govern the language. Unfortunately, adults often abandon their pursuit of a second language too early, that is before acquisition supersedes learning.

Various studies (Dulay, Burt & Krashen, 1982; Ellis, 1986; Krashen, 1981, 1982) have demonstrated that the acquisition of second language grammar follows a 'natural order' or sequence. For example, in the case of English as a second language, the 'ing' ending of words is usually acquired before the proper use of articles ('a' and 'the') while possessives and the third person singular are acquired later. As a result of this natural order of L2 acquisition, L2 learners (both children and adults) tend to make the same kinds of errors ('developmental errors') in a predictable sequence regardless of their native language or age (Dulay, Burt & Krashen, 1982). Although native speakers of a language may be irritated by the errors made by non-native speakers—and attribute them to a lack of study or carelessness—most errors made by L2 learners are a natural part of the language acquisition process.

Implications

Krashen's distinction between language learning and language acquisition helps to explain why two years in an ESL program does not automatically make college students fully proficient in English. Even if they have successfully memorized the rules of grammar and verb conjugations, and have developed an extensive vocabulary in English, the demands of mainstream classes do not leave much time for the application of this 'learned' information. ESL students are too busy trying to master new subject matter and keeping up with assignments. Reading, writing and speaking English are not yet automatic. Comprehension may still be limited and discipline specific vocabulary inadequate. Although ESL students enrolled in science classes are ostensibly learning science, we forget that they also are simultaneously both learning and acquiring proficiency in English.

Comprehensible input

For acquisition of a second language to occur, Krashen emphasizes the importance of 'comprehensible input'. This refers to messages that the learner receives in the new language that he or she can essentially understand. It does not mean that the input must be completely comprehensible. In fact, for language proficiency to improve, Krashen stresses that the messages or 'input' being received must be just 'a little beyond' the L2 learner's current level of competence. For example, if the message is very simple, the learner understands it effortlessly, thereby acquiring no new knowledge about the language. On the other hand, if the 'input' is too complex, then the message will not be understood and will remain meaningless. However, if the learner can comprehend most of the 'input', then the message will for the most part be understood, and the learner's mind will automatically attempt to make sense of the new or unknown part of the message. As a result, the individual's proficiency in the new language grows. Comprehensible input, according to Krashen, can be provided in a variety of settings including the language class, a 'natural' setting, or in a subject-area course. What is essential, however, is that the L2 learner remain focused on the meaning of the communication and not on its form or correctness.

What is especially interesting about comprehensible input is that it does not require that each and every word be understood. Actually, this is a phenomenon that we experience every day in our native language. If we are grading papers or quizzes while half watching and half listening to a television show, we can still follow the story line of the program without 'catching' every word. Or, if we hear only two-thirds of a conversation, we usually can figure out what was discussed in the part we did not hear. How do we 'fill in the blanks'? By considering the context and by drawing on previous experiences and knowledge. According to Krashen, the mind of the L2 learner works the same way, automatically using pre-existing information (linguistic, situational, etc.) to puzzle out what most likely belongs in those parts of a message which are just a 'little beyond' the individual's level of L2 language proficiency. As a result, what was once incomprehensible becomes comprehensible, and L2 language proficiency develops.

Two common forms of 'comprehensible input' are 'caretaker' speech ('motherese') and 'foreigner-talk' (Krashen, 1981, 1982; Dulay, Burt & Krashen, 1982; Ellis, 1986; Larsen-Freeman & Long, 1991).

Caretaker speech refers to the simplified way of talking that parents and others use to ensure that very young children can understand what is being said. Caretaker speech is both grammatically simple and based in the 'here and now', describing things that can be seen or events that are currently taking place. Without being aware of it, parents and caretakers provide comprehensible input; and, as the child's language proficiency increases, so does the complexity of the caretaker speech. As a result, children understand and respond to the 'messages' they receive, and at the same time they unconsciously acquire their first language.

As for foreigner-talk, perhaps you have noticed that sometimes when native language users are speaking to 'foreigners', they shorten their sentences, talk more slowly, try to use simple words, and gesture a lot. (Occasionally, they talk more loudly than necessary as if the non-native speaker were partially deaf.) Clearly, the purpose of foreigner-talk is to improve communication. In fact, not only does it make input comprehensible, but also it promotes the acquisition of the new language by the non-native speaker.

Implications

Clearly, no one would recommend that the science professor instructing LEP undergraduates adapt either caretaker-talk or foreigner-talk. Nonetheless, providing comprehensible input is relevant in the science classroom for both native and non-native English speakers. Students in general will learn less science if the instructor's explanations are confusing or if the textbook is incomprehensible. However, in the case of students of limited English proficiency, the way in which language is used for instructional purposes may be equally as important as the content of the lecture and the readability of the textbook. For example, if the professor uses long, complex sentences with many dependent clauses, then the input may not be comprehensible to the LEP student no matter how well organized the lecture. While native English speakers can focus on the new subject matter, automatically comprehending and interpreting most of the language of the lecture, ESL students may be dividing their attention between trying to understand the new subject matter and attempting to make sense of how the English language is being used. In fact, decoding the lecture may be a very tiring and energy intensive activity.

Instructors of classes that include students who are non-native speakers of English should make a serious effort to provide comprehensible input. This means presenting well organized lectures with clear explanations and using English in a way that can be understood by students who are still acquiring English. For example, an overview of the lecture should be given at the beginning of the class; periodically, the instructor should sum up the material he or she has just presented; new terminology should be written legibly on the chalkboard as well as defined; and several examples should be given to illustrate new concepts. Providing comprehensible input requires some effort on the part of the teacher but may yield large benefits to all students (native and non-native English speaking) in the course.

Comprehensible input applies equally as well to textbooks. Many introductory college science texts have become encyclopedic and are quite difficult to understand. For the instructor concerned with comprehensible input, careful selection of a textbook is just as important as well planned and worded lectures. The textbook should be one that an ESL student can read and understand. In addition, only the pages/chapters/sections actually being covered in the course should be required reading since it takes most ESL students much longer to read and study material in their second language. (See Chapter 6 for a more detailed discussion of textbook related issues.)

So far we have looked at three of Krashen's hypotheses: the difference between language learning and language acquisition, the role of the monitor, and the importance of comprehensible input in promoting L2 acquisition. While Krashen has divided the development of language proficiency along the lines of learned or acquired, we will see in the following section that Cummins dichotomizes language proficiency along different lines, distinguishing between conversational and academic language proficiency. While this classification scheme differs from that of Krashen, the two are not incompatible. Considered together, they help to explain many of the difficulties encountered by mainstreamed ESL students as well as some of the mistaken ideas that content-area instructors have about ESL students.

Conversational vs. academic English proficiency

According to Cummins, the level of English proficiency required for college coursework is much more complex than what is needed in daily conversation. For example, in a casual chat, an LEP student may be able to describe in English a part-time job or what he or she did while on vacation. However, when questioned orally in class or when taking timed, written exams, the same student may find it immensely difficult to explain scientific concepts in English. As a result, the teacher may be surprised when the student cannot express his or her ideas clearly or fails a test. After all, as far as the instructor is concerned, the student *speaks* English so language cannot be the problem in learning the subject matter. The instructor may conclude that the student has not studied sufficiently and/or is not capable of learning scientific material. These are plausible explanations. However, it could be that the instructor has unknowingly mixed up two different types of L2 proficiency, and as a result has mistakenly judged the student's *academic* language skills based on his or her *conversational ability* in English.

Cummins (1980) advises us that conversational English should not be used as a guide for predicting success in the classroom because the kinds of language skills needed to learn academic subject matter and to carry out the types of assignments demanded of students are much more complex than those used in everyday conversation. As a result, he hypothesizes that there exist two types of language proficiencies: BICS and CALP (Cummins, 1980, 1981; Cummins & Swain, 1986).

BICS stands for Basic Interpersonal Communicative Skills and refers to everyday conversational ability that is 'context embedded' (contextualized). During this type of communication, the conversation generally deals with familiar events or matters that require that the speakers react and respond to each other. Facial expressions, hand gestures, and the tone of the speaker's voice may contribute to the negotiation of meaning by the participants in the conversation.

On other occasions—particularly in the academic setting—language is 'context-reduced' (decontextualized). The events or topics being described to the listener are unfamiliar; there is little or no opportunity to negotiate shared meaning which in turn increases the likelihood of information being misunderstood. The college lecture, with the professor presenting a new topic, is an example of context-reduced language. Whether the subject is photosynthesis or covalent bond structure, the information is both abstract and unrelated to the students' everyday activities or life experiences. During the lecture, students may not even be particularly concerned with understanding what is being said. They may be too busy trying to write down the professor's every word since they cannot tell the difference between what is relevant and irrelevant. Since listening to a lecture and taking notes do not necessarily make the subject meaningful, how does the student eventually make sense of this decontextualized input? According to Cummins, this is done by using CALP—cognitive/academic language proficiency.

While BICS may allow an ESL student to chat casually with his or her professor and peers, it is CALP that students must utilize to find meaning in the context-reduced materials presented in the typical classroom. Compared to BICS, CALP requires much higher order language and cognitive skills. In other words, a student's ability to hold a context-embedded conversation (BICS) is not an indicator of his or her CALP. Consequently, when instructors are unaware of the differences between BICS and CALP, they may misjudge the actual level of preparation and ability of an ESL student to handle academically demanding, decontextualized coursework in English.

In Figure 2.1, the BICS/CALP distinction is represented by an iceberg. Above the waterline is conversational language proficiency (BICS) which depends on the surface features of language and lower levels of cognitive processing. Below the waterline is CALP which is related to the meaning of language as well as higher level cognitive processes.

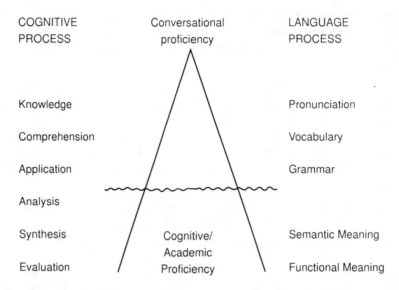

COGNITIVE   Conversational   LANGUAGE
PROCESS   proficiency   PROCESS

Knowledge   Pronunciation

Comprehension   Vocabulary

Application   Grammar

Analysis

Synthesis   Cognitive/   Semantic Meaning
                     Academic
Evaluation   Proficiency   Functional Meaning

Figure 2.1 Surface and deeper levels of language proficiency. (Reprinted by permission from Richard-Amato & Snow, 1992: 18.)

In their native or first language, all children develop BICS. (The only exception noted by Cummins is the severely retarded or autistic child.) He argues that in general it does not matter what IQ a child has or whether or not he or she has any special academic ability or language aptitude. All children learn to communicate in their native or first language. CALP, on the other hand, reflects a combination of language proficiency plus cognitive and memory skills, and it is CALP (not BICS) that will determine an individual's success in school (see Figure 2.2).

Language   CALP   Cognitive and
Proficiency   Memory Skills

Major Determinant of
Educational Progress

Figure 2.2 Relationship of CALP to language proficiency, cognitive and memory skill and educational progress. (Reprinted by permission from Cummins, 1980: 178.)

In the native language, BICS are acquired before a child enters school while CALP develops as schooling progresses. For second language learners,

Cummins postulates that BICS and CALP may develop separately and at different rates. Various studies have demonstrated that BICS—everyday conversational skills—in L2 may emerge in about two years while CALP—academic language skills—often take five to seven years to develop (Cummins, 1981; Collier, 1987; Collier & Thomas, 1989).

Before moving on to discuss the implications of the BICS/CALP dichotomy, there are two additional concerns that must be addressed.

First, after proposing the existence of these two kinds of language proficiencies, Cummins soon recognized that his original 'iceberg' model (which focused on the amount of contextual support) did not take into consideration sufficiently the cognitive demands of a particular task (Cummins & Swain, 1986). As a result, the 'iceberg' representation of BICS and CALP has been supplanted by a figure with four quadrants which portrays not only the degree of contextual embedding but also the cognitive demands of the task (Cummins & Swain, 1986: 153). While the 'iceberg' model is more than sufficient for the purposes of this book, readers who are interested in familiarizing themselves with the newer model are referred to the Cummins & Swain reference (1986: 151-156).

Second, there are a number of criticisms of the BICS/CALP distinction, and these are summed up by Baker (1993: 144-5). For example, one major concern is that the classification of language proficiency into BICS and CALP is an oversimplification and that if not properly understood, this dichotomy could lead to inappropriate forms of classroom instruction. Even with such reservations, the distinction between BICS and CALP remains useful and helps to explain some of the difficulties encountered by ESL students in mainstream courses.

Implications

Faculty members outside the fields of ESL and linguistics are often astounded by the timespan of five to seven years needed to develop CALP in a second language. However, this information does help to explain why two years in an ESL program cannot completely prepare all LEP students for the academic rigors of the mainstream classroom. It also indicates that poor test grades, ungrammatically written assignments and little participation in class discussions do not necessarily mean that ESL students are dumb, lazy, or not studying; rather, these students may still be developing BICS and/or CALP in English. In fact, when it comes to their academic coursework, many may be trying just as hard or harder to succeed than their native English speaking classmates even though their efforts may not manifest themselves in terms of achieving 'good' grades.

The separate natures of BICS and CALP also explain why some ESL students who can barely speak English excel on written exams and assignments while others who converse fairly well in English perform poorly in their classes. The former have well developed CALP, most likely reflecting a high level of education and literacy in the students' native language. The latter have well developed BICS but are lacking in terms of previous formal education and in the development of CALP in their native language.

Achievement in the sciences very much depends on CALP. In fact, BICS is of little importance in many undergraduate science courses since discussion and class participation are often quite limited or non-existent. Even when they do occur, expressing scientific concepts in English in front of an instructor and classmates is certainly not the same experience as an everyday chat in English with one or two friends. For the ESL student who fears making a mistake and/or being laughed at for his or her 'foreign' accent, class discussion may be quite anxiety provoking.

When evaluating ESL students in subject matter courses, instructors may find it hard to distinguish between an assignment or test poorly done because of a student's lack of academic English proficiency (CALP) and inadequate study and preparation. The instructor would certainly need to meet with the student, examine his or her notes, discuss what kind of preparation went into doing the assignment as well as how the student studied before drawing any kind of conclusion. Only in this way can recommendations be made which are appropriate for and helpful to a particular student. While one student may truly be struggling with the English language or the subject matter, another may be working 60 hours a week while enrolled full-time in college. The former may need tutoring while the latter might consider cutting back either his or her workload or courseload.

Linguistic interdependence

Besides the BICS/CALP dichotomy, Cummins has also hypothesized that CALP is transferable from one language to another (Cummins, 1980; Cummins & Swain, 1986). This is what he calls 'linguistic interdependence'. It means that a student who is well educated in his or her native language—be it Korean, Spanish or Farsi—will more easily acquire CALP in a second language because literacy and other cognitive skills transfer from one language to another. Of course, the converse is also true. The student who has poor native language skills and little formal education in L1 will have a much harder time developing CALP in L2.

Cummins explains that the transferability of CALP from L1 to L2 is made possible by the existence in all languages of 'common underlying proficiencies'. These are 'literacy-related functions of language' such as knowledge, concepts and skills which contribute to educational achievement. When developed in one's native language, they are readily usable when a second language is acquired. According to Cummins, it is only the 'surface' features of language—the alphabet, words, grammatical constructions, sounds, and syntax—that are different. Concepts are the same from language to language. (See Figure 2.3.)

Common underlying proficiencies intuitively make sense. For example, the words 'table' in English and 'mesa' in Spanish are symbols that we use to represent a piece of furniture which all of us can identify, regardless of whether it is made of wood, plastic or glass, has four legs or a central pedestal, or is round, square or octagonal. Although 'table' and 'mesa' do not look and sound alike, those differences are only superficial. The two words have the same meaning and evoke the same mental image. What this signifies in terms of linguistic interdependence is that once a concept has been mastered in one language, the language learner only needs to learn the new label in L2 (as well as any unique cultural attachments to the word). However, the concept does not have to be relearned.

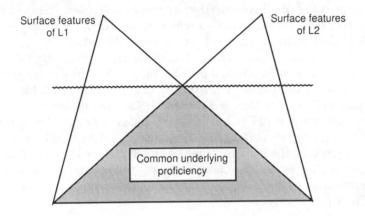

Figure 2.3 The 'dual iceberg' representation of bilingual proficiency. (Reprinted by permission from Cummins & Swain, 1986: 83.)

Implications

Linguistic interdependence strongly affects the performance of non-native English speaking students in the classroom. Some of these students may have received an excellent secondary and possibly college education in their homeland before coming to the United States. As a result, they will be able to transfer language and study skills as well as knowledge in subjects like history, math, science and geography from L1 (their native language) to L2 (their new language—in this case English). For them, learning the English names for concepts/objects may be relatively easy. The more difficult process will be expressing their thoughts and newly acquired knowledge in English.

Other ESL students, because of political or economic conditions in their countries, may have rarely attended school, resulting in less background knowledge in the academic disciplines, less well developed native language proficiency, and a lack of study skills. In other words, they will have little to transfer from L1 to L2. As a result, for students such as these, who gain entry into a college in the United States, failure and attrition may be likely outcomes if appropriate academic support is not provided.

L2 errors and error correction

Developing proficiency in a new language always involves making a lot of errors. When babies and small children babble and chatter, we allow them to do so without correcting their errors. Yet, errors made by adult L2 learners are often interpreted to mean that the person has not yet 'learned the rules' nor adequately studied the language. These notions are a misinterpretation of what is actually occurring.

Linguists distinguish between *errors* and *mistakes* (Larsen-Freeman & Long, 1991: 59–60). We all make mistakes when we are tired, for example, or in a hurry. Mistakes occur occasionally, but if we make them, we know how to correct what we have done wrong. Language errors made by L2 learners, however, cannot be self-corrected because they reflect the current state of L2 proficiency of the individual. The majority of errors made by L2 learners are 'developmental' (Dulay, Burt & Krashen, 1982). This means that the errors made by adult learners of ESL are the same kinds of errors that children make when learning English as their first language. Developmental errors are not due to inference by the student's first language nor are they due to a lack of study; rather they reflect the 'natural order' of language acquisition which was described on page 43. (For a discussion of interference errors see Box 2.1, pages 55–58.)

Implications

The unavoidability of L2 errors has some interesting implications when it comes to dealing with ESL students. Learning to communicate in a new language involves taking risks. The speaker (or writer) inevitably finds that there are thoughts that he or she cannot express as desired, words that are still missing from his or her L2 vocabulary, grammatical constructions that cannot readily be transposed from one language to another, and embarrassing blunders and *faux pas* that occasionally occur. Still, it is the person who is trying to master a new language who makes all these errors; indeed, the only way to avoid them is not to use the new language! As Krashen points out, 'learning' a language through memorization, repetition and drills, does not produce fluency. Rather, it is 'acquisition' that will eventually lead to an intuitive sense of what is correct and incorrect use of a second language, and it is acquisition of the language which invariably involves making a lot of errors.

For ESL students, much of their acquisition of English and many of the mistakes that they cannot help but make will take place in the mainstream academic classroom. These errors do not reflect stupidity, lack of study, or the absence of desire to become proficient in English. It is important for instructors to understand that making errors in L2 is both normal and unavoidable. Nevertheless, many teachers (and native language speakers) with the best of intentions tend to have an almost irresistible urge to correct the errors (both spoken and written) made by LEP students. When an ESL student talks, there is that desire to interrupt in order to correct verb tenses and sentence structure or to improve word choices. On exams and written assignments, the teacher gets out the pen with red ink to indicate spelling errors and faulty grammar. Although instructors mean well and sincerely believe that they are helping students to become more proficient in English, their corrections are not necessarily having that effect. Studies show that error correction, verbal and written, does not speed up L2 acquisition nor improve subsequent performance (Dulay, Burt & Krashen, 1982; Krashen, 1982).

As Krashen (1982: 75) explains: 'Error correction has the immediate effect of putting the student on the defensive. It encourages a strategy in which the student will try to avoid mistakes, avoid difficult constructions, focus less on meaning and more on form. It may disrupt the entire communicative focus on an exchange.' In other words, correcting the language errors of LEP students, no matter how well intended, may be counterproductive. In the classroom, for example, extensive error correction may cause the LEP student to write less and to participate (talk) less which in turn could inhibit learning.

Some faculty members get particularly annoyed by how ESL students write, even when the errors do not interfere with the reader's ability to comprehend what has been written. Studies have shown that how harshly instructors judge such errors depends on a variety of factors including their academic specialty. Apparently, science faculty (when compared to their colleagues in the social sciences, education, and humanities) are the least tolerant of the kinds of writing errors made by ESL students (Santos, 1988; Vann, Meyer & Lorenz, 1984; Vann, Lorenz & Meyer, 1991).

The implications of this observation are not known, but several questions do come to mind. Does this finding mean that science faculty hold their students to higher standards or are the science faculty just less flexible or tolerant? Does greater irritation by the errors in ESL students' assignments affect the grading of written assignments even if the errors do not interfere with comprehensibility? What happens when ESL students are in science courses that are part of a college's 'writing across the curriculum' program? Is any special training given to the faculty members teaching such courses or help provided to the ESL students taking them?

If error correction does not in general improve the language acquisition of the ESL student, the issue then becomes what should content-area faculty do about the language errors made by LEP students? Since most of us cannot just ignore them, we can follow some of Krashen's (1982: 118) advice. He recommends that corrections be limited to those which 'interfere with communication or impede the intelligibility of a message; errors that are the most stigmatized, that cause the most unfavorable reactions; and errors that occur most frequently.' For the instructor who insists on making corrections, addressing these three classes of errors will be much less time consuming and of greater assistance to the student.

What may be much more beneficial for the L2 student than error correction is modeling a better way of saying or writing whatever it was that the student did inappropriately. In this way, the student is exposed to the correct use of the English language but does not have to be made to feel embarrassed or stupid for having made an error. While error correction may contribute to language learning (and in this way may be quite helpful to some students), modeling appropriate language usage will promote L2 acquisition.

In the sciences, it is relatively easy to focus attention on content rather than on lexical or grammatical errors. Attention can be paid to whether or not the scientific information conveyed by the student is essentially accurate, given the student's level of proficiency in English. If the grammar or spelling of the student is truly disturbing to the instructor, corrections should be limited to the one or two most frequent or irritating types of errors.

The professor who demands perfect, standard, grammatically correct English on written assignments from all students (including LEPs) and who grades accordingly should be available during office hours to help students with the drafting or revision of assignments. If the instructor cannot or is not willing to do this, or if the class and/or the number of LEP students is large, then students should be referred to the appropriate learning resource facility or ESL tutoring center on campus.

For written, take-home assignments, students often have enough time to get help to correct their grammar, spelling and use of language. However, this is not possible during timed, written exams. In this case, LEP students should not be evaluated for grammar or spelling. Grading should be based on content. In addition, LEP students may need extra time when taking exams if what is being assessed is what they have learned and know, not the speed with which they can respond to questions in English.

The 'age' factor in second language acquisition

While some teachers are dismayed by the written work of their ESL students, others are equally as disturbed by their students' accents. What these instructors fail to appreciate is that as adult L2 learners, ESL college students will almost always speak English with an accent. Although an accent may be annoying to the listener, it does not necessarily impair communication. Accented English does not automatically mean that the speech is incomprehensible.

In general, only young children have the ability to make all the sounds appropriate to a given language; around puberty, that vocal flexibility disappears (Cummins, 1980; Harley, 1986; Singleton, 1989). As a result, most adult L2 learners do not and will not be able to sound like native speakers.

Although this connection between age of the L2 learner and pronunciation is well documented, the relationship between age and other aspects of L2 acquisition is extremely complex. For example, whether children or adults are 'better' L2 learners very much depends on the aspect of L2 proficiency which is being examined, e.g. 'global' level of achievement, effects of formal and informal learning environments, or mastery of grammar (Cummins, 1980, 1981; Cummins & Swain, 1986; Harley, 1986; Krashen, Long & Scarcella, 1979; Larsen-Freeman, 1991; Larsen-Freeman & Long, 1991; Singleton, 1989). For the purposes of this book, the specifics of each of the many investigations comparing younger and older L2 learners are unimportant. Rather, what is significant is that there is plenty of evidence that adults can become very proficient in a second language even if they can never lose their accent.

Implications

ESL undergraduates are adult L2 learners so that pronunciation may remain 'a problem'. For example, native Spanish speakers may always have trouble with the pronunciation of /i/ in words such as 'is' (saying something that sounds like 'ease') while native speakers of Japanese may tend to substitute /r/ for /l/ (saying 'retter' instead of 'letter'). (Box 2.1 describes some of the typical interference errors that affect L2 English.) Although students may

---

Box 2.1 The Pitfalls of English

I take it you already know
Of tough and bough and cough and dough?
Others may stumble, but not you
On hiccough, thorough, laugh and through?
Well done! And now you wish perhaps
To learn of less familiar traps?

Beware of heard, a dreadful word,
That looks like beard and sounds like bird.
And dead: it's said like bed, not bead,
For Goodness' sake, don't call it 'deed'!
Watch out for meat and great and threat
They rhyme with suite and straight and debt.

From Anonymous, *Hints on Pronunciation for Foreigners.*

The scientific study of languages, linguistics, reveals not only the differences between languages but also helps to explain why native speakers of a given language may have particular difficulties with a second language. To the native speaker of English, the linguistic characteristics of English are considered the norm. However, to a native speaker of Japanese, the linguistic characteristics of English are abnormal. In order to become proficient in a second language, the learner must be willing to relinquish his or her long-held linguistic norms based on the mother tongue. This is not necessarily easy to do. Sometimes, some of the structures and pronunciation of the native language interfere with appropriate production of the second language.

Consider the following examples which highlight some of the differences between English and the native languages of ESL students:

1. *In English, spelling and pronunciation are not always directly related.* This can be troublesome, particularly for students whose native languages are relatively phonetic, such as Spanish, Portuguese and Filipino. In those languages, most written symbols represent one sound, so that the way a word is spelled clearly indicates how it is pronounced and vice versa. Unfortunately, English is not at all so clear cut. For example, we have 'their', 'there', and 'they're'; these are three different words with three different meanings and three different spellings; nevertheless, they sound alike. Then too, we have pairs of words, such as 'bought/caught' and 'through/threw' that have similar sounds but are spelled differently and have different meanings. Next, consider the word 'sign'. It has only one pronunciation and one spelling, but it might be referring to a poster advertising a concert or to some kind of omen that something bad is going to happen. Clearly, the context (physical or linguistic) is important in providing the correct interpretation of the word's meaning. Moreover, some words change their pronunciation depending on their grammatical usage. Consider the word 'live' in the following sentences: 'This television show is brought to you *live* [adjective] from Los Angeles,' but, 'I *live* [verb] in New York City.' Or, 'I *refuse* [verb] to take out the garbage,' and 'Because of the garbage strike, there is a lot of *refuse* [noun] piling up in the streets.'

2. *The sounds of spoken English differ from those in some other languages.* For example, the 'th' sounds (as in <u>th</u>under or <u>th</u>en) do not exist in Farsi, Japanese, or many of the Indian languages. Native speakers of those languages may have difficulty producing 'th', thereby substituting a 't', 's', 'z', or 'd' sound, saying <u>t</u>under (for <u>th</u>under) or <u>d</u>en or perhaps <u>z</u>en (for <u>th</u>en). In Hindi there is only one sound for 'v' and 'w'. Therefore, an Indian student may have trouble with the pronunciation of words such as 'very' and 'wet', saying instead 'wery' and 'vet'. The Korean language has one symbol that represents the sounds of 'l' and 'r', and the pronunciation of this symbol varies with its position in the word. As a result, Korean speakers of English may have problems distinguishing between and correctly pronouncing 'r' and 'l'. This is especially true when these letters appear at the beginning of words, so that students may say 'retter' instead of 'letter' or 'lice' instead of 'rice'. Native Spanish speakers often have trouble with the pronunciation of the English vowel 'i'. In Spanish, this letter has one sound, the equivalent of the English vowel sound in sh<u>ee</u>p and s<u>ea</u>t. For this reason, Spanish speakers may pronounce English words such as 'is' and 'still' like 'ease' and 'steal'.

3. *Real life English usage may not resemble what ESL instructors and textbooks teach.* For example, learning the Roman alphabet may not be particularly difficult for most ESL students regardless of their native language. However, what they learn about the proper formation of English letters may only remotely resemble the professor's handwriting. If written sloppily, 'n' and 'h' look pretty much the same. So do 'l' and a 't' that does not get 'crossed'. Another example of

how real-life language usage differs from what is taught in the classroom is what happens when we speak: we run our words together so that 'I do not know' becomes 'I dunno' and 'What are you going to do?' becomes 'Watchagonna do?' For the non-native English speaker, figuring out what is being said becomes somewhat more difficult than decoding the measured words that may be used in the language classroom. As in all languages, English also has its own special idioms, colloquialisms, and slang that are used regularly whether in the classroom or in casual conversation. These expressions—when translated literally—often make no sense to the ESL student. Imagine the picture that comes to mind upon hearing the following idioms: 'Let's not beat around the bush', 'I need to pick his brains', or 'I want to bounce a few ideas off of them'.

4. *Grammar differs from one language to another.* For example, in English we can only use one negative in a sentence; however, Spanish grammar requires what we in English would consider 'double negatives'. In English we say, 'I am not going to talk to anybody.' The equivalent in Spanish is '*No voy a hablar con nadie,*' which when literally translated means, 'I am not going to talk to nobody'. This is the reason why native Spanish speakers may produce sentences with double negatives such as 'I no able to do nothing today,' or 'I no understand nothing in this textbook'.

In Korean, there are no words to distinguish the gender differences between the third person pronouns 'he' and 'she'. Therefore, a native Korean speaker may easily mix up the two, producing a sentence such as 'My sister, he is coming to visit.'

The rules for agreement between nouns and adjectives also vary from language to language. For example, in English we say 'blue dishes' or 'tall trees'; adjectives precede nouns, and they remain singular even when the nouns they describe are plural. However, in Spanish, adjectives have to be plural to agree with plural nouns and, in addition, adjectives follow nouns: *libros azules* and *árboles altos* (translated literally to 'books blues' and 'trees talls'). These differences in agreement between nouns and adjectives and/or in the position of adjectives may carry over from Spanish into English. For example, a native Spanish speaking student might say or write 'I saw the *bigs dogs*'.

A related phenomenon occurs, for example, with speakers of Cantonese. Their nouns usually do not show plurals, so when speaking or writing in English, a native Cantonese speaking student might produce 'four yellow pencil' or 'several tall tree'.

Correct word order in sentences can also be troublesome. Declarative sentences in English require the following sequence: subject-verb-object ('The dog bit him'). However, other languages arrange sentences differently. In Japanese, the word sequence is subject-object-verb, so that a Japanese ESL student might produce sentences in English such as 'He money steal'. or 'She dogs sees'.

In a language like Spanish, the endings of verbs indicate the subject pronoun so that it does not have to be written or spoken. For example, in English we would say or write: I talk, you (singular) talk, he/she talks, we talk, you (plural) talk, they talk. In Spanish, the I/you/he/she/we/you/they can be omitted since the verb endings mark the subject: *hablo* (I talk), *hablas* (familiar, singular, you talk), *habla* (he/she or formal you talk), *hablamos* (we talk), *hablan* (plural you or they talk). When native Spanish speakers are first learning English, they may omit the subject of the verb. For example, a student may write, 'Talked yesterday', and the reader cannot figure out who talked (I, you, he, she, we, they?) even though the student knows who did the talking.

The examples cited above only begin to touch upon the numerous differences that exist between English and the native languages of many of our ESL students. Yet, even this brief introduction to what linguists call 'contrastive analysis' helps explain why one ESL student writes a sentence that is missing a subject or another places the adjective after the noun it describes. Perhaps a more important point to consider is that even if these 'errors' are annoying, they do not necessarily interfere with the content or meaning of what the student is attempting to write or to say.

The bibliography that follows provides many more examples of the similarities and differences between English and other languages. These may be helpful in dealing with specific populations of ESL students.

CALIFORNIA DEPARTMENT OF EDUCATION 1992, *Handbook for Teaching Korean-American Students*. Sacramento, CA: California Department of Education.

CALIFORNIA STATE DEPARTMENT OF EDUCATION 1989, *A Handbook for Teaching Cantonese-Speaking Students*. Sacramento, CA: California State Department of Education.

CALIFORNIA STATE DEPARTMENT OF EDUCATION 1987, *Handbook for Teaching Japanese-Speaking Students*. Sacramento, CA: California State Department of Education.

CALIFORNIA STATE DEPARTMENT OF EDUCATION 1986, *Handbook for Teaching Pilipino-Speaking Students*. Sacramento, CA; California State Department of Education.

CALIFORNIA STATE DEPARTMENT OF EDUCATION 1989, *A Handbook for Teaching Portuguese-Speaking Students*. Sacramento, CA: California State Department of Education.

LEKI, I. 1992, *Understanding ESL Writers*. Portsmouth, NH: Boynton/ Cook.

SWAN, M. and SMITH, B. (Eds) 1987, *Learner English*. Cambridge, England: Cambridge University Press.

be embarrassed by speaking with an accent, the latter is usually of little consequence in the science classroom. This is because speaking accented English has nothing to do with the kinds of abilities (e.g. Cummins' CALP) that promote science learning. Indeed, what adult L2 learners lack in verbal proficiency may be more than compensated for by the skills and knowledge that they bring to the academic setting. The latter, however, is dependent on the individual's having had several years of formal schooling in his or her native language prior to attempting academic work in L2 (Collier, 1987; Cummins, 1980; Cummins & Swain, 1986). For examples of this, one need not look any further than the international students who are successfully pursuing advanced degrees in math, science, and engineering in US graduate schools in spite of any difficulties they may have with spoken English.

Native English speakers sometimes presume that accented English indicates that a person really does not 'know' the language, perhaps lacks intelligence, or that what he or she is saying contains incorrect information (Carranza, 1982; Edwards, 1982; Gallois & Callan, 1981). Clearly, these assumptions may be quite mistaken. Although an accent may slow down verbal communication (because the listener is having trouble understanding what is being said), it in no way reflects the cognitive/academic ability of the speaker.

The significance of 'ethnic speech markers' (including pronunciation, the use of grammar, and tone) and the relationships that develop between members of ethnic groups and speakers of dominant and subordinate languages can be explained in social and psychological terms (Giles, 1979). For example, native English speakers react differently to the accented speech of various ethnic groups. While the accents of Europeans speaking English are often perceived as being charming, quaint, or cultured, this is not the case with many of today's immigrants especially those from Central and South America and Asia. Their accents are interpreted to mean that the speaker is not only deficient in English but also lacking in education. Linguistic preju-dice of this type is even experienced by immigrants who were professionals in their native lands—physicians, veterinarians, lawyers, dentists—who may end up working in factories or doing much lower level jobs in the United States until and if they can master English, earn enough money, and get recre-dentialed and relicensed to practice their professions in the US.

Concerns about their verbal proficiency may motivate non-native speakers to select majors and courses where the least amount of spoken English is required. Although some LEP students are not particularly embarrassed by having an accent, others are. The latter rarely participate voluntarily or speak up during class, and they may be reluctant to seek the help of faculty members during office hours. ESL students admit that it is very disturbing and discouraging when native speakers almost reflexively respond to the sound of their accented English by saying, 'What?'

It is ironic to note that many Americans blame their failure to learn a foreign language in high school, college, or later in life on their being 'too old' when they began their language studies. However, if age were the cause of such failure, then most undergraduates enrolled in ESL programs would never become proficient in English. Clearly, other factors besides age come into play in the L2 learning/acquisition process. For example, what about that oft referred to special 'gift' or 'aptitude' for language learning?

Is there a special gift or aptitude for languages?

Although some adults learn foreign languages more easily and more rapidly than others, researchers have found it difficult both to prove the existence of and to measure an 'innate linguistic aptitude' (Baker, 1993; Ellis, 1986; Krashen, 1981; Larsen-Freeman, 1991; Larsen-Freeman & Long, 1991). Language apti-tude (what is sometimes called a 'gift' for languages) may actually reflect many factors including motivation to become proficient in the target language, the methods of language instruction, the intelligence of the learner, as well as the learner's formal study skills. In addition, the student's self-confidence, level of anxiety in the learning environment, personality, attitude toward the teacher and classroom, as well as degree of identification with the new language and culture may also influence the learner's apparent 'aptitude' for his or her new language.

Implications

For the ESL undergraduate, the existence of a special 'gift' or 'aptitude' for the acquisition of English might be helpful, but it is not necessarily relevant. Proficiency in English must be developed in order to do well academically and to earn a college degree. Interestingly enough, ESL students struggling with the language may say that English is 'hard' or that they get embarrassed speaking English in public. They may be frustrated with how long it takes to master English or by the fact they will never be as proficient in English as in their native tongue. Nevertheless, in spite of their difficulties, you will not hear them saying that they cannot learn English because they are 'too old' or because they lack some special linguistic 'aptitude'. They cannot give up on English unless they want to give up on their education and career goals.

The affective filter

Not surprisingly, emotions, motivation, and anxiety affect L2 acquisition. For example, comprehensible input will not be processed by the learner who is anxious, upset, or intimidated. Although Duley & Burt (1977) were among the first to refer to the relationship between 'affective delimitors' and L2 acquisition, it was Krashen (1981, 1982) who championed the connection. He postulated that an 'affective filter' exists that can decrease or increase the intake of comprehensible input. When the affective filter is high/strong, intake is blocked and L2 acquisition reduced; when the affective filter is low/weak, intake is facilitated, promoting second language acquisition (see Figure 2.4).

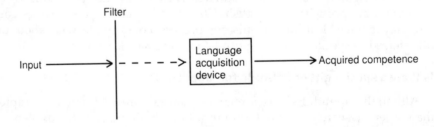

Figure 2.4 Operation of the 'affective filter' (Reprinted by permission from Krashen, 1982: 32.)

Implications

Classroom conditions can raise and lower the affective filter. For example, continuously correcting L2 errors will raise the affective filter for ESL students while a classroom environment that boosts self-confidence and reduces anxiety will lower the affective filter. When the latter happens, both L2 acquisition and content learning increase.

The concept of the affective filter is applicable in two ways to the introductory science course because it can promote (or inhibit) both science learning by all students as well as the acquisition of English by LEP students. Many students, particularly non-science majors, are especially afraid to take science courses; science has the reputation of being a difficult subject, demanding a lot of work but not necessarily yielding good grades. Science as traditionally taught raises the affective filter for many students. Therefore, whatever science instructors can do to lower the affective filter—perhaps by reducing the competitive atmosphere and building a sense of community in the classroom, or by organizing cooperative learning and study groups—will increase how much science all students learn. Furthermore, by providing necessary academic support and by paying closer attention to how they use English as the language of instruction, faculty members can promote the acquisition of English by the non-native speakers enrolled in the course.

Some Comments on Mainstream ESL Students

Second language acquisition is a complex process, and the principles described here only skim the surface. However, the issues discussed above do provide some insight into why non-native English speaking students taking mainstream courses may experience difficulties.

As the number of ESL students increases on campuses across the nation, there is a growing need to somehow bridge the gap between what is known about the process of L2 acquisition and the expectations of content-area instructors. As a result, researchers are beginning to take a closer look at two important issues. One is how mainstream faculty perceive the academic abilities and performance of ESL students; the other is the gap that exists between what an ESL program can provide its students and the demands of content-area courses taught in English (Russikoff, 1994; Snow & Kinsella, 1994; Swartley, 1994).

ESL students are usually very much aware of their lack of proficiency in English. Even those who have successfully completed an ESL program still do not feel ready to compete with native speakers of English in the mainstream college classroom. In a study conducted by Smoke (1988), 198 ESL students enrolled at a four-year City University of New York college were asked if they felt prepared for mainstream college courses when their 'remediation' was completed. Eighteen per cent said 'yes', 57% responded 'somewhat', and 25% indicated that they were 'not prepared'. About a quarter of these students recommended the addition of more ESL coursework in pronunciation and speech, and in writing research papers. The majority indicated that they had problems with 'understanding how to read and study from textbooks' (92%), 'writing research papers' (87%), 'talking to the professors' (81%), 'taking notes from lecture classes' (74%), and with 'answering exam questions' (71%).

Ostler (1980) in an earlier study had noted that advanced ESL students who were already taking mainstream courses felt very unprepared. Her subjects were 133 ESL students with 27 different majors at the University of Southern California. Seventy-two per cent were undergraduates and the rest were graduate students. Ostler found that almost all the students regardless of their majors felt they most needed help with reading texts (90%), taking notes in class (84%) and with asking questions in class (68%). Fifteen students in her sample were studying the 'hard sciences'. Their top four areas of 'need' involved reading their textbooks (100%), taking class notes (86%), asking questions in class (67%), and laboratory experiments (60%).

In terms of what is known about the rate of L2 acquisition, Ostler's and Smoke's findings should not be surprising; it generally takes five to seven years to develop cognitive/academic language proficiency (Collier, 1987; Collier & Thomas, 1989; Cummins, 1981) while a college ESL program typically lasts two years and may emphasize BICS over CALP. As a result, ESL students in the mainstream classroom face the extremely difficult task of learning new content in a language they are still trying to master. This is why what the content-area instructor does or does not do can strongly influence the achievement of such students.

Conclusion

Larsen-Freeman (1991: 335-8) in a recent review of L2 acquisition literature noted ten issues of particular relevance for teachers who work with LEP students:

1. 'The learning/acquisition process is complex.' There are many ways to teach and learn a second language, and what works for one student may not work for another.
2. 'The process is gradual.' Developing L2 proficiency takes a long time.
3. 'The process is nonlinear.' It involves making errors and a lot of 'backsliding' as new structures are acquired. Memorizing a new word or grammatical structure does not mean that the student will use it correctly at all times in the future.
4. 'The process is dynamic.' As they become more proficient in the new language, learners change their cognitive strategies.
5. 'Learners learn when they are ready to do so.' Students can only master

aspects of the new language for which they are prepared, and this follows a natural progression that generally cannot be altered.

6. 'Learners rely on the knowledge and experience they have.' Individuals use what they already know about language(s) as they actively engage in developing proficiency in another language.

7. 'It is not clear from research findings what the role of negative evidence is in helping learners reject erroneous hypotheses they are currently entertaining.' Error correction may be helpful or harmful depending on how it is done.

8. 'For most adult learners, complete mastery of the L2 may be impossible.' Pronunciation may remain accented, and certain aspects of the new language may be especially difficult to master.

9. 'There is tremendous individual variation among language learners.' Students develop proficiency in a new language at different rates and achieve different levels of mastery.

10. 'Learning a language is a social phenomenon.' For most individuals, language is a means of oral and written communication, and it is acquired by interaction with other members of society. Much of what happens in the classroom is attributable to the teacher's and learners' social needs.

These ten characteristics of L2 acquisition need to be kept in mind by all instructors who teach ESL/LEP students, and that includes science faculty. Confronted with the changing undergraduate demographics and the dwindling number of science majors, professors have a choice to make. They can continue to say that the language difficulties of LEP students do not concern them; their job is to teach science. However, such an attitude may lead to further attrition from the science pipeline. Or, faculty members can modify how they teach to better meet the needs of students who are learning science through a new and unfamiliar language. By selecting this second option, we might find that more students, both majority and minority, native and non-native English speaking, end up majoring in the sciences. Isn't this one of the goals of science education reform?

3 The Many Cultures of the Science Classroom

While the topic of 'culture' may seem out of place in a book about teaching science to language minority students, there are many aspects of culture that strongly affect the science classroom. Examples include the course content (what is and is not taught), how and from what perspective information is presented, and the attitudes, behavior, and language of the teacher and of the students. The effects of culture in the classroom may not be particularly noticeable when teachers and their students share a common language and culture. However, with an increasingly multilingual and multicultural student population, cultural differences may manifest themselves in a variety of unexpected ways. It is for these reasons that this chapter addresses a variety of culture-related issues. Among these are the culture of the science we teach, students' prior knowledge about science, classroom culture, the characteristics of the 'successful' science student, and the omission of cultural considerations from plans to reform science education. In subsequent chapters additional culture-related topics are discussed including learning styles (Chapter 4) and rhetoric and writing styles (Chapter 6).

What Does Culture Mean?

The word 'culture' evokes many images. It may make us think of the anthropologist doing fieldwork, studying the marriage customs, housing arrangements, and the economic system of a group of 'exotic' people in a distant land. On the other hand, we may associate the word 'culture' with those educated and refined members of society who listen to classical music, read serious literary works, and who frequent art museums.

There is, however, another interpretation of the meaning of 'culture'. As described by Bennett (1990: 47), culture is:

> 'a system of shared knowledge and belief that shapes human perceptions and generates social behavior ... where we happen to be born, and when, largely determines the culture we acquire.'

From this perspective, culture defines the world view, value system, and what is considered appropriate behavior within a given society. It also molds how group members communicate, determining the appropriate use of both the native language and nonverbal communication. In other words, culture is a learned way of life which is transmitted from generation to generation. (See Box 3.1 for further discussion of nonverbal communication).

Box 3.1 Nonverbal Communication

From studies of two-person interactions, Birdwhistell (1974: 213–214) estimated that more than 65% of communication is nonverbal. To many people this figure is quite startling, particularly considering all the years spent in school studying verbal and written language as a means of communication. Often, we are unaware of the large amount of information transmitted from one person to another through gestures and behavior.

According to Dr Annette Lopez (the Director of the Center for Bilingual Education at Kean College of New Jersey, Union, NJ):

'Each culture has its own nonverbal system which is learned totally out of awareness. By the time children reach age five, their communication system includes oral language and nonverbal behavior, and both are culturally determined. Each individual actually learns to 'speak' two languages, a verbal one and a nonverbal one. Schools give us overt lessons in the development of our verbal language, but our nonverbal language is acquired unconsciously. Usually, we are unaware of it until we come across someone whose nonverbal messages clash with or differ from our own.'

Nonverbal communication includes many components such as the frequency of touching; the use of interpersonal space; gestures and body movements; eye contact; pitch, tone, and voice intonation; and the use of time. How each is used and its importance varies from culture to culture. Thus, when individuals from two different cultures try to communicate, more than the use of each other's language is involved. Difficulties may arise not only in understanding what each other is trying to say but also from misinterpretation of nonverbal forms of communication. Depending on the situation, the results of misreading nonverbal cues may be comical, embarrassing, or outright offensive. For example:

- An American in Brazil or Germany may quite unwittingly offend his or her host by the use of the hand gesture that involves touching the tip of the thumb to the tip of the index finger with the other three fingers of the hand extended. While the American intends to signal that everything is 'okay', the German or Brazilian is appalled by this vulgar and obscene gesture (Axtell, 1993: 47).
- Or, as Lopez points out, 'Our ears become attuned to the sounds of our native language, and often we will interpret the sounds of other languages based on our own system of pitch, tone, and intonation.' For this reason native English speakers sometimes conclude that speakers of Arabic and Chinese are always angry. This is because the sounds of those languages seem harsh to American ears.

All sorts of nonverbal miscommunications can and do occur in the classroom when the teacher and students come from different cultures:

- When an instructor asks students, 'Do you understand?', an American student might request that the instructor re-explain the entire topic. In contrast, a student who has recently arrived from Vietnam may not respond at all (implying that he or she does understand) or may say 'yes' even though not one word or idea was understood. Why would a student fail to avail himself or herself of the help that is offered? According to Vietnamese custom, the student is showing respect for the teacher (Garner, 1989).

- In the United States, students are expected to look directly at their teachers when asking and answering questions. The student who fails to look at the teacher is thought to be unprepared or hiding something. This presents problems for Asian and American Indian students who have been taught to show respect and courtesy by looking down and keeping their eyes averted (California Department of Education, 1991: 31; Garner, 1989).

Lopez advises us that 'Although we may not always be able to prevent such misunderstandings, we can increase our awareness of the importance of nonverbal communication. Recognizing that there are differences without being judgmental is essential in order to live within our very multicultural/multilingual society.'

Additional information about nonverbal communication can be obtained by contacting Dr. Lopez at the following address:

Dr Annette Lopez
Director, Center for Bilingual Education
Kean College of New Jersey
Morris Avenue
Union, NJ 07083
Phone: 908-527-2477 (or 2405)
Fax: 908-355-5143

Most people remain unaware of how strongly culture influences all that they do. As Hall (1959: 70) pointed out. 'Entire systems of behavior made up of hundreds of thousands of details are passed from generation to generation, and nobody can give the rules for what is happening. Only when these rules are broken do we realize they exist.'

Because culture is so deeply engrained, each of us tends to think that our own culture (the culture in which we were raised) is the correct one and that those who do not share it must in some way be different, abnormal, or even inferior. For example, isn't it 'normal' to greet people by shaking hands? When eating lunch with a friend, don't we sit opposite each other? Aren't we taught to avoid using double negatives when we speak and write? However, if we had been born and raised in other parts of the world, we might bow when greeting others, sit side-by-side with a friend at the lunch table, or our native language might require the use of double negatives.

The effects of cultural differences in the classroom range in magnitude. For example, an immigrant student trying to express his or her appreciation may give a gift to the teacher. Often it is some memento from the student's homeland. Misunderstanding the intent of the gift, the teacher refuses to accept it thinking that perhaps the student is trying to use the gift as a bribe to influence his or her grades. The end result is that the teacher has misjudged the student's actions, and the student is left bewildered and hurt. While we might classify this incident as a relatively small (though still disturbing) cultural misunderstanding, other effects of culture in the classroom may be longer lasting and may affect generations of students. Examples of the latter include the absence of certain information and alternative perspectives from the curriculum; prejudice against or low teacher expectations for minority students; and the attitude that the study of a foreign language is enrichment while the study of English as a second language is remediation. In a science classroom, there rarely is any explicit reference to culture, yet students must contend implicitly not only with the classroom culture but also the culture of science. As Hall (1976: 180) points out: 'In certain contexts, the structures of culture and education are synonymous, and we can learn about one by studying the other.'

The Culture of the Science We Teach

Quite often, basic science texts and teachers of introductory science courses introduce their subject by presenting the scientific method(s). This invariably includes discussion of the characteristics that make science different from (and superior to) all other 'ways of knowing': it is objective, based on observations that can be reproduced, and is universal and culturally neutral. Scientists are described as making every effort to keep their personal biases out of their research; it is explained that the methods of science are the same in research laboratories all over the world, and that the theories and laws of science are equally as valid in one part of the world as in another.

Science, as taught today, begins with the premise that through observation and investigation, we (that is, scientists) can learn why things happen in the world around us. With this knowledge we can then predict, possibly modify, or even change the course of future events so that progress will take place and the quality of human life improve. Indeed, by means of science, nature can be understood and sometimes controlled (Samovar, Porter & Jain, 1981; Stewart, 1972).

Not everyone, however, agrees with this image of science. For example, many have argued that science cannot possibly be objective or neutral since it is practiced by humans who often are totally unaware of their own cultural biases (Banks, 1993; Gordon, Miller & Rollock, 1990; Hall, 1959; Kelly, Carlsen & Cunningham, 1993; Locke, 1992; Maddock, 1986; Middlecamp, 1989; Rosser, 1990; Saville-Troike, 1978; Stanley & Brickhouse, 1994). Thus, *which* 'scientific' issues are studied, *how* they are investigated and interpreted, and *who* carries out such studies are all culturally influenced.

Similarly, the use of science to understand and eventually control nature is not esteemed by all cultures (Anderson, 1988; Banks, 1993; Gallagher & Dawson, 1986; Hall, 1959; Locke, 1992; Samovar, Porter & Jain, 1981; Sitaram & Cogdell, 1976; Stewart, 1972). Rather, it has been described as being primarily characteristic of modern, 'Western', technologically oriented societies in which individuality, efficiency and progress are valued, and people look toward and work for a better future. In contrast, other cultures (generally portrayed as 'non-Western') revere the past, search for the truth by spiritual means, place the well-being of the group before that of the individual, and believe that humans should attempt to live harmoniously with nature.

Clearly, the classification of world views into 'Western' and 'non-Western' is an oversimplification. Members of any society show considerable variation in their beliefs, and stereotyping all members of any culture should be avoided. Consider the following example: The 'Western' world view is typically associated with the United States and its citizens. Yet, in terms of their values and beliefs, many American Indians are more 'non-Western' than 'Western'. This is particularly true when it comes to attitudes toward science and nature. As a result, cultural conflicts may develop when Native Americans study traditional science. (See Box 3.2 for a more detailed description of Native Americans in higher education and the study of science.)

Box 3.2 Native Americans and the Study of Science

Native American college students who earn a Bachelor's degree most often major in business and management, education, the social sciences, health sciences, and psychology (National Center for Education Statistics, US Department of Education). Very few study science. For example, in 1990 American Indians/Alaskan Natives earned 4,212 Bachelor's degrees; however, only 73 were in the physical and 130 in the biological sciences (National Science Foundation, 1992). With such a small pool of potential graduate students, it is not surprising to learn that in 1990 American Indians/Alaskan Natives earned 9 Master's degrees in the physical and 14 in the biological sciences. As for Doctorates, the National Center for Education Statistics reports that in 1990, American Indians/Alaskan Natives were awarded five Doctorates in the physical and four in the life sciences.

The obstacles faced by Native American students who attend college have been well documented, and poverty, inadequate financial aid, high drop-out rates from high school, and lack of academic preparedness are frequently cited (Hill, 1991; Hodgkinson, 1990; Levy, 1992; O'Brien, 1992; Tierney, 1991, 1993). However, cultural conflicts contribute significantly to the problems encountered by American Indian students (Dunn, 1988; Haukoos & Satterfield, 1986; Locust, 1988; More, 1987; O'Brien, 1992; Ovando, 1992; Pipes, Westby & Inglebret, 1993; Reyhner, 1992; Robinson Shade, 1989; Tierney 1991, 1993). Tierney (1993: 320) refers to 'cultural disruption', Pipes, Westby & Inglebret (1993: 139) to 'cultural dissonance', and others (California Department of Education, 1991: 33) to a feeling of being 'cultural dislocated'. Consider the following examples:

- Native students may be absent from class and from exams because of family and tribal obligations.

- To succeed in college may require unwanted assimilation into mainstream American society.
- Traditional college instruction often depends on learning by listening to lectures. Nevertheless, many Native American students prefer to learn by watching and then doing (Haukoos and Satterfield, 1986; More, 1987; Pipes, Westby & Inglebret, 1993; Reyhner, 1992; Robinson Shade, 1989).
- The nonverbal behavior of Native American students (such as a lack of eye contact or silence) may be misinterpreted by faculty members (Pipes, Westby & Inglebret, 1993; California Department of Education, 1991).
- 'American Indian English' (Leap, 1992, 1993) does not provide students with the kinds of academic language skills that are required to succeed in the college classroom.
- Native beliefs about the importance of living in harmony with nature and respect for all living things may come into conflict with the teachings and practice of modern day science and technology (Levy, 1992; Locust, 1988).

When all of the above are considered together, it is not surprising that so few Native Americans major in the sciences. Nevertheless, there are organized efforts to increase American Indian participation in careers in science and technology. These include AISES (The American Indian Science and Engineering Society, based in Boulder, Colorado), AIRO (American Indian Research Opportunities Program at Montana State University, Bozeman, Montana), and the ASSIST Program (Alliance of States Supporting Indians in Science and Technology, an eight state regional network headquartered at Montana State University, Bozeman, Montana).

Equity and increased employment opportunities are not the only reasons for encouraging American Indians to study science, technology, or engineering. Professionally qualified Native Americans are needed to manage the natural resources found on reservations (Hill, 1991).

It is exceedingly difficult to find specific information on how to adapt college science courses to meet the needs of American Indian students. Haukoos & Satterfield (1986: 199), after examining the learning style preferences of Native American students enrolled in introductory college biology, recommend changes that will produce 'a student centered classroom climate that is congruent with Native American custom and learning style'. Dunn (1988) describes a non-majors course entitled *People and the Environment* that is taught at Oglala Lakota College in Kyle, South Dakota; this is one of the 24 tribally controlled community colleges in the United States. The course, text, laboratory, and field work focus on biological and ecological issues pertinent to reservation life, directly relating to the needs of the students and their community. Although Ovando (1992) does not specifically address college science, his chapter includes many resources and ideas that might be of interest to science faculty teaching American Indian students.

Dr Jon Reyhner, Associate Professor of Curriculum and Instruction at Montana State University, Billings, has written extensively about American Indian students (Reyhner, 1992) and is the column editor on American Indian Bilingual Education for *NABE NEWS* (published by the National Association for Bilingual Education, Washington, DC). He believes that:

'Many Native students need specialized support programs staffed by individuals who are knowledgeable about the experiential background of

American Indian students. The work of AISES, various Indian centers at colleges and universities, and Native American/American Indian studies programs can help supplement the extended family support structure that Native students often must leave behind in order to obtain a college education. These groups can become advocates for the offering of more Native-oriented course content and courses that better target Native student needs. Even recognizing Native American languages as meeting university language requirements helps students get through their programs and reaffirms the importance of their cultural background.

Special Native support programs not only encourage students to utilize mainstream support services (such as tutoring) available on campus but also can help train and sensitize college staff and faculty to the needs of Native students. If a college is going to recruit Native students, it is important to try to get a large enough population of students and staff so that together they can form a supportive community. For this reason, it is probably best to target one or two nearby tribes because of the tremendous diversity, both cultural and linguistic, from one tribe to another. Colleges and universities also should sponsor summer programs to help Native American students ease the transition from high school to college. Students can use this time to acclimatize themselves to the demands of college work and to begin adjusting to life away from home and family.'

Two-thirds of the Native American population (which according to the 1990 Census totals just under two million) resides in just ten states (California, Oklahoma, Arizona, New Mexico, Alaska, Washington, North Carolina, Texas, Michigan, and New York). According to 1991 figures, there were 114,000 American Indians enrolled in institutions of higher education. Of these, 106,000 (93%) were undergraduates; 63,000 (55%) were attending 2-year colleges and 100,000 (88%) public institutions (*The Chronicle of Higher Education Almanac,* August 25, 1993: 13). In 1989, almost three-quarters of American Indian college students were enrolled in just 79 colleges (O'Brien, 1992).

Although the majority of Native students are studying at a limited number of institutions of higher learning, others are struggling in isolation, far away from family, friends, and accustomed ways of life. Such students cannot help but benefit from the mentoring and support provided by caring faculty and staff members.

Increasing the representation of Native Americans in the sciences presents many challenges. However, faculty members who are aware of the cultural and linguistic needs of such students are much more likely to provide suitable forms of instruction as well as appropriate academic and emotional support.

For additional information about American Indian students, Dr. Reyhner can be reached at:

Dr Jon Reyhner
Department of Curriculum and Instruction
Montana State University, Billings
1500 North 30th Street
Billings, MT 59101-0298
Phone: 406-657-2315
email: edci_reyhner@vesper.emcmt.edu

The ties between culture, science, and education are deep and often unexamined. It is easy to forget that when science faculty are delivering lectures and teaching laboratories, they are not just transmitting objective knowledge nor are they solely instructing students about a particular method for observing and investigating natural phenomena. Rather, they are imparting culturally based values and beliefs. As a result, much of what professionally trained scientists and science educators take for granted as being logical, true, and important may not be nearly so obvious to students, especially those who were raised, socialized, and previously schooled in 'non-Western' cultures and other parts of the world. They may be challenging some of the students' most deeply held beliefs and contradicting what the students already have been taught by their previous teachers and family members.

Students' Prior Knowledge About Science

Students, whether in elementary school or college, enter the science classroom with pre-formed explanations to describe and predict what happens in the natural world. As remarked by Kessler & Quinn (1987: 61): 'All cultures have well-developed theories about how the physical world operates without studying formal science.' Often these alternative conceptions are referred to as misconceptions, preconceptions, ethnoscience, naive beliefs, naive theories, alternative frameworks, erroneous ideas, or folklore (Champagne, 1986; Helm & Novak, 1983; Kessler & Quinn, 1987; Wandersee, Mintzes & Novak, 1994). What they are called is not, however, at issue here. What is important is that students are very reluctant to give up such beliefs in spite of what they are taught, observe, and experience in formal science courses (Champagne, 1986; Fisher et al., 1986; Helm & Novak, 1983; Kessler & Quinn, 1987; Meyer, 1993; Soyibo, 1993; Wandersee, Mintzes & Novak, 1994). For example, students sometimes believe that respiration and breathing mean the same thing, that all fruits taste sweet, and that fertilizer is plant 'food'. Although this information is scientifically incorrect, it nonetheless provides the non-scientist with a satisfactory way of understanding the physical world.

While we might want to think that such erroneous beliefs are found only in cultures less developed and less scientific than our own, that is clearly presumptuous on our part. Alternative conceptions cut across age, ability, gender, and cultural boundaries (Wandersee, Mintzes & Novak, 1994), and numerous examples have been cited in the literature involving students in elementary school as well as college (Fisher et al., 1986; Helm & Novak, 1983; Meyer, 1993; Wandersee, 1985; Wandersee, Mintzes & Novak, 1994; also see *Private Universe*, distributed by Pyramid Film and Video, Santa Monica, CA). For rapid verification of just how common are alternative scientific conceptions, ask some of your students (or friends) why it is cold in the winter and hot in the summer, or in which part of the human body most of digestion occurs. Chances are the responses you receive are not what is taught in the science classroom nor written in science textbooks.

Students can hold on to their alternative conceptions about science while earning good grades. They do this by keeping separate what they believe from what the teacher expects them to know (Edmondson & Novak, 1993). Apparently, this can be done successfully in spite of contradictions between prior beliefs and the new information presented in class (Meyer, 1993).

For students to 'overcome' their scientific misconceptions, instructors must do more than teach the course content. They must also provide opportunities for students to discover and confront their misconceptions for only then can learning be meaningful and accurate (Atwater, 1994; Meyer, 1993).

Classroom Culture

Nothing in the classroom escapes the effects of culture: what is taught and how it is taught, the language of instruction, the textbook and the information it includes, the approved kinds of classroom behavior, the roles of and relationship between teacher and students, teaching and learning styles, and the process of assessment (Andersen & Powell, 1991; Apple, 1992; Hall, 1976; Saville-Troike, 1978, 1979). Culture shapes and defines the educational system, which in turn, transmits, maintains, and reinforces mainstream values, beliefs, language, and culture, teaching them to generation after generation of students.

The pervasiveness of culture in the academic setting has been described by Adams (1992: 5–6) as follows:

> In academe as in any culture, many of the most sacrosanct practices remain unstated, unexamined, and unacknowledged unless or until they are challenged by divergent beliefs from outside the predominant culture. While most faculty and students who have been socialized into the traditional classroom culture are scarcely aware of its existence, those students who have not already been socialized into this culture by previous schooling or a congruent home or community culture often become painfully aware of it. They find that their values and beliefs are in conflict with many traditionally sanctioned classroom procedures that constitute an implicit or hidden curriculum, the *how* of teaching as distinct from the *what*. For example, classroom engagement in competitive or assertive behavior, 'talking up' in class, and acceptance of grading curves by which one's gain is another's loss are likely to be in conflict with cultures that do not endorse individual success at the expense of one's peers or that value modesty over assertiveness and cross-age tutoring over competitve inter-peer debate.

Furthermore, recent advocates of multicultural classrooom practice (M.F. Green, 1989) note that traditional instructional models have not even served traditional students all that well. Despite the belief (held by many faculty) that their own college classrooms are culturally neutral and that cultural neutrality is itself an academic norm, the assumptions and values that characterize [American] higher education mainly derive from aspects of European culture shared by nineteenth- and twentieth-century European immigrants to this country, who benefited from higher education to the degree that they already shared a common history and could thereby understand the norms and participate in the behaviors of its educational systems … But to those not socialized, acculturated, or familiar with the ways of higher education, traditional classroom practices seem impersonal, competitive, and off-putting.

With culture playing such a prominent role in the academic setting, cultural misunderstandings can and do occur. This is especially true with a multilingual, multicultural student population (Adamson, 1993; Border & Van Note Chism, 1992; Claxton & Murrell, 1987; Damen, 1987; M.F. Green, 1989; Peitzman & Gadda, 1991; Richard-Amato & Snow, 1992; Robinson Shade, 1989; Saville-Troike, 1978, 1979). Here are some examples of the kinds of cultural misunderstandings that might occur in a college classroom:

- A student copies an entire passage from a text without citing a reference. Is this plagiarism?

- Another defines what something is by describing all the things it is not. Does this mean the student is incapable of logical thinking?.

- A student refuses to look the instructor in the eye and will not answer or ask questions. Is he or she necessarily unprepared or in some way trying to deceive the instructor?

- Pairs of students chatter away in their native language while the professor is trying to lecture. Are they being rude?

As annoying, impolite, or inappropriate as these behaviors may seem, in each case what the students are doing may very well represent the norms for the societies in which they were raised and previously schooled. Nevertheless, their American teachers may not know this. Likewise, the students may be totally unaware that what they are doing is considered 'wrong' or 'inappropriate' in a college classroom in the United States.

In the long run, it is the instructor who determines what is expected in his or her course, and it is the student who must adapt. Students raised in other cultures often need time to make the necessary accomodations to the belief and value systems that define a classroom, a particular course, or an academic discipline. This will not take place instantaneously and certainly will be slowed down if the 'rules of the game' are not made as explicit as possible.

What instructors normally see taking place in their classrooms is only a tiny part of the acculturation process through which immigrant and foreign students pass. It is easy to forget that these students are not just learning chemistry, math, or history; rather, they are becoming accustomed to an entirely new way of life which encompasses values, beliefs, behaviors, and a language different from what they have previously experienced and known. Therefore, whatever their instructors can do to facilitate this transition will reduce both 'culture shock' and 'education shock'.

The Successful Science Student

Each academic discipline defines what should be taught, how it should be taught, as well as the characteristics of a successful learner of that discipline. In the case of science, good students traditionally have been described as those who persist, earn good grades, work well on their own, thrive in a competitive atmosphere, and who excel at analytical thinking and abstract reasoning. Clearly, if these are the hallmarks of good science learners, then other kinds of students must in some way be 'unfit' for science.

Another way of defining successful science students is that they are the easiest ones to teach! They are 'teacher-proof, curriculum-proof, and competition-proof enough to survive traditional undergraduate training' (Lipson & Tobias 1991: 95). According to Tobias (1990: 10), 'top tier' science students are those who already share the values and characteristics of scientists.

So, what message is being sent to 'second tier' students who are interested in and capable of doing science but differ from 'top tier' students in their preferred ways of learning or ability to tolerate traditional science classroom practices (Tobias, 1990; Lipson & Tobias, 1991; Seymour, 1992a, b)? Are they in some subtle way being told that science is only for a select few and that they are not suited for science majors? Tobias sums up the situation by stating that *'unless they are younger versions of the science community itself*, many otherwise intelligent, curious, and ambitious young people have reason to conclude there is no place for them in science' (Tobias, 1990: 11).

Often the qualities that promote success in the traditional college science classroom are not those that characterize many women and minority (African-American, Hispanic, Asian, and Native American) group members. Just like the majority students who choose not to study science, many minority students prefer global rather than sequential learning, do better in a supportive rather than a competitive classroom environment, and learn more when working collaboratively/cooperatively rather than competitively (Anderson, 1988; Border & Van Note Chism, 1992; Claxton & Murrell, 1987; M.F. Green, 1989). It is therefore not at all surprising that minorities remain underrepresented in the sciences in spite of numerous programs and efforts to remediate this situation (Massey, 1992; National Science Foundation, 1992; Office of Technology Assessment, 1988; Sims, 1992).

Stimulating an interest in science in elementary and secondary students does not change what they will experience when and if they enroll in college and start taking traditionally taught science courses. While much of the science education reform movement in the United States has focused on grades K-12, Tobias emphasizes (Hoots, 1992; Lipson & Tobias, 1991; Tobias, 1992a, b) that this is not sufficient. Undergraduate faculty also have a significant role to play in recruiting and retaining capable students in the sciences. 'Good students may be lost at the college level not because they fail their science education but because their science education is failing them' (Lipson & Tobias, 1991:92-3).

The Omission of Cultural Considerations in Science Education Reform

Many reasons have been proposed as to why fewer students are majoring in the sciences. These include:

- inadequate elementary and secondary math and science preparation,
- outdated equipment and laboratory facilities,
- cookbook laboratory experiments,
- a need to change from the lecturing mode to a more student-centered form of pedagogy including more hands-on instruction,
- a lack of mentors and role models for minority students,
- the general underfunding of science education,
- science classes that are too large and impersonal,
- graduate teaching assistants who often are 'foreigners' with poor mastery of English, and
- science as a career has lost its appeal.

Unquestionably, all of these variables in some way are contributing to the loss of science majors so that addressing them is important. Nonetheless, focusing on them may actually be diverting attention from two interrelated and possibly more important issues: the changing undergraduate demographics and the growing cultural disparity between teachers and their students.

As discussed in Chapter 1, an extraordinary demographic change is taking place in the United States, affecting enrollments in public schools and colleges. The percentage of Hispanic and Asian and Pacific Islander students has been increasing much more rapidly than that of Whites, Blacks, and American Indians/Alaskan Natives (see Tables 1.2, 1.3 and 1.5). As for the United States as a whole (see Table 3.1), demographic projections (Edmonston & Passel, 1992: 39) indicate that between the years 1990 and 2090 the following changes will take place: Asians will increase from 2.9% to 15.1% of the US population, and Hispanics from 9.0% to 24.3%. On the other hand, Whites will decrease dramatically (from 75.2% to 48.8%) as will American Indians (from 0.8% to 0.4%). The Black population will decrease very slightly (12.1% to 11.3%).

Table 3.1 US Population for race/ethnic groups: 1990-2090

Year	All Races	White Non-Hispanic	Asian	Black	Hispanic	American Indian
*Population (in millions)**						
1990	248.8	187.1	7.3	30.0	22.4	2.0
2000	276.8	198.4	12.0	34.1	30.3	2.1
2010	299.4	204.2	17.1	37.4	38.6	2.1
2020	320.5	208.4	22.7	40.2	47.1	2.2
2030	340.1	211.1	28.5	42.5	55.8	2.2
2040	355.5	210.5	34.5	44.1	64.2	2.2
2050	369.4	209.1	40.6	45.2	72.4	2.1
2060	385.8	209.8	46.8	46.4	80.7	2.1
2070	402.7	211.0	53.1	47.6	89.1	2.0
2080	419.1	211.6	59.5	48.5	97.4	2.0
2090	436.7	213.2	66.0	49.6	106.1	1.9
Percentage						
1990	100.0	75.2	2.9	12.1	9.0	0.8
2000	100.0	71.7	4.3	12.3	10.9	0.8
2010	100.0	68.2	5.7	12.5	12.9	0.7
2020	100.0	65.0	7.1	12.5	14.7	0.7
2030	100.0	62.1	8.4	12.5	16.4	0.6
2040	100.0	59.2	9.7	12.4	18.1	0.6
2050	100.0	56.6	11.0	12.2	19.6	0.6
2060	100.0	54.4	12.1	12.0	20.9	0.5
2070	100.0	52.4	13.2	11.8	22.1	0.5
2080	100.0	50.5	14.2	11.6	23.3	0.5
2090	100.0	48.8	15.1	11.3	24.3	0.4

*All figures rounded independently.
(Reprinted with permission from Edmonston & Passel, 1992: 39)

In other words, as a result of changing demographics, students and teachers, undergraduates and their professors, are gradually but significantly growing apart in terms of native culture and language. Why does this matter? It matters because the teaching styles of instructors may be incompatible with the learning styles of the students. It matters because it increases the likelihood of verbal and nonverbal miscommunication. And, it matters since all teachers bring to the classroom a set of culturally based expectations as to which kinds of students will do well and which will not (Good, 1987). These expectations, in turn, affect not only how teachers interact and relate to students but also student behavior and achievement.

Mainstream or 'regular' teachers usually receive little training in how to deal with diverse kinds of students especially those of limited English proficiency. As a result, expectations may be raised or lowered without any concrete basis. For example, based on popular images it may be assumed that all Asian students will automatically do well in science while Hispanics will do poorly.

Several studies have confirmed this type of stereotyping. For example, Ford (1984) found that teachers give lower evaluations to the written work and hold lower expectations (as to socioeconomic status, intelligence, ability to communicate, and pleasantness) of children who speak English with a Spanish accent. Similarly, Penfield (1987) noted that mainstream teachers feel burdened or angry about having LEP students in their classes, sometimes blaming the academic problems of such students on their being lazy or not making a sufficient effort. Although these findings are based on studies at the public school level, professors sometimes can be overheard in college hallways expressing similar sentiments.

College Environments and the Educational Pipeline in the Sciences

The results of a recent Higher Education Research Institute (HERI) study suggest 'that the typical environment for science education in American colleges and universities tends to be impersonal, competitive, and authoritarian. Such an environment may well serve to discourage many students from studying science, especially those who may feel underprepared or who may have doubts about their ability to succeed in science' (HERI, 1992: 9-14).

In examining how the 'culture' of science affects undergraduate science education and practice, the HERI study documents (1992: 9-15) that college science professors are predominately male (biological sciences 77.3%; physical sciences 88.9%), white (biological sciences 92.7%; physical sciences 92.4%) and over the age of forty (biological sciences 79.6%; physical sciences 77.6%). In other words, minority students and women 'have limited opportunities to find faculty role models' (HERI, 1992: 9-14).

Other findings of this study suggest a variety of areas of conflict between the needs of today's students and the attitudes of science faculty. For example when compared to their colleagues in education, the humanities, and the social sciences, faculty in the biological and physical sciences are considerably less satisfied with the quality of their students, less likely to attend workshops on racial/ethnic awareness, and least likely to use student-centered pedagogy (HERI 1992: 9-16 to 9-20). Participation in racial awareness workshops is of special significance because it was found to be one of the characteristics of faculty members who were most likely to adapt student-centered pedagogy (HERI, 1992: 9-12). The unfortunate conclusion that can be drawn from these findings is that in spite of rapidly changing student demographics, persistent attempts at educational reform, and a stated goal that science should be made accessible to all students, cultural considerations have barely influenced the nature of undergraduate science education.

Conclusion

In *Teaching for Diversity* (Border & Van Note Chism, 1992: 1) five reasons are given as to why colleges and universities must address diversity issues:

1. *The Moral Argument:* Given that all humans are equal, then all students deserve to participate equally in higher education;
2 *The Demographic Argument:* If institutions of higher education are going to survive, then they must be willing to educate a much more diverse student population.
3. *The Civic Argument:* Since we live in a democracy, we need educated citizens and skilled workers.
4. *The Enrichment Argument:* Student diversity will bring new viewpoints into the scholarly dialogue.
5. *The Political Argument:* The rise in incidents of racism and intolerance on campus must be dealt with.

What needs to be added to this list is *'The Cultural Argument'*: that is, the many ways that culture affects every aspect of the instructional process must be examined and considered in order to effectively and appropriately educate today's increasingly diverse student population.

Perhaps at some hypothetical point in the past, cultural considerations in the science classroom may have been unnecessary. But that is not the situation in the United States as we enter into the twenty-first century. The demographic shifts currently taking place are outpacing the rate of science education reform. Multicultural and multilingual classrooms are found across the nation—from grade school to graduate school. Science can no longer be taught as if all students were the same. Those days, if they ever did exist, are gone, and the needs of today's students must be recognized and addressed.

Box 3.3 Categories and Culture

Dr Catherine H. Middlecamp is the Director of the Chemistry Learning Center at the University of Wisconsin-Madison. She credits her students as her 'teachers' and has written and made presentations about what they have taught her (for example, Middlecamp, 1989, 1994, 1995; Middlecamp & Moore, 1994). The following anecdote is about one of her students, and according to some recent articles (Shea, 1994; Wright, 1994), this is not an isolated incident:

In Dr Middlecamp's words:

'Our campus registration form gives students the option of identifying their cultural heritage. Students may select from the categories of African American, Asian, Native American, Hispanic, Caucasian, or Other, with subcategories available in some cases. Ernesto, a student from Nicaragua, reacted to the form with both dismay and indignation. '*All* of these apply to me,' he pointed out. 'Which one am I supposed to pick?'

Ernesto grew up in Nicaragua. Although he at first may be presumed to be Hispanic, his mother was from one of the indigenous groups in the country (Native American). Furthermore, his grandfather had immigrated to the west coast of Nicaragua from China (Asian). Among Ernesto's ancestors were African-Americans who were brought as slaves to Nicaragua's east coast. Thus, Ernesto's cultural roots lay in many parts of the globe. When confronted with the ethnic categories listed on the registration form, he could not decide which box to select.

Some cultures and groups of people are more inclined toward the use of categories than others. Western scientists seem to be major 'category users'. For example, in chemistry, students are taught to distinguish between numerous classes of chemicals, often on an either/or basis: there are metals and non-metals, acids and bases, and alpha, beta, and gamma emitters. Chemistry as a discipline is broken down in subcategories: organic, inorganic, analytic, bioinorganic, biophysical, etc. Although such categories may seem to be objective and culture-free, in reality they are not. Both the very act of *using* categories and *defining* what gets placed in them have a cultural basis.

The world has no inherent categories; its boxes and boundaries appear only if we draw them. The extent to which people define and employ categories varies, and many cultural groups rely far less on categories than do Western scientists. Ernesto, in the earlier example, would not have constructed a situation where his ethnic background was defined by picking one of a number of categories. Like Ernesto, many people tend to first view things as a whole, rather than carving out parts of them, or separating them from their larger context. A native American woman comments, ' "All things, All things, All Things are Related" is not just a charming chant … it is a profound evaluation of the nature of the Universe.' (Spencer, 1990: 17).

Even if two cultures are similar in their tendencies to categorize the world, there is no guarantee that the lines will be drawn in the same places. For example, some groups of people will view humans as separate from nature (and able to control it); others will view humans as part of nature. One culture may view a chemical as a healing drug; another may view the same chemical as a harmful drug. Some educators may see their students as majors or non-majors; others may see these same students as first-year or upperclass students. The point here is not if using categories is 'good' or 'bad', although this question is also worthy of debate. Rather, science instructors need to be aware that a bias towards using certain categories may be built into the subject matter. Categorizing things is certainly a useful way of coming to know the world. It is not, however, the only way.'

For addition information, Dr. Middlecamp can be reached at:

Dr Catherine H. Middlecamp
Chemistry Learning Center
The University of Wisconsin-Madison
1101 University Avenue
Madison, Wisconsin 53706
Phone: 608-263-5647; Fax: 608-262-0381; email: middleca@macc.wisc.edu

4 Learning Styles, Science Instruction, and Ethnicity

One of the ways that diversity manifests itself in the classroom is in the varied approaches that students use in order to 'learn'. For example, some students like to study alone while others prefer working in small groups. Some students are very competitive; others are not. There are students who seem instantaneously to grasp abstract concepts and others who need exposure to numerous, concrete examples before concepts can be understood. Some students easily absorb information from listening to lectures while others must read and write about the subject matter in order to learn it. There are students who can work independently and others who want and need direction and encouragement from the instructor. In other words, although instructors may teach as if all students learned the same way, there do exist real differences in how students take in and process new information. These are what are referred to as 'learning styles'.

Several aspects of learning style theory and research are related to the content of this book:

- Certain learning styles are characteristic of students who have traditionally done well in the sciences.
- Students' learning styles apparently influence their choice of major.
- There are learning styles that facilitate the learning/acquisition of English as a second language.
- Cultural upbringing strongly influences learning styles.

It is for all these reasons that a discussion of learning style theory and some learning style classifications are presented here.

This chapter begins by looking at what is meant by 'learning style' and how, in general, learning styles affect classroom performance. Several learning style classifications are then discussed in more detail including field independence/dependence (field sensitive/insensitive), global/analytic (simultaneous/sequential), competition/cooperation, ambiguity tolerance, need for structure, preferred perceptual modes, and impulsivity/reflectivity. How each of these learning styles might affect student achievement and behavior in science courses is considered, as well as the various relationships that have been noted among learning styles, choice of major, and ethnicity. At the end of the chapter reasons are presented as to why diverse learning styles should be considered in science education reform efforts.

What is Meant by 'Learning Style'

There seem to exist as many definitions of 'learning style' as there are articles and books written on the topic. For example, learning style has been described as 'The characteristic or usual strategies of acquiring knowledge, skills and understanding by an individual' (More, 1987: 19) and as the 'cognitive and interactional patterns which affect the ways in which students perceive, remember, and think' (Scarcella, 1990: 114). Learning styles have been depicted as 'moderately strong habits rather than intractable biological attributes' (Reid, 1987: 100) and as being relatively 'stable over time' yet alterable (Witkin *et al.*, 1977: 15).

Learning styles are often presented in terms of bipolar or contrasting characteristics. For example, a student might be classified as being collaborative or competitive, visual rather than auditory. Yet, most of the time a student's preferred way of learning falls somewhere between the extremes. In other words, it would be more accurate to describe the aforementioned student as more collaborative than competitive and more visual than auditory. In addition, students do not have just one learning style. Rather, they utilize several, some better developed and more strongly preferred, others rarely used and/or less well developed.

Theoretically, one learning style is not inherently better than another. Yet, our own experiences, first as students and for some of us as teachers, have taught us that what works successfully in one learning situation may not suffice in another. Consider the following: There is a student who learns easily by listening to lectures and by reading the textbook; as a result, this student does very well in many college courses. However, the same student may encounter difficulties in a public speaking class that requires oral presentations or in a studio art course in which he or she must create and then critique drawings and paintings. The broader and more flexible a student's learning style repertoire, the more likely he or she is to be able to meet the demands of different teachers, courses, and disciplines.

While there seems to be a biological basis for an individual's preferred learning style, the environment in which a person is raised is clearly a major determinant (Anderson, 1988; Bennett, 1990; Claxton & Murrell, 1987; M.F. Green, 1989; Hilliard, 1989; Hofstede, 1986; Keefe, 1987; National Association of Secondary School Principals, 1979; Robinson Shade, 1989; Scarcella, 1990). The socialization process, previous schooling experiences, and the values, beliefs, and world view of the culture in which a person grows up strongly affect how he or she organizes and conceptualizes information. Consequently, it is not at all surprising that researchers have found that certain learning styles are characteristic of or preferred by many members of particular ethnic and cultural groups. For example, a number of studies have shown that American Indians tend to be visual rather than auditory learners (Haukoos & Satterfield, 1986; More, 1987; Reyhner, 1992; Robinson Shade, 1989) and that many Mexican-American students work more cooperatively and are more field sensitive than their Anglo-American peers (Ramirez, 1973; Saracho, 1989; Shade, 1989). These and similar findings do not mean that all members of an ethnic group learn in precisely the same way; considerable variation in learning styles does exist among the members of any group. Nevertheless, it does appear that certain ways of learning are more highly valued and used more frequently in different societies (Anderson, 1988; Bennett, 1990; Claxton & Murrell, 1987; M.F. Green, 1989; Hilliard, 1989; Hofstede, 1986; Scarcella, 1990).

International, immigrant, refugee, Native American, and LEP undergraduates who have been raised, schooled, and socialized in other countries and/or cultures may find that their preferred styles of learning differ significantly from those expected of 'typical American' students. Their previous educational experiences may have emphasized memorization rather than critical thinking skills; participation in class discussions and challenging the teacher's ideas may have been unheard of. Such students are not going to say to themselves, 'My learning style is different from that of my classmates', or 'My learning style is incompatible with the teaching style of my instructor'. Instead, what is more likely to happen is that a student may study hard yet earn poor grades, or feel bored or turned off by the class and, perhaps, withdraw from the course.

There do exist numerous assessment procedures for determining an individual's preferred learning style(s) (Bennett, 1990; Claxton & Murrell, 1987; Cornett, 1983; Keefe, 1987; National Association of Secondary School Principals, 1979). However, such instruments are not routinely administered to students. As a result, neither they nor their instructors are aware of how the students learn best. In introductory science courses with a multicultural/multilingual student population, one is left to conclude that instructors who can use a variety of teaching styles—in response the many ways in which students learn—will be more effective as teachers.

Some Examples of Learning Styles

For those who teach science to undergraduates, it is not necessary to be familiar with all the learning styles that have been identified. Rather, it is more important to examine a few learning styles in order to get a feel for the various kinds of strategies that different students use to learn the same material.

The learning styles discussed below are just a small sample of those described in the literature. In no way is this listing meant to be comprehensive. It does, however, provide an introduction to some learning style classifications along with descriptions of how each can affect the achievement and performance of undergraduates in traditional science courses.

Field independent/field dependent

Probably the best known of the learning styles is field independent/field dependent which is sometimes referred to as field insensitive/field sensitive (Bennett, 1990; Castañeda & Gray, 1974; Scarcella, 1990; Witkin *et al.*, 1977). The terms field independent and field dependent were developed by Herman Witkin (see Witkin *et al.*, 1977: 6–7) to describe how individuals perceive various items in relationship to the surrounding environment (field). The field independent individual sees the items as discrete from the surrounding field while the field dependent person cannot distinguish the items embedded in the field. Others (for example, see Castañeda & Gray, 1974), have used a slightly different nomenclature, field insensitive and field sensitive, which emphasizes the relationship between how the individual perceives (discrete parts versus global perspective) to other learning style characteristics. The latter includes the degree of sensitivity and responsiveness to social situations and to the emotions of others.

Field independent (insensitive) students are often described as self-motivated learners, needing little outside reinforcement from their peers or from their teachers. They work well on their own, are task oriented, and are good at abstract, analytical thought, and at learning details. In contrast, field dependent (sensitive) learners prefer a more global perspective, have more difficulty with problem solving, and are more sensitive to the social environment in which learning takes place. They like working in groups, need more guidance and encouragement from their teachers, and typically learn information in the same way it is presented to them.

Based on even this brief description of field independent/dependent learner characteristics, it is readily apparent that the traditional lecture/laboratory format used in many college science courses favors the field independent student (Anderson, 1988; Higher Education Research Institute, 1992; Kolb, 1981; Seymour, 1992a,b; Tobias, 1990; Witkin *et al.*, 1977). The classroom environment is often competitive and lacking in personal encouragement from either the instructor or peers. Students typically are left to work and to struggle alone.

Both science majors and their professors are often field independent learners; thus, science faculty will teach in a way that appeals to other field independent learners. In contrast, field dependent individuals are more likely to be interested in the social sciences and humanities, the helping professions, business, or elementary education (Anderson, 1988; Claxton & Murrell, 1987; Kolb, 1981; Witkin *et al.*, 1977).

Global/analytic and simultaneous/sequential

Similar to field independence/field dependence are the learning style classifications of global/analytic and simultaneous/sequential (Kirby, 1984;

More, 1987; Scarcella, 1990). Global or simultaneous learners tend to see the whole picture and the relationship between the parts as 'one'. Analytic or sequential learners begin by identifying the individual parts, building up step-by-step to the 'big picture'. We might say that global learners see the forest, and analytic learners, the trees.

College science instruction has traditionally had an analytic/sequential orientation. Numerous, seemingly unrelated facts must often be learned before their relevance to a particular topic ever unfolds. Abstract theories are described in detail long before any practical applications are examined (Anderson, 1988).

In a principles of biology course, for example, the sequence of topics often presented in textbooks and lectures is: elements, atoms, molecules, cellular organelles, and, lastly, cell structure and function. For analytic/sequential learners, the introduction of the subject matter in this order is quite logical. Material is learned, moving from lower to higher levels of organization. However, global/simultaneous learners sitting through the same classes and reading the same textbook might be asking themselves, 'What is the point? What do atoms, elements and molecules have to do with cells and living things?' For them, the mass of detail that they must memorize first obscures the final message or meaning. In fact, class may seem incredibly boring or pointless. For this reason, global/simultaneous learners in a science course would benefit by beginning with a 'top down' overview of the topic (including several interesting examples) before taking a 'bottom up' approach.

Competition/Cooperation

For some students, competition is an excellent motivator, causing them to study and learn more. Competitive students may be testing the limits of their own abilities, may want good grades to help them get accepted into graduate or professional school, or perhaps they are striving to please their parents or teachers. Whatever the reasons, competition enhances their academic performance. Other students, however, become extremely anxious in a competitive environment, so much so that learning actually is reduced. The latter often do better working cooperatively in small groups, which draw less attention to the individual and which allow the learning process and its outcome to be shared among the group members (Bennett, 1990; Johnson, Johnson & Smith, 1991; Scarcella, 1990).

A correlation seems to exist between a preference for cooperative/collaborative learning and field dependence as well as between competition and field independence (Bennett, 1990; Scarcella, 1990).

In recent studies of the reasons why well qualified students get 'turned off' to science, the competitive nature of the science classroom has been cited frequently (Lipson & Tobias, 1991; Seymour 1992a,b; Tobias, 1990).

Apparently, there are talented and capable students who enter college planning to major in the sciences who could benefit from a more collaborative mode of classroom instruction and a more supportive classroom atmosphere. While this applies to many 'majority' students, as will be discussed later in this chapter, it is especially true for many women, minorities, and students of limited English proficiency.

Ambiguity tolerance

Another way in which students differ is in their ability to feel comfortable and to cope with ambiguity (Budner, 1962; Chapelle & Roberts, 1986; Damen, 1987; Frenkel-Brunswik, 1949; National Association of Secondary School Principals, 1979). Some learners would prefer that all knowledge fall into discrete categories so that questions could be answered by a simple 'yes/no' or 'right/wrong'. However, as subject matter becomes more advanced and problems more complex, there may be several ways to interpret information and more than one right answer. While one student may feel at ease when challenged by an ambiguous situation, another may feel threatened or confused.

Science is somewhat deceptive to novice students who may at first think that all that is involved is learning facts, formulas, definitions and vocabulary. Ambiguity may not be much of a problem at the introductory level; what is essential is a good memory and attention to detail. However, as the coursework progresses, students soon discover that the subject matter does not remain so clear-cut, that there may be alternative ways to solve problems, various interpretations of the results of experiments, and that many scientific questions remain unanswered. Those students who can tolerate ambiguity find the new complexity of the subject matter manageable and stimulating. Those uncomfortable with ambiguity grow frustrated and confused. The latter, searching for predictable solutions, are probably the ones most likely to ask questions such as 'Will this be on the test?' or 'Would this be a correct/acceptable answer on the exam?'

Although professors might like students to arrive at college with the ability to deal with uncertainty, not all of them do. Fortunately, there are many ways that instructors can help them. For example, lectures should be well organized so that students do not get unnecessarily confused; the instructor should periodically sum up what has been covered and where the lecture is headed. As new topics are presented, students might be told how this new material is related to information that was previously presented. Instructors might model problem solving techniques especially when there is more than one way to reach the answer or more than one correct answer. Students who have always been taught that there is only one way to solve problems or only one correct answer to any question will need practice and encouragement when learning to deal with new levels of complexity and ambiguity.

Need for structure

While some students with the briefest of explanations can carry out assignments correctly from start to finish, others require considerable supervision and step-by-step directions. In a science class, the former are quickly classified as 'good' students; teachers like them because they are smart and easy to teach. In contrast, those students who are always in need of help are often called 'bad' students. This may mean that according to the instructor, they are unprepared, not too intelligent, and/or unable to work independently. From the teacher's perspective, it takes much less effort to teach the 'good' students than the 'bad' ones.

The classification of 'good' and 'bad' students in many instances may really be a reflection of how these two groups differ in their need for external structure: the extent to which they require assistance in planning and executing assignments (Bennett, 1990; Holland, 1989). The greater the need for structure, the more help the instructor will have to provide if students are to succeed. This is especially relevant in the case of students who are field dependent/global/simultaneous learners who have the greatest need for structure and have the most difficulty with traditional science instruction (Anderson, 1988; Bennett, 1990; Witkin *et al.*, 1977).

In college, students are expected to work independently, and professors often presume that a description of an assignment and an announcement of the due date are all the information that students require in order to complete an assignment. However, many students—often freshmen, the 'underprepared', and those who are learning English as a second language—may need more structure. Written, step-by-step directions, a schedule of due dates for each part of the assignment, and regularly scheduled meetings with the instructor may be necessary so that projects get carried out in the proper sequence and completed on time.

Providing external structure to students does require more time and extra effort on the part of the instructor. Yet, if students are enrolled in college courses and do not already have the necessary skills, when and where else are they going to learn them? By putting into practice the planning and organizational skills that they will need, under the supervision of their instructors, students will begin to internalize the process so that eventually they will be able to provide their own 'structure'. In many ways, the situation is analogous to that of teaching students how to tolerate ambiguity. By modeling the desired behavior, the instructor will be helping students to expand their learning style repertoire and to become more successful students.

Preferred perceptual modes

Individuals vary considerably in terms of the type of sensory (perceptual) input that best promotes learning (Bennett, 1990; Keefe, 1987; National

Association of Secondary School Principals, 1979; Reid, 1987; Scarcella, 1990). Thus, students can be classified as visual learners (who learn by reading and/or seeing); as auditory learners (who learn by listening and hearing); as kinesthetic learners (who learn by 'total physical involvement with a learning situation' [Reid, 1987: 89]), or as tactile (who learn via hands-on activities, such as performing laboratory experiments and building models, or by writing about or 'mapping' the information under study).

Mainstream US schooling and conventional college classroom teaching rely heavily on auditory input: teachers talk and students sit and listen. In such an environment, learners whose preferred perceptual modes are visual, kinesthetic, or tactile are at a disadvantage. Not only will they probably learn less than their auditory classmates, but also they may become bored. For this reason, the instructor who presents material in ways that appeal to the auditory, visual, kinesthetic and tactile perceptual modalities will be helping more students to learn. In a science course, this can be done by supplementing the lecture/lab format with additional reading and writing assignments, with videos, films, demonstrations, slides, model building, and with class and small group discussions.

Impulsive/reflective

In this learning style classification, students are categorized according to how long they reflect about the accuracy of a response before answering a question or trying to solve a problem (Claxton & Murrell, 1987; Damen, 1987; Kagan, 1966; Keefe, 1987; Messner, 1976; Scarcella, 1990). Impulsive individuals value speed of response which may reduce the accuracy of their answers; reflective learners proceed more slowly since providing the correct answer is most important to them.

One way that impulsivity and reflectivity affect student performance is in the taking of timed exams, particularly multiple choice tests (Claxton & Murrell, 1987). Impulsive students may finish exams quickly but not spend enough time considering the appropriateness of their answer choices. Reflective students who take a long time to ponder over each multiple choice item may never reach the last test question before the class period ends. In either case, the exam will not conclusively demonstrate what either kind of student actually knows or has learned. Concerned instructors try to help students deal with their impulsive and reflective tendencies and make every effort to design tests that leave enough time for all students to answer the questions and to review their answer choices for correctness.

Teachers are often unaware of how their own actions influence the impulsive/reflective behavior of their students. Consider the following example: In the American classroom, students are expected to respond to the questions presented to them by their teachers. If students are unsure of the correctness of an answer, many teachers would like students to offer responses even at the risk being wrong. Participation supposedly indicates that the student is interested in the topic and is trying to learn or already knows something about it; silence on the part of a student indicates lack of preparation, disinterest, and/or that the student does not know the correct answer.

Rowe (1974a, b) was the first to document the relationship between teacher 'wait-time' and student responsiveness. She found that teachers typically give students just under one second to begin answering a question. If the student does not start responding during that brief interval, the teacher will repeat the question or ask another student for the answer. When students do respond within that first second, teachers immediately comment on the response, ask another question, or introduce a new topic. Through controlled studies, Rowe found that by increasing teacher wait-time to three to five seconds, more students offered longer, appropriate responses. Longer wait-times apparently increase both cognitive processing and student learning (Tobin, Tippins & Gallard, 1994).

Increased wait-time benefits both impulsive and reflective learners. The former can use those few extra seconds to reconsider the accuracy of their responses; the latter would be more likely to offer an answer since they would have more time to evaluate its correctness.

However, lack of student responsiveness may have many other causes which have nothing to do with reflectivity/impulsivity or with teacher wait-times. Shy students may become very nervous at the thought of speaking up in front of the class. Not wanting to draw attention to themselves, they will not raise their hands to offer an answer even if they know the correct one. Students who speak English with a 'foreign' accent may be afraid of being misunderstood or laughed at, thereby choosing not to join in the discussion. For others, the reasons for remaining silent are culturally determined. Many Japanese, Korean or Thai students will not answer a teacher's question if they have any doubt as to the correctness of their response (California State Department of Education, 1987; California Department of Education, 1992; Garner, 1989).

In those science classrooms in which the instructor uses questioning to promote critical thinking and discussion, extending the wait-time is one way to encourage more students to participate. If there is a sense of community in the classroom, then the instructor may want not only to provide extended wait-time but also specifically to call on individual students. This is especially necessary when there are several students who otherwise tend to dominate the class discussion. To help students overcome their reservations about answering questions in front of a class, practicing in the context of a small group may be helpful.

Implications of Learning Style Diversity

This brief overview of various learning styles is designed to illustrate and emphasize how learning style differences can significantly influence the achievement and performance of college students taking science courses. Science as traditionally taught is partial to the field independent/ analytic/competitive/auditory learner who needs little structure and who can answer questions and solve problems both quickly and accurately. Nonetheless, this does not rule out the fact that other 'kinds' of intelligent, talented students with alternative preferred learning styles are also interested in science. However, to successfully recruit and retain the latter would require some changes in undergraduate science instruction particularly at the intro-ductory level. These would include a more student-centered pedagogy, cooperative/collaborative small group projects, a warmer, more supportive classroom atmosphere, and improved relations and communication between science faculty and students.

Incompatibility of learning style (e.g. field-dependent students taking a science course taught by a field-independent instructor) may influence students in their choice of a major. Witkin *et al.* (1977: 49–50) reported that 'shifts out of mathematics and science were especially common among the more field-dependent students; the shifts serve to bring about a better fit between students' cognitive styles and their career choices'. Kolb (1981) who developed a learning style classification based on experiential learning theory found that individuals in the sciences and math favor abstract conceptualiza-tion and reflective observation; those in other fields such as business, the humanities, agriculture, nursing, and engineering demonstrated different patterns of strength along the concrete/abstract and active/reflective dimen-sions.

Tobias and Seymour independently have been looking into the reasons why capable students, who are interested in the sciences, turn to non-science majors (Lipson & Tobias, 1991; Tobias, 1990; Seymour, 1992a, b). Seymour's 'switchers' and Tobias' 'second tier' students often leave the science 'pipeline' because affectively and cognitively they get 'turned off' by how science is taught. These findings, along with those of Kolb (1981) and Witkin *et al.* (1977), suggest that incompatability between students' learning styles and the instructors' teaching styles may be a major source of attrition from the sciences.

Learning style issues are of growing importance as the undergraduate student population becomes more diverse ethnically and linguistically. There are numerous studies to document the relationship between culture and learning styles. For example,

•   Hispanic, Native American, and African American learners have been found to be more cooperative/field dependent/global/simultaneous than their Anglo American counterparts (Anderson, 1988; Bennett, 1990; Border and Van Note Chism, 1992; More, 1987; Ramirez, 1973; Reyhner, 1992; Robinson Shade, 1989; Scarcella, 1990).

- Preferred perceptual modalities also are culturally linked. Reid (1987) found that the preferred sensory modality of ESL students was kinesthetic while that of native English speakers was auditory. However, among the ESL students, those who were native speakers of Korean were the most visual, Chinese and Arabic the most auditory, Arabic and Spanish the most strongly kinesthetic, and Arabic, Chinese and Korean the most tactile. Numerous studies have shown that Native American students are visual learners (Haukoos and Satterfield, 1986; More, 1987; Reyhner, 1992; Robinson Shade, 1989).
- For students who are not native speakers of English, learning style preferences may affect the ease of English learning/acquisition. In particular, tolerance for ambiguity and field independence seem to enhance the development of English proficiency (Chapelle & Roberts, 1986; Larsen-Freeman, 1991; Larsen-Freeman & Long, 1991; Oxford 1989).

Conclusions

One of the aspects of learning style theory that remains unresolved is the importance of matching students' learning styles to the teaching styles of their instructors (Anderson, 1988; Bennett, 1990; Claxton & Murrell, 1987; Scarcella, 1990; Shade, 1989; Tharp, 1989; Witkin et al., 1977). For the purpose of this book, this is an interesting issue but not necessarily relevant. First, we generally do not test for student learning styles in science courses. Second, with an increasingly diverse undergraduate population, the likelihood of ever 'matching' students' learning styles with faculty teaching styles grows even more remote. Third, learning styles should not be used to stereotype students. It is no more correct to presume that all white males are competitive, field independent learners, and all Hispanics collaborative, field dependent learners, than it is to believe that all Asian-Americans are destined to become scientists and engineers and all Hispanics great writers of fiction. Such generalizations are just not true, and in the case of learning styles, there is wide variation within any group of individuals.

Top-down, large-scale efforts to reform science education are taking place slowly and have only reached a limited number of college campuses. Therefore, whatever individual instructors can do to teach in ways that tap into the wide range of learning styles of today's students is a more realistic 'bottom up' approach to make science more accessible to more students. Best of all, such efforts do not usually require any major grants, revision of the curriculum, nor departmental approval.

As Clarke (1993, 1994) has suggested, the likelihood for success of educational reform begins with individual initiative. This is because systems inherently resist change. Science instructors who are willing to broaden their teaching styles, to use a more student-centered pedagogy, and who will work with today's students and not complain about their deficiencies are much more likely to bring about dramatic, immediate, and positive results than those who want to change the students or the educational system.

5 How Instructors Can Help Limited English Proficient Students in Traditional Science Courses

It is the start of a new semester. You are standing in front of your class. First you scan the room, looking at the faces of your new crop of students. Then you glance down at your class roster. You smile at your students and say, 'Welcome to Bio/Chem/Physics 101' and give a brief description of what you intend to cover in the course and what you expect the students to learn. You look professional, prepared, experienced and self-confident. The students are impressed; they already have heard through the 'grapevine' that you are a tough but fair instructor. They listen intently to your words.

Fortunately, the students cannot see into your head! Behind your facile smile and calm air, a 'private' conversation is running through your mind. It goes something like this: 'Help! What country am I in? Where did these students come from? Does anyone speak English in this class? Are they going to understand me? How am I going to teach them science? Oh boy, I am in trouble.'

Rest assured. This chapter is designed to answer those questions and to reduce anxiety. There are numerous strategies which faculty members can use to facilitate the instruction of science to LEP students. In fact, not only will the LEP students benefit, so too will many native English speaking students who find science to be a particularly difficult discipline.

There are four key points to be emphasized about the information that follows:

1. Faculty members can pick and choose what best suits their own particular style of teaching as well as the needs of their students.
2. Most of the techniques described here do not require any specialized training in order to be put into practice.
3. The recommendations that follow in no way suggest, nor should they be interpreted to mean, that academic standards be lowered, that content be watered-down, or that expectations be reduced for language minority students.
4. These suggestions are derived from the principles of good teaching and

successful ESL practices and will benefit LEP students in two ways: they will facilitate the learning of science and also increase the students' proficiency in English.

The recommendations that follow are based on opinions expressed by LEP students to this author and on suggestions contained in many of the references cited in this book (for example, see Bennett, 1990; Cochran, 1992; M.F. Green, 1989; Peitzman & Gadda, 1991; Richard-Amato & Snow, 1992; Rosenthal, 1992/1993; Scarcella, 1984; Simms & Leonard, 1986; Sutman, Allen & Shoemaker, 1986). Whether you are concerned about the lecture, the text, the laboratory, written assignments, testing, your interaction with students, the resources available on your campus, and/or other approaches to helping improve science instruction for LEP students, you should find some helpful ideas in what follows.

The Lecture

The lecture remains central to science instruction (Higher Education Research Institute, 1992), allowing the teacher to present a large amount of information to students in a relatively short period of time. From the instructor's point of view, it does not really matter if the class has 30 or 800 students. The subject matter is addressed explicitly, in a time and cost efficient manner. Lectures simplify the work of instructors and enable them to sum up in an hour's time the contributions and findings of many researchers from the past and the present. While some students learn well from lectures, others do not. The latter, for example,

- may not be able to identify what is important from what is not,
- may have trouble listening to new information and simultaneously taking notes,
- may get confused by unfamiliar vocabulary,
- may get bored from just sitting and listening, and
- if they do not understand a particular concept or idea, may get 'lost' (tune out) for the rest of the lecture.

Engrossed in the topic of the day, anxious to cover the subject-matter without omitting one detail, the instructor may be quite oblivious to whether or not the learning needs of the students in the class are being met.

There are, however, many ways to enhance a lecture so that it becomes not only more interesting but also more comprehensible to students. The instructor who can answer 'yes' to many of the following questions is well on his or her way to helping today's diverse students to understand and learn science; this is especially true for those students who are still learning English.

- Do you speak clearly?
- Do you maintain a moderate and reasonable pace?

- Do you look at your students, talking to them, not at the lectern or the chalkboard?
- Do you present an overview of what is going to be covered before delving into the details? (This can be accomplished orally and/or by briefly outlining the topic on the chalkboard.)
- Do you take into consideration that not all students enter the course sharing the same background knowledge?
- Do you present new terms and definitions both orally and in written form?
- Do you write the most important concepts or points on the chalkboard or present them via transparencies or handouts?
- Do you make sure that your handwriting is legible?
- Do you provide students with handouts that summarize what was or will be covered in class?
- At various times during the lecture, do you briefly summarize the information that has just been covered?
- Do you try to make connections between what you are teaching and the personal lives of your students?
- Do you relate the new information you are presenting to topics covered earlier in the course?
- Do you try not to ramble too far afield? And, if you are in the habit of wandering off the subject, do you explicitly relate the digression to the main topic of the lecture as you get back on track?
- Do you watch the faces of your students to determine if they are following what you are saying?
- Do you frequently remind yourself to keep your language simple?
- Do you teach in a variety of ways in order to appeal to the diverse learning styles of your students?
- Do you repeat and rephrase the most important points of the lecture?
- Do you use a lot of synonyms and/or give the definitions of words that LEP students may not otherwise understand?
- Do you present well-organized lectures so that all students can more easily take notes and follow your presentation?
- Do you emphasize those points which are most important?
- Do you present new concepts step-by-step?
- If a concept is abstract, do you give several concrete examples?
- Do you periodically stop and ask if there are any questions and answer them if there are?
- Do you encourage students to submit questions in writing if they are too anxious about speaking up in front of the class?
- Do you model critical thinking skills by asking questions and then leading the students to the answers?
- Do you use videos, slides, films or whatever materials are available— either in class or as additional assignments—to visually and aurally reinforce the information covered in lecture?

- Do you discuss and/or demonstrate effective note-taking skills?
- Do you allow students to tape-record lectures or make available through your college's resource center audio- or video-tapes of the lectures?
- Do you prepare and distribute vocabulary lists that include key terms, their meanings, and sentences that show each word used in context?
- Do you try to stay away from excessive use of jokes, slang or idioms, and if you use them, do you briefly explain what they mean for the sake of the students who do not understand?
- If you use references to popular American culture, do you also explain what you mean for the sake of the non-native students?
- If the class is small enough, do you try to use cooperative/collaborative group learning, mixing together native and non-native speakers of English?
- Do you incorporate writing-to-learn activities? (For some examples, see Chapter 6.)
- If there is information that students do not understand, do you explain it in another way, giving examples and/or making analogies?
- Do you try to maintain a sense of humor?
- If there is too much material and too little time left near the end of the semester, do you resist the urge to rush through everything? In other words, do you teach what you reasonably can and plan to make appropriate changes in your syllabus for the following semester?

The Text

Although no one knows the exact figure, it has been estimated that on some college campuses 20–50% of the students do not purchase their assigned texts (Lichtenberg, 1994). Evidently, there are students who do not consider the textbook nearly as essential as the instructor(s) responsible for its selection.

In the case of introductory science courses, there invariably is a companion textbook. Its selection is sometimes done with great care, other times in great haste. It can be done by the individual instructor or by a committee. However it is done, the selection process should take into account not only the content, organization, and cost of the text but also its comprehensibility and reader friendliness. These last two factors are particularly important when the class includes students of limited English proficiency. Although they may have completed a program of study of English as a Second Language, various studies have shown that these students often still have difficulty reading and studying from textbooks (Ostler, 1980; Sheorey & Mokhtari, 1993; Smoke, 1988).

The instructor who can answer 'yes' to the following questions will be helping all students, especially those of limited English proficiency, to benefit from the textbook and any other additional reading assignments. (See Chapter 6 for further discussion of introductory science texts.)

- Do you deliberately select a readable textbook and only assign relevant pages?
- If there is a choice of texts, do you consult with an ESL specialist about the selection of the one most suitable for your students?
- Do you discuss with your students the layout and organization of the text and how to find information in it?
- If there are additional reading assignments beside what is in the text, do you provide students with study guides that explicitly indicate what information they should be looking for in these articles/readings?
- If there are several LEP students who speak the same native language, do you try to obtain a textbook in their language that can be put on reserve in the library and can be used by the students as an additional reference?

The Laboratory

As Reid (1987) has shown, many ESL students when compared to their American peers are much more tactile and kinesthetic in terms of their preferred learning styles. The laboratory therefore offers these students the opportunity to learn science by 'doing' science. In addition, while working in the lab, they can practice their English when reading directions, writing down observations, and talking to their lab partners and instructor. By doing all that is possible so that they can answer 'yes' to the following questions, instructors will be helping to optimize the laboratory experience for non-native English speaking students:

- Do you provide written instructions which are easy to read and understand?
- If students work in pairs or small groups, do you mix native and non-native English speakers?
- Do you circulate through the laboratory, stopping to talk to students, including the non-native speakers of English, to ask them about the experiment, results, etc?
- Do you make available additional videos, slides, models, and/or demonstrations to reinforce what the students are doing in the laboratory exercises?
- Do you have students work in small groups when analyzing and interpreting their results?
- Have you considered making laboratory reports a small group project with each student assigned a particular part of the report such as the introduction, materials and methods, results and their analysis, or discussion and conclusions? In this way, who does each part is rotated from week to week, and two grades are assigned each student for a given report: an individual grade for the part he or she prepared as well as an overall group grade.

Written Assignments

The kinds of written assignments required in a science course, such as laboratory reports, short essays, and research papers, may be some of the easiest forms of writing in English for ESL students. Usually, there is a particular format required for the assignment, and its content is based on data, research findings, and factual information (Ballard & Clanchy, 1991; Johns, 1991a, b).

Nevertheless, as described in Chapters 2 and 6, non-native speakers of English do encounter many difficulties when writing in their second language including grammar, punctuation, organization of ideas, word selection, and spelling. This is true for many ESL students even if they have successfully completed an ESL program (Ostler, 1980; Russikoff, 1994; Smoke, 1988; Snow & Kinsella, 1994; Swartley, 1994).

Some science faculty believe very strongly that their job is to teach science, not writing. However, they invariably give students graded, written assignments. Thus, writing does become an integral part of the science course, allowing students to demonstrate what they know and have learned. Writing is also useful to help students learn science, and examples of such activities are described in Chapter 6.

Many students encounter difficulties with the writing process. This is as true for native English speakers as for non-native speakers. As mentioned previously in Chapter 2, several studies have shown that science faculty are less tolerant of the writing errors made by ESL students than are their colleagues in the social sciences, education, and humanities (Santos, 1988; Vann, Meyer & Lorenz, 1984; Vann, Lorenz & Meyer, 1991). This is true even though the science faculty can readily distinguish between content and form.

There are many ways that instructors can help their students with written assignments. Those who can answer 'yes' to the following questions are already providing the kind of support that many students need, particularly those who are still learning English.

- Do you supply written instructions that describe what you want done and how you want it done?
- Are your handouts and written instructions models of the quality of writing you expect from your students?
- Do you make available sample assignments that illustrate the kind and quality of work you are expecting?
- Are you available during office hours if students need additional assistance with organizing or revising their assignments?
- Do you refer students to the appropriate writing centers on campus if they need additional help?
- If you insist on correcting spelling, syntax, lexical, or grammatical errors, do you try to concentrate on the one or two types of errors that are the most annoying?

- For term papers and major written assignments, do you set specific deadlines for each of the following: selection and approval of the topic; submission of an outline/first draft along with references; date the final version must be turned in?
- When grading, do you focus on content?
- Do you consult with an ESL specialist if one of your students is having a specific writing problem?

Testing

Certain difficulties may arise when ESL students are taking tests (Ballard & Clanchy, 1991; Johns, 1991a). For example, they may lack the words in English to adequately express what they actually know and have learned. With limited time available, they may become nervous, forgetting some of the English they have already learned. The format of the test may be unfamiliar; and they may not understand the wording of test questions and may misinterpret what is being asked of them.

To alleviate these and other difficulties encountered by ESL students during the testing process, an instructor should consider the following:

- During timed exams, do you go out of your way not to penalize LEP students for grammar, spelling, syntactical, or lexical errors?
- When grading, do you focus on content, not form?
- Do you allow LEP students to use bilingual dictionaries?
- Do you include a variety of types of questions on exams (such as short answer, fill in the blank, problem solving, essay, multiple choice, true/false, sequencing, and matching)?
- Do you ask an ESL specialist on your campus to look over your exam questions to help you eliminate ambiguous items and grammatical constructions that might confuse ESL students?
- Do you give students extra time if they need it to complete their tests?
- Do you encourage students to make pictures and diagrams to help clarify their written responses?
- If a student does poorly on an exam, do you ask the student to meet with you at office hours to determine what went wrong and how to prevent it from occurring again?
- Do you place copies of exams from previous semesters on reserve in the library so that students who do not belong to sororities or fraternities and who do not have friends who have already taken the course will have the same opportunity to find out in advance what your tests are like?
- Have you considered alternative forms of assessment such as individual or group projects or research papers?

Interacting With Students

Good faculty/student relations and a pleasant classroom climate have been emphasized in the discussion of various topics in this book. First, in Chapter 2, the affective filter (Krashen, 1981, 1982) was described and how emotions influence L2 acquisition. Second, the inaccessiblity of science instructors as well as the competitive classroom atmosphere were mentioned in Chapter 3 as conditions that 'turn off' students to science (Seymour, 1992a, b; Tobias, 1990). And third, as mentioned in Chapter 4, many of today's students are relatively field dependent; for them to learn science, a supportive instructor and a collaborative classroom are helpful.

Making a science classroom pleasant for students does not mean that the content is watered-down nor that standards and expectations are lowered. It does indicate that instructors are aware that affect has an impact on learning and that how they interact with students can increase or decrease students' interest in and learning of science.

There are many ways that a teacher can influence the classroom climate. While some instructors like being buddies with their students, having their students call them by their first name, and socializing together, other faculty members would find such a relationship very awkward. Moreover, students who have been raised in cultures in which teachers are honored and respected might find such chumminess quite disconcerting. Therefore, the recommendations that follow (once again in question format) indicate how an instructor can make a science classroom more supportive for *all* students, while maintaining whatever distance is necessary to keep the instructor and students most comfortable.

- During the first week of the semester, if the class is small enough, do you carry out some 'ice breaker' activities so that the students will feel more comfortable with each other and with you? Do you make sure that you, the instructor, participate along with the students?
- As part of the 'ice breaker' activities, do you have students exchange phone numbers (if they are willing) so that should they miss a class or be confused about some of the material presented in class, they can call up a classmate to find out what they missed or to get help?
- Do you help organize the students into study groups?
- Do you inform students about academic support services available on campus such as writing or tutoring centers?
- Are you available to assist students during office hours?
- Do you encourage LEP students to participate in class and small group activities and praise their efforts?
- When LEP students ask questions in lecture or the lab, do you paraphrase the question before responding so that you can verify that you correctly understood the question and/or so that the whole class will hear the question you will be answering?

- Do you try to make the classroom atmosphere both pleasant and intellectually stimulating?
- Are you patient and supportive when LEP students speak up in class, remembering that they may be self-conscious about their accents and unsure of their ability to express themselves clearly in English?
- When you see that a student is in academic trouble, do you invite him or her to meet with you at office hours so that the problem(s) can be diagnosed and a plan of corrective action implemented promptly?
- From the beginning of the term, are you explicit about your grading system, and do you periodically provide the students with feedback on how they are doing?
- Do you try not to prejudge students and/or their abilities based on their accent, skin color, culture, religion, handicap, manner of dress, or country of origin?
- Do you try to treat all students fairly?
- If workshops and training are provided on campus on topics such as diversity in the classroom or how to teach ESL students, do you make every effort to attend?

Taking Advantage of Resources Available on Campus

Between teaching classes, carrying out research, serving on committees, advising students, writing grant proposals and articles for publication, a professor can work at a college or university for many years and remain unaware of the resources available on campus to help students. The questions that follow provide some useful prompts for science instructors who want to investigate not only what might be helpful to themselves but also to the students enrolled in their courses:

- Have you tried to find out if your college has an ESL program or specialist who you can call with questions pertaining to language difficulties ESL students may experience in your course?
- Have you determined if your college has a tutoring service and/or writing center where LEP students can receive assistance?
- Have you inquired if there is a Supplemental Instruction (SI) Program on campus and if it can be attached to your course? (See Box 5.1.)
- Do you find time to go to the library to browse through journals such as *College Teaching* or *The Journal of College Science Teaching* to look for new ways to assist your students or to enhance your teaching?
- When the opportunity arises, do you attend faculty development workshops that address effective teaching?

Other Recommendations

The final set of recommendations which is given below goes a bit beyond helping to recruit and retain LEP undergraduates in the sciences. The instructor who pursues these avenues fully recognizes the changing demographics of the undergraduate population and is willing, both professionally and personally, to meet the needs of today's multicultural and multilingual students:

- In your introductory science classes or through advisement, do you provide students with information about careers and graduate study in the sciences, the Graduate Record Exam, what is involved in earning a Master's and/or Doctorate, graduate fellowships, and special opportunities in the sciences for minority students?
- Are you willing to increase your awareness of issues pertaining to the education of immigrants and language minority students and to the changing demographics of the United States? Are you reading newspaper and journal articles on these topics?
- Have you considered the possibility of organizing some workshops in your department or for content-area faculty to discuss and learn about issues related to the instruction of LEP students, the process of second language acquisition, or matters pertaining to student diversity?
- Are you aware of the resources available through the ERIC Clearinghouse on Languages and Linguistics, the Center for Applied Linguistics, the National Clearinghouse for Bilingual Education, Teachers of English to Speakers of Other Languages, and the National Association for Bilingual Education? The addresses and phone numbers of these organizations appear in the Appendix at the end of this book (page 180).
- Have you started studying a 'foreign language' and decided to stick with it until you are fluent? Only then will you truly understand the difficulties faced by LEP students!

Conclusion

Faculty members who can answer 'yes' to many of the questions listed above are already helping the ESL students enrolled in their science courses. Those who answered with more 'no's' than 'yes's' now have some ideas, some guidelines, about the kinds of things they might do to enhance science instruction for students who are still learning English.

Clearly, there is a lot that individual instructors can do without any specialized training to improve how science is taught. Many of these techniques reduce linguistic barriers for non-native speakers of English, thereby enhancing both the acquisition of English and the learning of science. Other students, including many native speakers of English who are afraid of science and find it 'hard', will also benefit from the recommendations presented in this chapter. For the instructor who is most comfortable teaching in the lecture/lab mode, this chapter offers activities and course enhancements that can be put into effect without major alteration of the traditional course format.

Box 5.1 Supplemental Instruction

One of the most effective academic support programs used at approximately two hundred colleges and universities across the United States is Supplemental Instruction (SI). It was developed in the mid-1970's at the University of Missouri-Kansas City (UMKC) to provide academic assistance to students enrolled in high risk courses. High risk courses are those in which—semester after semester—thirty percent or more of the students withdraw and/or receive grades of 'D' or 'F'.

What makes SI unique is that it changes the perspective taken on the source of 'the problem'. It is not the students who are considered high risk. Rather, certain courses are high risk, meaning that all students (those who we consider 'good', 'average' and 'poor') are likely to encounter difficulties.

At regularly scheduled times (generally three or more) during the week, students enrolled in high risk courses voluntarily meet with their SI leader. During these SI sessions, the leader serves as a facilitator and models how a successful student goes about studying and mastering the course content. Skills such as note-taking, how to study, and how to prepare for an exam are developed and practiced. The SI leader helps the students to help themselves and to help each other by working together cooperatively.

Who are the SI leaders? They are usually students who have successfully completed the course to which they are assigned, and they are trained in how to organize and run the SI sessions. Even though the SI leader has already passed the course, he or she continues to attend both lectures and labs, taking notes and doing the reading assignments.

At colleges and universities that operate SI programs, there is an experienced professional supervisor who selects and trains the SI leaders and who helps to identify high risk courses. The supervisor encourages instructors of such courses to attach SI to their sections, but participation is always voluntary. If a faculty member agrees that SI is a good idea, he or she approves the selection of the SI leader. Often it is the faculty member who nominates a former student for the position.

Supplemental Instruction is not remediation, and participation by students enrolled in high risk courses is voluntary. SI is generally available from the start of the semester and can therefore be of assistance before students encounter difficulties. In other words SI is 'proactive' rather than 'reactive'.

There is more than a decade of research demonstrating the effectiveness of SI. SI participants obtain higher course grades, receive fewer grades of 'D', 'F' or withdrawal, and reenroll and graduate from college at higher rates than non-SI students. SI is a welcome addition to introductory science courses which are notoriously high risk (even for students who enter college liking science and with good high school preparation in the sciences and math). In a study that included 304 sections of introductory biology and 329 of chemistry (at 146 institutions during the period of 1981-1993), SI participants received higher final course grades, more final grades of 'A' and 'B', and lower percentages of 'D's', 'F's' and 'withdrawals' than students who did not participate in SI. All results were statistically significant at the $p<0.01$ level. (Data obtained from the National Center for Supplemental Instruction, University of Missouri-Kansas City.)

Readers interested in more information about SI can contact:

Center for Academic Development-Supplemental Instruction
University of Missouri-Kansas City
Student Support Services Building
5100 Rockhill Road
Kansas City, Missouri 64110-2499
Phone: 816-235-1174
Fax: 816-235-5156

In addition, the National Resource Center for the Freshman Year Experience, University of South Carolina (Columbia, SC) has published an excellent monograph (Martin *et al.*, 1992) describing the theory behind and the practice of Supplemental Instruction.

6 Issues Related to Rhetoric, Writing and Reading

Language is essential for the teaching of science. Oral language is used to lecture, to ask and answer questions, to conduct discussions, and to direct classroom and laboratory activities. Written language is used to place information on the chalkboard, to prepare exams and quizzes, for laboratory directions and reports, to record experimental results, and to respond to test questions. Without written language there would not be any science textbooks or journals, nor Master's or Doctoral dissertations, nor a detailed historical record of scientific discoveries, developments and methodologies. Language is so central to the teaching of science that it is impossible to imagine a 'language free' science classroom.

This chapter includes discussion of three language-related issues which are relevant to both science instruction and to language minority students. The first has to do with the written work in English of ESL students and how it may reflect both the style and pattern of argumentation of the students' native language. The second is writing to learn science which is a process that can help both native and non-native speakers of English. The third is the science textbook: its selection, readability, actual usefulness, and implications for bilingual students. These three topics—rhetoric, writing and reading—highlight the relationship between language and culture, so that this chapter is an extension of the discussion about culture which began in Chapter 3.

Language and Culture

Language is an integral part of culture, and the words that we have and how we use them reflect our values and belief system. The native language we speak (and eventually write) and how we use language to communicate are determined by the culture in which we are raised and schooled (Connor & Kaplan, 1987; Damen, 1987; Gadda, 1991; Hall, 1976; Kaplan, 1966; Lemke, 1990; Liebman, 1992; Richard-Amato & Snow, 1992). Babies and toddlers not only acquire the vocabulary, sounds and syntax of L1 but also the culturally determined 'rules' about 'what can and should be said, and how, and when, (Gadda, 1991: 55). Similarly, ESL students studying in the United States are learning both American English and American culture. Although native speakers rarely give this a thought, language reveals a lot about a culture. Consider the following:

- Certain colloquial expressions reflect a particularly Anglo-American world view. For example, 'Time is money,' and 'Cleanliness is next to godliness'.
- In the United States, indirect speech acts are often used for the sake of 'politeness'. At home, someone might say to a child or spouse, 'Would you mind taking out the garbage?' However, what is really meant is, 'Take out the garbage!' In class, an instructor might quizzically ask a student, 'You did not finish the assignment?' However, the real meaning of this rhetorical question is, 'That assignment is due today. What are you, stupid or lazy? Another 'F' won't help your grade!' For the ESL student such 'polite' or indirect forms of language may elicit literal (and possibly inappropriate) responses.
- Another example of the influence of culture on American English has to do with the abundance of sports analogies and sports related idioms. You can say all of the following and never once be referring to sports: 'grab the ball and run with it', give 'ballpark' figures, 'bounce around a few ideas', 'wrestle' with the facts, cry 'foul ball', describe your 'gameplan', play 'hardball', 'sit on the sidelines', and 'tackle' the job. For the individual who is still learning English (and/or is not particularly interested in baseball, football and basketball), the meaning of such remarks might be more than a bit confusing!
- Culture also determines how things are classified and categorized. Examples of this are presented in Box 3.3, pages 78–79.
- Argumentation patterns are shaped by language and culture. This can create difficulties for ESL students when the rhetoric of their native language (L1) carries over into their written English (L2) producing discourse style which is considered inappropriate.

Effects of L1 Reasoning on L2 (English) Writing

When it comes to L2 learning, relatively little attention is paid by either teachers or students to the kind of reasoning that is typically used by native speakers of the target language. Therefore, ESL students may become quite proficient in the grammar, vocabulary and sentence structure of English, yet unwittingly bring to it the logic and rhetoric characteristic of their native culture and language. As a result, the written work of ESL students sometimes seems 'out of focus', disorganized, or may contain what is considered to be irrelevant information (Ballard & Clanchy, 1991; Connor & Kaplan, 1987; Damen, 1987; Gadda, 1991; Kaplan, 1966; Leki, 1992; Lemke, 1990; Liebman, 1992; Reid, 1992).

Each academic discipline also has its own discourse style. For example, scientific reasoning is linear and inductive. The basic facts are first laid out, and from there a case is built. All extraneous information and unnecessary words are omitted producing a tightly knit argument and a style of writing which is concise and precise. This style, however, does not come naturally to most individuals including both native and non-native speakers of English.

Kaplan (1966) was the first to note how the native languages of students influence their writing in English. He found that when native speakers of Semitic languages write in English, their paragraphs are characterized by parallel constructions (which produce considerable repetition); that the English writing of native Chinese and Korean speakers is marked by 'indirection', 'tangential' references to the subject, and by descriptions of what things are not (rather than what they are); and that native French and Spanish speakers include digressions and introduce extraneous information when they write in English.

According to Kaplan (1966:15), paragraph development can be graphically presented in the various language groups as shown in Figure 6.1.

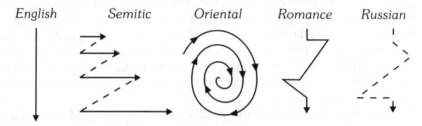

Figure 6.1 Kaplan's graphical representation of paragraph development in various linguistic systems. (Reprinted with permission from Kaplan, 1996:15.)

As a result of these different L1 styles of writing, ESL students may produce written assignments in L2 that are totally inappropriate for the discourse style of a given academic discipline. For example what is considered good writing in a creative writing course would be unsuitable in a science course.

It is easy to forget that one rhetoric is not necessarily better than another, but that particular forms of rhetoric are more or less appropriate to particular situations. Leki (1992: 90) reminds us that rhetorical logic is 'socially *constructed* rather than a reflection of innate thought processes' and that we need to remember 'the relatively arbitrary nature of rhetoric because all rhetorics seem to want to claim for themselves that they are self-evidently logical.'

As for science, students are not born knowing how to think and write scientifically; they must be taught these skills. For ESL students, scientific writing and its argumentation patterns may be among the easiest to develop (Ballard & Clanchy, 1991; Johns, 1991a, b). Compared to other academic disciplines, the topics are specific; personal interpretations and opinions generally are not required; the writer does not have to be familiar with American history and culture; the appropriate vocabulary comes directly from the lectures and text;

and creativity and imagination are much less important than the presentation of evidence from which conclusions can be drawn.

While ESL teachers and linguists might be prepared to recognize and deal with alternative reasoning and writing styles that appear in the L2 writing of ESL students, science professors often are not. Yet, they grade and evaluate a variety of written assignments (e.g. essay exams, laboratory reports, term papers) prepared by ESL students enrolled in their courses (Russikoff, 1994; Snow & Kinsella, 1994). Since many of the reasoning and writing skills needed in science go far beyond the reaches of what an ESL program can provide, it is therefore up to the science faculty to help students develop these abilities. They may need to explicitly instruct students about how to:

- present a reasoned and scientifically acceptable argument (Ballard & Clanchy, 1991);
- write in a way that takes into consideration the 'cultural norms and expectations of their audience' (Scarcella, 1984: 684)
- provide the type of evidence and documentation appropriate to scientific discourse, and
- distinguish between what is considered relevant and irrelevant information in terms of scientific reasoning.

Not only will ESL students benefit from this type of instruction, so will many native English speaking students who are not accustomed to the conventions of scientific thinking and writing.

Writing to Learn in Science

In a traditional lecture/lab science course, students are expected to learn by listening to lectures, reading the text, studying their class notes, doing experiments, writing laboratory reports, and solving sets of problems. For some students this works well, but for many it does not. Differences in learning styles as well as students' prior preparation in science may be contributing to some of the difficulties they encounter in science courses. This does not mean, however, that the situation is hopeless. While all students will benefit, it may be especially useful and important for students such as these to use various kinds of writing activities to help them learn science and mathematics (Connolly & Vilardi, 1989; Madigan, 1987a; Strauss & Fulwiler, 1987).

Writing? You can almost hear the chorus of science faculty and students exclaiming, 'Writing is for English class; it has nothing to do with science!' Instructors balk, concerned with having even more papers to grade. Students fret. Will they have to pay attention to spelling and grammar? After all, this is a science course! And, what about the students of limited English proficiency? Might writing exercises be too difficult and scare them away from science?

Reactions such as these reflect some of the misunderstandings about the nature of writing to learn science. However, as Susan Kirschner (former Director of the Core Program and Professor of English at Lewis and Clark College in Portland, Oregon) points out:

> Ordinary language, especially written language, is often overlooked in the teaching of science. Yet, when students bring their own language to what they initially experience as an arcane and/or exclusive set of specialized, 'artificial' languages (such as the language of science), they learn how to make complex concepts their own. Written language, even more than spoken language, is a tool of considerable power in learning abstract concepts well enough for them to become useful. Writing strategies can be used to think about any problem or topic, and students need not concern themselves with getting it—their writing—'right'. In fact, writing to learn science activities are not the place to work on spelling, punctuation, or sentence structure. Thus, ESL students as well as their native English speaking classmates should be advised not to worry about making mistakes. Furthermore, if ESL students cannot express their ideas in English, they can even try using their native tongue, and when necessary, translating into English later.

Writing to learn science helps students clarify their thoughts, relate new information presented in class to previous knowledge, and can provide the instructor with feedback on what students do and do not understand. It helps all students overcome a variety of 'barriers to learning' such as difficulties with comprehending the text or making sense of their lecture notes. ESL students stand to gain even more from this opportunity to practice writing informally in English.

The kinds of writing activities used to promote the learning of science differ in both form and function from 'professional' scientific writing (such as the articles that appear in scientific journals). When students use writing to learn science, form (grammar, spelling, syntax, etc.) is not important. They are not writing to demonstrate what they already know; instead, the purpose of this kind of writing is to help students to understand new information. Only when instructors are able to make this distinction can they comprehend the value of writing to learn science.

Examples of writing to learn science activities

Two excellent sources of information on writing to learn science are a series of articles that appeared in the *Journal of College Science Teaching* (1987) and Connolly & Vilardi's *Writing to Learn Mathematics and Science* (1989). The following examples of the kinds of writing activities that can be used in science courses come from those two sources.

Tobias (1989: 51) describes the 'divided-page exercise' to help students solve problems. On the right-hand page of their journals, students carry out their calculations and try to solve assigned problems. On the left-hand page they record their responses to two questions: 'What is making the problem difficult for me?' and 'What could *I* do to make it easier for myself?' By answering these questions, students help clarify their thinking, often over-coming whatever is blocking their ability to solve the problem.

Another instructor mentioned by Tobias (1989: 54) uses 'minute papers'. Several times during the semester, toward the end of a class, he asks his students to react to two questions. These are, 'What is the most significant thing you learned today?' and, 'What question is uppermost in your mind at the conclusion of this class session?' The students' responses provide feed-back to the instructor as to what they do and do not understand. The instructor can use this information in planning future lessons.

Martin (1989) makes two important points that relate to the need for writing to learn activities in science. First, she notes that some students seem to truly understand the subject matter but cannot break it down into the bits of information that they must recall for objective type exams (Martin, 1989: 113). Second, she describes how students often have trouble studying from their lecture notes because rereading their notes does not necessarily help them identify the concepts they do not understand (Martin, 1989: 114-115). Lecture notes, as she aptly points out, reflect how the instructor organizes and thinks about the subject matter. However, through writing activities, students can put that information into their own words, thus coming to 'own' it.

Martin (1989) describes a series of optional 'microthemes' which students can write in the *Human Biology* course that she teaches. Points earned on microtheme assignments can substitute for points allotted on objective exams. Many of the microtheme topics require that the students draw analogies to help explain the science they have learned. As an example, she mentions (page 114) how a student compared covalent bonds to 'two jugglers each with three balls sharing a fourth ball between them'. In one of her microtheme topics, she asks the students to make up a story that includes an analogy to explain how the kidney gets rid of the 'dastardly molecule urea'. The story/analogy had to include the various parts of and the processes that occur in the kidney. Microthemes are limited to one typed page and are graded on the basis of scientific accuracy. Students may rewrite unsatisfactory microthemes.

Analogies are also emphasized in some of the physics writing activities at the University of Massachusetts, Amherst (Mullin, 1989). In physics, some students memorize formulas and equations in order to solve problems but have no intuitive feel for the principles or concepts they are supposedly learn-ing. By means of writing, they are asked to turn quantitative into qualitative descriptions. Often, this is best done by the use of analogies. Concepts that students could not grasp from lectures, from the text, or from formulas, may actually begin to make sense when put into the students' own words and when comparisons are made to objects and phenomena with which they are familiar.

Strauss & Fulwiler (1987: 256) describe coming 'to view writing as central to helping students learn chemistry under the sometimes adverse conditions of a large lecture class'. They placed boxes by the exits of their lecture hall to collect students' 'thoughts, questions, concerns, critiques, and commentary'. Students would drop in questions pertaining to the lecture, or those that developed while studying the text, reviewing for an exam, or while working with some of their classmates. After sorting out the candy wrappers, graffiti and jokes, the instructors typically were left with 20 to 30 'fragments of writing' contributed by students who had something they needed to comment on or to clarify about the course. Questions that occurred frequently were presented on overhead transparencies (in the students' own handwriting) and then responded to. Others are answered using dittos. If students so requested, their questions were answered personally and privately, during office hours or by phone. The 'exit box' approach provided the instructors with immediate feedback, and as Strauss & Fulwiler noted, in the process of writing their questions, students sometimes discovered the answers they were looking for.

Ambron (1987: 263) describes using journals, freewriting, and microthemes in an introductory cell biology course with students who had 'shown poor language skills in traditional college writing assignments.' She mentions that 'the creativity and scientific accuracy in the students' responses [to the freewriting activities] made me rethink many of my former beliefs about their language skills (page 265).'

Additional writing to learn science activities are to be found in the selected, annotated bibliography that appears in Madigan (1987b); see also Box 6.1.

Box 6.1 Writing to Learn Science: The Unknown Object

One of the writing activities Professor Susan Kirschner (former Director of the Core Program and Professor of English at Lewis and Clark College in Portland, OR) recommends combines writing and collaborative learning to inquire into the identify an unknown object. This is a technique she and others developed at the Bard Institute for Writing and Thinking (The Bard Center, PO Box 5000, Annandale-on-Hudson, NY 12504-5000; phone 914-758-7432). Professor Kirschner has been an associate of the Institute for the last ten years. (For readers who are not familiar with the Institute's activities, it is worth mentioning that the Institute regularly offers a series of writing workshops and conferences including one entitled 'Writing to Learn Math and Science'; the Institute also provides on-site consultations.)

In Kirschner's words:

The process of inquiry into an unknown object involves both informal writing and collaborative learning. It also uses some of the habits and practices important to good scientific inquiry including:

- using language to describe and name things,
- building consensus, that is deciding the points that the members of the group agree upon as well as those issues about which the members 'agree to disagree',
- valuing differences in opinion and testing all possible interpretations, especially those that challenge consensus,
- learning how differences of opinion even more than agreement promote scientific inquiry,
- observing closely and carefully and asking questions based on those observations, and
- appreciating how collaboration and the sharing of information stimulates and advances science.

In addition to learning science by means of the activity to be described, non-native speakers of English have the opportunity in a science class to use their new language in an authentic setting and to practice both written and oral forms of English. They may need reminding that this work will not be graded and that it is their ideas and not the form of their writing which are important. Let all students know that what they write will be shared with a partner, but that they need not worry about spelling, punctuation, or any other constraints having to do with appearing 'correct' in public. Each student will need a worksheet or page in a notebook which is divided into four columns.

Part I

Step 1: An unknown object (even the teacher may not know what it is) is placed where the students can see, touch, smell and observe it. (If some students think that they can identify the object, they are asked to contribute within the 'fiction' of not knowing, or an alternative object can be provided.)

Step 2: In the first column of their worksheet or notebook page, the students describe the object in as much detail as possible. Tell them that you want the description to be so precise that someone entering the room could recognize the object based on their description.

Step 3: In the second column, ask the students to write down their hypotheses or guesses about what the object could plausibly be and also what its functions might be. (What might it 'do'?) Also in column 2, they should jot down what else they would need to know in order to be more confident about their guesses.

Step 4: Students then pass their notebooks (or worksheet) to the person sitting to the left and receive a notebook (or worksheet) from the person sitting on the right. They read what their partners have written in columns 1 and 2. Then, in column 3 (of the partner's worksheet or notebook), each student holds a 'written conversation' with his or her partner. In this collaboration, partners share additional information that one or the other may have overlooked, generate ideas neither had previously considered, and question and give reasons why some the guesses or hypotheses appear dubious.

Step 5: Students then pass the notebooks (worksheets) to the right, returning them to their original owners. After reading what the partner has written, students write further thoughts and responses in column 4.

Part II

Step 6: At this point, divide the students into small groups of four to six. Make the groups as diverse as possible and mix the students of limited English proficiency with native English speakers. Ask students to read each other's notebooks and to talk about the various guesses or hypotheses, evaluating which ones seem most plausible and why.

Step 7: Next, the group's task is to form consensus as to what the object is and does. One member of the group should serve as a recorder, taking notes, keeping track of how consensus is negotiated, and recording those points about which people agree to disagree.

Explain that consensus involves negotiation of differences, not domination by the majority view or by the strongest or loudest voice. Encourage the group to find the largest areas of agreement and also to identify those points on which they disagree. Actually, it is the latter, the areas of disagreement, which will stimulate further inquiry and learning, while it is the effort to agree, to try to build consensus, that sharpens differences.

Step 8: One member of each small group then reports back to the entire class on the hypothesis or guess it found most plausible. Members of the larger group ask questions, express doubts, and offer additional reasons for believing the hypothesis under consideration. Discussion then centers on which of the hypotheses put forward seems most plausible to the whole class. Is one more believable than another? If so, why? If there are competing hypotheses, see if consensus develops around one.

Step 9: Point out that when the group agrees on what to name an object then any member of the group can refer to the object with assurance that everyone else in the group will understand what he or she means. In contrast, outsiders might well not understand unless told or unless they somehow figure it out. Other discourse communities, disciplines, traditions, fields, experts, and cultures would try to understand and claim to know the object in different ways and would probably give the object a different name. See if students can give you some examples. (For example, the term 'artifact' can have very different meanings for archeologists and biologists. For the former, it may refer to an ancient object made by humans, while for the latter, an artifact is an artifically produced abnormal structure or appearance in a cell or specimen. Similarly, a 'bond' means one thing to a chemist in terms of chemical structures but refers to something completely different when a psychologist is describing the relationship between mothers and their offspring.)

Step 10: Also ask what remains mysterious about the object — either because the group is not confident of its identification or because there is something that remains inexplicable or puzzling. Students invariably want to know what the object is: the right answer. The teacher can counter such queries with questions such as, 'Why would you believe me if I told you?'; 'I got it from my friend, daughter, taxi driver...' or 'I found it on the beach and haven't the foggiest idea what it is either.' Inquiry, scientific and other, involves questioning anything and everything, including authority.

Step 11: The instructor may also point out the role of consensus building in the construction of scientific knowledge; how the process of science involves building consensus about what is true, false, and marginal, and how these definitions change and are reinterpreted over time (Banks, 1993; Locke, 1992).

Step 12: Finally, ask students to write informally to help them understand their own learning behaviors throughout this exercise. They should take five minutes or so to respond to the following questions:

• What did you learn and from whom?
• What was your role in the group and how did you feel about it?
• Did you change your mind about the unknown object, what it might be and its function? When? In response to whom or what?
• What was the effect of being asked to try for consensus?

Conclusion

When this exercise is over, students will have been asked to observe, describe, infer, form hypotheses, consider and record the hypotheses of others, provide reasons (both supportive and critical), analyze and reflect, share their writing and ideas with other students, reach consensus, and to stand back and reflect critically about the entire process they have just experienced. Each of these activities is an integral part of scientific inquiry. This exercise simulates skills and processes of scientific inquiry that stretch far beyond memorization of facts and formulas.

For additional information contact:

Professor Susan Kirschner
Department of English
Lewis and Clark College
0615 SW Palatine Hill Road
Portland, OR 97219
Phone 503-768-7353
Fax: 503-768-7359
email: susan@lclark.edu

Reading and the Introductory College Science Textbook

While not every introductory college science course incorporates writing to learn activities, most require students to purchase a specific textbook. The content of the text reinforces and supplements the instructor's lectures, and students are presumed to benefit by reading the assigned pages/chapters and perhaps by answering the end-of-chapter questions.

While textbook selection is sometimes done with immense care, this is not always true. An instructor may pick a book in haste, when he or she remembers that book orders are long overdue; another professor may be influenced in the choice of a text by a persuasive publisher's representative. A selection committee may reach a compromise, picking the book that least offends the most members of the committee. However, it is important to note that no matter how much a textbook may appeal to the instructor or a selection committee, that does not mean it is necessarily the best book for all students. Skilled, novice and L2 readers interact differently with their texts (Brown, Armbruster & Baker, 1986; Duran, Revlin & Smith, 1992), and they may differ significantly in how much they benefit from doing the assigned reading in the required text.

Scientific writing generally is straightforward and factual, and to the student it may seem especially boring and impersonal. Although a science textbook, newspaper article, or novel may be written in the same language— English—students often talk about how much harder it is to read and understand science. Unlike other materials that they read, the content of the science textbook is for the most part unfamiliar; the vocabulary is strange, and new words are introduced at a very rapid rate. There is no temporal or predictable sequence to the unfolding of information nor are there familiar themes to which the reader can relate. The bottom-up presentation of information (details before general ideas and concepts) often requires that the text be read several times (Westby & Rouse, 1993). The information is dense and is presented with little repetition or paraphrasing. The emotion, drama, and chronological unfolding of events that characterize many other forms of writing and other subject areas are absent from the science text, often making the reading tedious and slow going.

Another concern about scientific writing is that it has been growing more complex. Hayes (1992) in examining the text difficulty of scientific journals such as *Nature, Science, Cell, Scientific American*, and *Physics Today* found that many are becoming increasingly inaccessible and incomprehensible to anyone outside the specialty discussed in a given article or journal. He also reports on 'major college textbooks' for the introductory sciences, stating that those in physics and astronomy are written at lower levels, and those for biology, chemistry and geology are increasingly difficult.

Over the years introductory college science textbooks seem to have been 'growing': in length, breadth and depth of coverage, overall reading complexity (and cost). With the rapid rate of scientific discovery, some of these changes are to be expected. Nevertheless, many of these *introductory* books have become encyclopedic, and it is not possible for the instructor to 'cover' the content in a one (or even two) semester course. While the texts are beautifully illustrated and comprehensive in scope, there is so much detailed information packed between the covers that to call them introductory is an oxymoron.

In order to meet the curriculum demands of the many introductory courses taught on college campuses across this nation, every possible topic must be included. This increases the marketability of the text, as do the bountiful color illustrations and photographs. Whether or not the text is readable and comprehensible from the student's perspective may be forgotten by the instructor who is dazzled by the wide range of topics that is included and by the visual attractiveness of the book (Britton, Woodward & Binkley, 1993). In other words, the features that sell the book may have little to do with how helpful it actually will be to the students who are supposed to read and learn from it.

Science instructors rarely have time nor the occasion to think about what students get out of and are actually doing when reading the textbook. For example, are students:

1. Actually purchasing and reading the textbook? (And if they aren't, what are the reasons?)
2. Benefiting more by doing assigned readings before or after the lecture?
3. Searching for the main ideas or looking for the information for which the instructor will hold them accountable?
4. Learning facts or attempting to make sense of new concepts?
5. Trying to relate what they read to previously learned information or waiting for the book or instructor to do this for them?
6. Taking notes, underlining, or highlighting the text? And, do these techniques actually help students to learn and remember information?
7. Studying the formulas, graphs, diagrams, illustrations, and photographs or sticking to the written text? And do these visual aids help them to learn the material?
8. Slowing down when reading difficult passages, rereading sections of the text that are particularly troublesome, or skipping over the parts they do not understand?
9. Noting down what they do not understand so that they can ask for help later?
10. And, if the student is reading a text in his or her second language, how are all of these processes affected? Advanced ESL students in various studies (Ostler, 1980; Sheorey & Mokhtari, 1993; Smoke, 1988) often express concern about their ability to read and to understand their academic texts; they would like to be able to read more rapidly in English.

Dornic (1980) provides a summary of the effects of bilingualism on reading. Apparently, decoding (comprehending the meaning) in the nondominant (second) language is slower. In addition, 'prolonged verbal and intellectual activity' in the nondominant language causes mental fatigue and impairment of the short-term memory. Even on tasks in which bilinguals performed equally well in their dominant and nondominant languages, they *perceive* more difficulty, stress and fatigue when using their second language.

Thus, it is not surprising that ESL students claim that it takes them two or three times as long to read something in English than in their native language. However, it apparently is not just the time that is required but also the psychic energy expenditure that makes reading in a second language particularly difficult. This is especially true when the subject matter and vocabulary are unfamiliar.

In order to obtain more information about some of today's introductory science texts, Dr Linda Hirsch, Associate Professor of English at Hostos Community College of the City University of New York, carried out a reading level analysis. Dr Hirsch has conducted considerable research on identifying and addressing the needs of ESL students in content-area courses taught in English (Hirsch, 1988, 1991; Hirsch, Nadal & Shohet, 1991), and she is familiar with the various tests for assessing readability levels. (Clearly, text comprehensibility depends not only on how the book is written but also on characteristics of the reader, and these issues are discussed below.)

The selection of the specific texts analyzed by Dr Hirsch was not comprehensive. It included a total of six introductory science texts (two each in biology, chemistry, and physics) which were readily available in the science departments at Kean College of New Jersey in the summer of 1993. The readability test that was selected and performed by Dr Hirsch was that of Fry (Fry, 1977; Zakaluk & Samuels, 1988).

For each text, three 100-word passages were selected, and the number of syllables and the number of sentences counted and averaged. The averages were then plotted on the Fry Graph to determine the approximate grade level. As Dr Hirsch succinctly puts it, 'For uniformity and to make meaningful comparisons, reading selections were on equivalent topics'. Table 6.1 includes Dr Hirsch's findings.

According to the Fry readability test results, the biology and physics texts are somewhat easier to read than the two in chemistry, and five of the six books are written at the college-level (grades 13 and above). According to Dr Hirsch:

> Almost all of the textbooks examined require reading skills at the college level or beyond, levels difficult to attain for many ESL or post-ESL students. The high readability levels of college textbooks is one reason why many ESL students fare so poorly in English-language content courses. It is apparent that the transition from ESL class to academic coursework in English is a huge jump in the complexity of the material to be comprehended.

The high readability levels of college science texts indicates that ESL students may need help in learning how to effectively read and use the books assigned to them (T.W. Adams, 1989; Dubin, Eskey & Grabe, 1986). As indicated in the case studies in Chapters 7 and 9, some science instructors and ESL teachers, concerned with this issue, have written and developed their own instructional materials for science courses that include ESL students. Instructors cannot assume that all students who have completed an ESL program can comprehend their texts with the same facility as their native English speaking peers. In fact, many of the latter are required to take remedial reading courses and also have difficulties with reading their texts.

Table 6.1 Six introductory science texts: Fry readability levels

Subject matter Author(s) of text	No. of sentences	No. of syllables	Readability by grade level*
Biology			
Mader (3rd edn, 1990)			
Anaphase (p. 150)	6.5	163	11
Small Intestine (p. 552)	5.0	169	14
Gills (p. 565)	6.5	153	9
Average readability Mader			11
Starr & Taggart (6th edn, 1992)			
Anaphase (p. 144)	6.8	182	17+
Small Intestine (p. 646)	6.1	176	15
Gills (p. 702)	5.8	152	9
Average readability Starr & Taggart			13
Chemistry			
Brady & Holum (1993)			
Molecular Orbital Theory (p. 293)	6.0	181	17
Avogadro's Principle (p. 323)	4.5	162	12
Polyprotic Acids (p. 739)	3.0	180	17+
Average readability Brady & Holum			16
Ebbing (1993)			
Molecular Orbital Theory (p. 398)	4.3	167	14
Avogadro's Law (p. 175)	3.0[1]	197	17+
Polyprotic Acids (p. 676)	6.0[2]	207	17+
Average readability Ebbing			17+
Physics			
Cutnell & Johnson (2nd edn, 1992)			
Decibels (p. 453)	5.1	183	17+
Coulomb's Law (p. 505)	6.1	156	10
Magnetic Field (p. 599)	3.0	159	13
Average readability Cutnell & Johnson			13
Serway & Faughn (3rd edn, 1992)			
Decibels (p. 462)	5.8	172	14
Coulomb's Law (p. 506)	4.5	173	15
Magnetic Field (p. 630)	5.8	167	13
Average readability Serway & Faughn			14

* The Fry readability grade levels were determined by Dr. Linda Hirsch, Associate Professor of English at Hostos Community College of the City University of New York.
 1. The same readability (17+) is obtained whether or not the equation is counted as a sentence.
 2. If the three equations are counted as additional sentences, no grade level is calculable.

Faculty members whose classes include students of limited English proficiency (as well as underprepared native English speakers) should be discriminating in both the selection of a text and in terms of required reading assignments. No matter how comprehensive or well illustrated a text, no matter how famous its author, or how recent its copyright, the book serves no purpose if students won't and don't use it.

When a course includes students of limited English proficiency, whoever is selecting the textbook might want to consult with an ESL specialist on campus in order to determine the appropriateness of the books under consideration. Students might be enlisted in the selection process since they are relatively accurate judges of textbook learnability (Britton et al., 1991).

Selecting a suitable text means taking into consideration many factors including the background knowledge and experiences of the students, their reading ability in English, the difficulty of the subject matter and vocabulary, and how the information in the text is organized (Chall & Conard, 1991). The ideal science text for an ESL student would not only be comprehensible in terms of the subject matter but also just slightly more advanced than his or her current reading level in English. Under these conditions, the student will be able to understand and learn the science, and his or her ability to read in English will also improve (Chall & Conard, 1991; Krashen, 1982).

Conclusions

Rhetoric, writing and reading are issues that many content-area instructors feel should be left in the capable hands of their colleagues in the English department. The chemist has enough chemistry to teach and the biologist enough biology to fill every minute of the scheduled lectures and laboratories. Nonetheless, as Mohan (1986: 1) reminds us, 'Language is the major medium of instruction and learning'. Consequently, how language is used in the classroom is relevant to teachers and their students whatever the subject matter.

Language issues are of growing importance as the population of students of limited English proficiency increases. Their reading, writing, listening and speaking skills in English are developing at the same time they are studying different content-areas. They are also being introduced at a very rapid rate to new vocabulary, both general and subject-specific.

While the language-related issues discussed in this chapter — scientific reasoning in English, writing to learn science, and reading the science textbook—may not necessarily be foremost in the minds of science instructors, they do affect student achievement in science and should not be overlooked. In the long run, the science teacher who is aware of the importance of language in the instruction of science and who integrates meaningful reading and writing activities into the course will be helping all students, both the non-native speakers of English as well as the many native English speaking students who find science to be an especially difficult subject.

7 Case Studies I: Providing Academic Support to Science Students Who are Still Learning English

The case studies presented in this chapter include both the efforts of individual faculty members as well as campus-wide initiatives to improve science instruction for LEP students. Each includes general information about the college or university: its students' ethnic and linguistic backgrounds, the college's ESL program, plus a relatively detailed description of the kind of academic support provided to LEP students enrolled in science courses. Members of the faculty, staff, and/or administration at the institutions contributed this information, and their names and addresses are included at the end of each case study should readers want to learn more about a particular program.

In the first and second case studies, a geology professor at Brooklyn College (which is part of the City University of New York) and an assistant professor of biology at National-Louis University (Chicago, Illinois) describe in their own words not only how they teach but also their thinking about teaching when their courses include both native and non-native speakers of English.

Next are a series of case studies that involve college-wide programs at institutions that serve large numbers of language minority students:

- At Hostos Community College (which is part of the City University of New York) located in the Bronx, New York, there are 'language integration' activities involving faculty training and curriculum revision to make content-area courses more accessible to ESL students.
- Project LEAP (Learning English-for-Academic-Purposes) at California State University, Los Angeles, is designed to improve the academic language skills of high risk language minority students enrolled in general education courses. The project has involved faculty training, curriculum and teaching enhancements, plus the use of Supplemental Instruction.
- Cooperative learning study groups have been introduced into math and science courses at Our Lady of the Lake University (San Antonio, Texas).

- At Glendale Community College (Glendale, CA), Supplemental Instruction is being used to improve student achievement in high risk courses and to increase student retention and persistence.

Although these case studies reveal a variety of strategies for providing the academic support needed by students of limited English proficiency, they all share two common features. First, science instruction, with only a few modifications or enhancements, remains 'traditional' with a basic lecture/lab format. Second, the language of instruction is English. These characteristics are what distinguish the case studies presented here in Chapter 7 from those that will appear later in Chapter 9. In the latter, practices such as learning English through science instruction (which is called 'content-based ESL') as well as science coursework involving the use of the students' native language are described.

Efforts on the Part of Individual Science Instructors

Brooklyn College (City University of New York): How one geology instructor tries to meet the needs of diverse students

Brooklyn College (BC) is one of the many institutions that comprise the City University of New York (CUNY). A 1990 survey of first-time, full-time freshmen at BC showed a diverse student population: 49% White, 21% Black, 12% Asian, and 9% Hispanic. Twenty-three percent of these students are non-citizen, permanent residents, and 32% speak English as a second language.

The multilingual and multicultural nature of Brooklyn College students is typical throughout the CUNY system. In fact, it was reported that in the academic year 1988-89 there were 12,000 matriculated undergraduates enrolled in CUNY's various ESL programs (Cochran, 1992: 1).

In an attempt to help faculty (and also counselors and administrators) to educate such a linguistically diverse student population, CUNY's Instructional Resource Center prepared and published a handbook with guidelines for teaching language minority students (Cochran, 1992). In it is the following description of a geology professor who had developed very effective strategies for teaching diverse students when the content includes difficult or technical language:

> For a lecture at Brooklyn College on the 'geologic processes affecting biological evolution,' a geology professor begins by asking the students just to listen and think along with him as he talks. He discourages them from taking detailed notes during the lecture itself, though he encourages written 'after the fact' summaries (on index cards) of the salient points of a lecture or a reading assignment. He gives them a choice of doing the assigned reading either before or after the lesson, thus allowing for individual learning styles, and (for those who choose 'before') neutralizing apprehension over arriving at class 'unprepared.' This teacher also, at the

outset of his lecture, places on the chalkboard a diagram illustrating the highpoints of his talk. Miraculously, when the students are routinely tested on the content of the lecture at a later date, their understanding and factual recall surpass what one would expect from a class of copious note-takers (Cochran, 1992: 8).

It took a little 'digging' to track down this previously unnamed geology professor. He is Dr David Seidemann who for more than 15 years has been 'informally' involved in the teaching of minority students. Over the years, at Brooklyn College, he has noted the increasing number of ESL students. As a result, he has attempted to develop a way of teaching that will 'help every-body'.

Dr Seidemann tries to set the 'context of the course' by showing how 'science is connected to life'. He encourages students, even in large lectures, to ask questions, and he holds a lot of office hours. As for the ESL students, he does 'correct their grammar on written assignments but does not deduct points for errors'.

In Dr Seidemann's words:

Over the years I have developed a few tricks that seem to help in teaching science to non-science majors. At the beginning of the semester I explicitly set the context for the whole course. Generally, students take my course because they are *required* to. I tell students the reasons why they should regard the science requirement as justified. These justifications range from the narrowly selfish (geologic knowledge is helpful in buying homes), to the broadly selfish (a scientifically literate public can help shape rational public policy), to the purely abstract (understanding how the earth works can be fun in the same way that one might enjoy tinkering with old radios). As the semester proceeds I set the context for each of the topics that I introduce. Students are more receptive to learning when they understand why I feel the lesson that I am teaching is valuable.

I have also come to appreciate the value of encouraging some discussion in my lecture class. While the class is primarily lecture (90%), I 'seed' the class with provocative questions or challenges to the students' expectations. Quite often this leads to lively discussions of religion and science, public policy and science, tolerance, etc. For example, when I discuss our current belief in conti-nental drift, I first note the evidence that Alfred Wegener cited in his model. I then ask if Wegener's many observations are consistent with a belief in conti-nental drift. Typically, the students respond in the affirmative. I then tell them about the ridicule Wegener endured from the scientific community. I attempt to initiate a discussion of the tolerance of novel ideas, intellectual arrogance, etc. Sometimes the students respond, sometimes not. But if I use enough examples of this sort during the semester, I am guaranteed to engage the students' interest in one of the 'seed' topics.

On a more mundane note, in my first lecture I tell students that I do not care how they use the text in the course: they may read the text before or after my lecture on the subject. In this way, I try to let students know that there is not a right way for learning and that they should do whatever works for them.

Also early in the semester I explicitly tell students that I have organized my lectures systematically and that my blackboard notes represent a good outline of my thoughts. In this way, I try to demonstrate to the students the value of organizing and summarizing as a means of learning. In this discussion of learning methods, I also note that it may be useful for students to listen to what I am saying and summarize it in their notes rather than to record what I say verbatim.

In lab classes I explicitly tell the students the philosophy that underlies the labs, i.e. that we want students to observe and reason. Although the geology course uses rocks and minerals to get across this lesson, the skills of observation and reasoning that we are attempting to hone are applicable to anything in life. By citing the reason why I believe labs to be important I diffuse much of the students' resistance to learning from the lab experience. In lab, I am a minimalist: I give a scant introduction to each lab and allow the students to bumble towards answers. I often answer their questions during lab (in one-on-one encounters) by questioning the students in order to let them think their way towards the answer. This method can be extremely useful for some students. I have seen students gloat with joy when they finally arrive at an answer: they recognize that they have earned the answer and deserve the credit. A well-taught lab can be a lesson in empowerment for students.

I do nothing in my labs or lectures designed specifically for ESL students. However, over the years ESL students who have sought my help during office hours discover that I will not only explain geology to them, but I will work with them on improving their English. I have learned how rewarding these encounters can be: often in the course of these tutorials the students share their viewpoints and personal histories with me. In this way I have been taught about the Cultural Revolution in China from a student who experienced it; I have learned to see the issue of Puerto Rican nationalism through the eyes of an Hispanic student; and I have been constantly entertained by the attempts of ESL students to understand idiosyncratic American customs. In sum, in return for the informal English lessons that I give during office hours, I get lessons in world history and culture that go beyond what can be learned from books.

Dr David Seidemann
Professor of Geology
Brooklyn College of CUNY
2900 Bedford Avenue
Brooklyn, NY 11210-2889
Phone: 718-951-5761

National-Louis University (Chicago, Illinois): One instructor's experience teaching General Biology when many of the students are non-native speakers of English

National-Louis University in Chicago is typical of most American colleges and universities; in order to graduate, all undergraduates are required to complete a laboratory science course. Nonetheless, National-Louis is not exempt from the changing US demographics, and its students are increasingly diverse ethnically and linguistically. In this case study, Dr Ofra Peled, an Assistant Professor in the Science Department of National-Louis University, describes how she manages to teach *General Biology* when many of the students are still learning English.

In Dr Peled's words:

National-Louis University (NLU) serves more than 16,000 students in its three Chicago-area campuses and at academic centers in five US and two European locations. It offers Bachelor's, Master's and Doctoral degrees. In the Chicago area there are two suburban campuses and an urban campus in downtown Chicago. The Language Institute at NLU is located on the downtown Chicago campus and provides both undergraduate and graduate students with five levels of English instruction. The Institute is growing rapidly: In 1980 there were about 75 students enrolled while in 1993 that figure had increased to 500.

We have a very small Science Department. There are four full-time faculty members and a few adjuncts, and like our students, faculty may have to travel among the campuses each quarter. I mainly teach at the urban campus. All undergraduate programs at NLU require at least one laboratory science course, and most students choose *General Biology* (LAN110). I have been teaching one or two sections of *General Biology* on the urban campus every quarter for the past five years. The course meets twice a week for three hours; each session includes two hours of lecture and one hour of lab. The topics covered during the ten weeks include cell structure, transport, cell division, genetics, molecular gene expression, and evolution. *General Biology* is taken by both science and non-science majors.

It seems to me that the number of ESL students in my classes has, in general, been increasing. However, the actual number of students of limited English proficiency enrolled in *General Biology* varies from semester to semester. For example, in the Fall 1993 quarter, in a class of 20, there were only three students whose native language was English! Of the remaining 17 students, 11 had started learning English two to four years ago. Their native languages included Polish, Russian, Spanish and Chinese. Six students, who are native Spanish speakers, mostly learned English as children. In the Spring 1994 quarter, in the afternoon section of *General Biology* there were eight ESL students (all Polish) in a class of twenty-one; in the evening section of 19 students, eight were non-native English speakers (five Polish, two Hispanic, and one Russian).

I have not observed a significant difference in the level of performance of native and non-native English speakers in the biology course. Perhaps this can be attributed to the following: I find that many of our ESL students have a strong background in math and science. This is especially true for Eastern European students. They tend to have good study skills and are often young and have time to study. Their language difficulties, I think, are balanced by the limited background in math and science of our students who are graduates of the Chicago public high schools. The latter also tend to be older, to work full-time, and to have less time to devote to their studies. Both of these groups do well in our courses. It is the few students who have difficulties in English, as well as being less well prepared academically, who find it hardest to cope. For example, I have taught a few refugee Vietnamese students who had not had regular schooling in the past; their academic struggles belie the 'model minority' stereotype.

There are many ways in which I try to help ESL students. I intentionally speak a bit more slowly. I always encourage the students to tape the lectures so that they can listen again and fill out sections they may have missed when taking notes during class. I also write a lot on the chalkboard including new terms, their meanings, and basic concepts. Although writing on the board takes more time, I prefer that students copy from the board rather than write the information from memory (which could lead to errors such as misspellings or misunderstanding of complex information). When students are given assignments to answer review questions, I make sure that they use full sentences and do not copy from the textbook. I also help students with corrections and revisions of their written work. I am in the process of compiling a list of the words and their definitions that seem to be the most troublesome for the ESL students; I would like to be able to distribute this to the students ahead of time along with translations into their native languages.

My exams include multiple choice and short essay questions. I find that ESL students can usually write essay questions quite well, and I encourage them to use a dictionary if they need one. They do, however, have special difficulties with multiple choice questions. Generally, they are not used to multiple choice items and have never learned the strategies for solving them (such as narrowing down the answers and guessing between the remaining two choices or looking for clues in words such as 'always', 'never' or 'only'). In addition, they may need guidance in answering multiple choice items when the choices include possibilities such as 'both "a" and "b" are correct' or 'all of the above are correct'. For the ESL students, it may be difficult to distinguish very subtle differences in meaning in the various answer choices.

Something new that we are trying out at NLU is adding more newspaper and magazine articles about science to the reading, writing and debate activities in the 'Bridge' course that students take following completion of the ESL program in preparation for Freshmen Composition. However, it is too early to tell if this kind of introduction to science will make a difference in more advanced courses.

The text that we use in *General Biology* is *Biosphere: Realm of Life* by Wallace, King & Sanders (Glenview, IL: Harper Collins College Division). It does not seem to present any particular difficulties to the students. What I have noticed, however, is that ESL students who have not advanced their knowledge of English sufficiently have problems both reading and comprehending texts in upper division science courses.

In spite of any extra work that may be involved, I enjoy teaching such a variety of students, and I find that the diversity in student experiences enriches the classroom a great deal.

Dr Ofra Peled
Science Department
National-Louis University
18 South Michigan Avenue
Chicago, IL 60603-3202
Phone: 312-621-9650 (ext. 3409)

College-wide Programs to Assist Language Minority Students in Science Courses

Hostos Community College, City University of New York (Bronx, NY): Language integration across the curriculum

Eugenio Maria de Hostos Community College of The City University of New York (commonly known as Hostos Community College or HCC) is a public, two-year institution that grants Associate's degrees in the arts and sciences. The information about its student population and 'language integration' activities was contributed by Dr Diana Diaz (Instructional Development Coordinator, Office of Academic Affairs). Dr Peter Castillo Monteza (Professor of Chemistry) provided the description of *Environmental Science I*.

The student population at Hostos is 80% Hispanic, 13% Black, and 7% Other; the College enrolls 5,000 FTEs (full-time equivalent students). During any given semester, approximately 1,000 students are taking courses in the four-level ESL program; another 350 are enrolled in a developmental writing course specifically designed for ESL students. (HCC also offers some academic courses in which Spanish is the language of instruction. The use of the native language to teach content-area courses is discussed further in Chapter 8.)

In the fall of 1991, HCC began planning and implementing 'language integration' activities to linguistically and methodologically enhance content courses, thereby making them more accessible to ESL students. This has involved both curriculum revision and a series of faculty development workshops. As of the fall 1993 semester, approximately 35 full-time faculty had received training, and 60 or so courses had been 'enhanced'. Two grants (Title III and Vocational Education) provided the necessary funding for these activities.

One of the enhanced courses in this program is *Environmental Science I* (ENV 4014); it is taught in English by Dr Peter (Pedro) Castillo Monteza, a Professor of Chemistry in the Natural Sciences Department. Usually, 25 students enroll per semester, and they must have reached at least an intermediate level of English proficiency. Upon satisfactory completion of *Environmental Science I*, students earn four credits toward their Associate's degree.

ENV 4014 meets twice a week for one hour and 20 minutes for lectures, and there is a weekly, two hour lab. The text, selected by a departmental committee, is Hill's *Chemistry for Changing Times* (New York: Macmillan), and the topics that are covered in the course include matter and energy; atoms, elements and periodicity of elements; compounds and chemical bonds; organic chemistry; energy; air pollution; and water pollution. In the laboratory there are a wide variety of activities such as how to measure the volume, mass and density of solids and liquids; the separation of components of a mixture using paper chromatography; study of the properties of acids and bases; the synthesis of chemical compounds, and the purification of water by precipitation and filtration.

With funding from the grants, Dr Castillo (along with Dr Alfredo Villanueva, Professor and Chairperson of the English Department) prepared a workbook of supplemental readings and exercises to complement the lectures and text in ENV 4014. This workbook was piloted in the fall 1993 semester and is entitled *Workbook and Reading Exercises for Environmental Science I*; it is available through Hostos' bookstore. As explained in its preface:

> Each unit of the workbook corresponds to a topic in the course syllabus and includes a summary and sample exercises (multiple choice, true-false, short answer, and essay) along with the answers to the multiple choice questions. There also are quantitative problems to be solved (and their answers). Additional reading assignments (in English) in the workbook further expand upon what is taught in lecture.

Spanish translations and vocabulary of key terms are included in each unit for Spanish dominant students as are multiple choice, true-false, and short answer questions in Spanish.

Besides co-authoring the workbook, Dr Castillo has made other modifications to meet the needs of the many students in ENV 4014 who are non-native English speakers. For example, he includes more class drills and exercises including writing short paragraphs and essays. The course syllabus was rewritten to add more information. The classes are taught in English, and Spanish is used only if a word needs to be translated for a particular student.

Since the course enhancements were added only recently, information is not yet available on student outcomes. However, already there are plans to enhance *Fundamentals of Chemistry*, CHE 4000.

For further information about language integration activities or *Environmental Science I* at Hostos Community College contact:

Dr Diana Diaz
Instructional Development Coordinator
Hostos Community College
500 Grand Concourse
Bronx, NY 10451
Phone: 718–518–6588/99

Dr Peter (Pedro) Castillo Monteza
Professor of Chemistry
Natural Sciences Department
Hostos Community College
500 Grand Concourse
Bronx, NY 10451
Phone: 718–518–4136

California State University, Los Angeles: Learning English-for-Academic-Purposes

At California State University in Los Angeles (CSLA) an interdisciplinary approach is being taken to help underprepared language minority students enrolled in mainstream courses. Project LEAP (Learning English-for-Academic-Purposes) was initiated in the fall of 1991. Its costs have been shared between the University and a grant from the US Department of Education, Fund for the Improvement of Postsecondary Education (FIPSE).

The following information about CSLA, its students and Project LEAP was provided by the co-directors of Project LEAP, Dr Ann Snow (Associate Professor, School of Education) and Dr Janet Tricamo (former Director of the Learning Resource Center at CSLA and now Vice-President for Students at Highline Community College, Desmoines, Washington).

In Dr Snow's and Dr Tricamo's words:

CSLA is a public institution that primarily grants Bachelor's and Master's degrees; it also has a joint PhD program with the University of California. There are approximately 14,600 undergraduate and 4,800 graduate students, and the student body is extremely diverse: 31.7% Latino, 28.8% Asian, 23.5% White, 10.1% African American, and 0.4% Native American. Sixty-seven percent of the entering freshmen are non-native speakers of English (mainly Hispanics and Asians), and more than 60 languages are spoken on campus by both native and foreign-born language minority students. In spite of the large number of language minority students, CSLA does not have a formal ESL program. However, there is an American Culture and Language Program to prepare recently arrived international students for academic study in the United States. In addition, the Special Services Program of the Learning Resource Center employs a half-time ESL specialist who teaches two pre-Baccalaureate courses each quarter for non-native speaking Educational Opportunity Program (EOP) students.

The purpose of Project LEAP is to improve the academic literacy skills of high risk language minority students (both native and foreign born) in the general education curriculum. For these students, the high level reading, writing and oral communication skills emphasized in the general education curriculum are particularly demanding. Project LEAP provides a cost-effective, equity conscious, and pedagogically sound alternative to traditional ESL instruction. Through Project LEAP, mainstream faculty are trained to *enhance* the curriculum and teaching methods of popular general education courses; the goal is to improve the academic literacy skills of language minority students as they learn new subject matter.

EOP language minority students concurrently enroll in a language-enhanced general education course and a paired supplemental instruction course which is co-led by a professional language specialist and a peer study group leader. The EOP students participating in Project LEAP are primarily first generation, ethnic minority students, mainly from Latino and Asian backgrounds.

The content-area faculty members who teach the language enhanced general education courses as well as the language specialists and peer study group leaders attend a quarter-long seminar to introduce them to L2 acquisition issues and techniques to integrate language and content instruction. This training takes place in the fall quarter. Then the enhanced general education classes and their paired supplemental instruction courses are taught during the winter quarter. During the spring quarter, the course teams document their work and contribute to the annual Project LEAP manual which is intended for use by future instructors and peer study group leaders of the targeted courses.

Upon successful completion, students earn four units of Baccalaureate credit for each enhanced general education course and two units of 'sub-Baccalaureate' credit for the concurrent study group course.

Two science courses for non-science majors have been included in the language enhanced general education curriculum. In the winter of 1992, the enhanced version of Bio. 165, *Humans and Their Biological Environment*, was taught for the first time; 97 students enrolled including 14 who also registered in the Project LEAP study group course. The text was Cunningham & Saigo's *Environmental Science: A Global Concern* (Dubuque, Iowa: W.C. Brown). In the winter quarter of 1994, Bio. 155, *Natural History of Animals* was also offered, with 13 of the 90 students co-registered in the study group course.

Course enhancements in *Humans and Their Biological Environment* include:

- providing students with detailed handouts
- presenting lecture notes as overhead transparencies
- forming in-class study groups of four to five students; the students enrolled in the Project LEAP supplemental course formed their own small groups while the rest of the class divided itself into additional groups. The members of each group worked together to critique and advise each other on drafts of written assignments (peer editing); to prepare for tests, and to write questions that might be incorporated into exams. The study group membership was intentionally culturally and racially diverse
- focused reading assignments: students were directed to specific sections of the text that contained the most important definitions and concepts and were provided handouts listing this information
- submission of student generated exam questions
- provision of very explicit directions for the written assignment as well as instructions for the 'peer reviewers'
- an explicit explanation of course grading in the syllabus.

The 14 students enrolled in the Project LEAP two-unit supplemental instruction course participated in additional activities such as techniques for familiarization with their textbook and for understanding the organization of the chapters of the textbook; guidance in how to go about reading the chapters including making an outline and answering questions; learning the use of connectors (for example, words that indicate comparison and contrast); how to check their grammar; how to write a formal letter and how to write a summary; how to use office hours wisely; how to make an oral presentation; and how to take written notes. (These activities as well as the course enhancements are described in Snow, 1992.)

Bio. 155, *Natural History of Animals*, is an introductory course in organismal animal biology designed for non-science majors. There are two 75-minute lectures per week plus a weekly laboratory of 2 hours and 50 minutes. The textbook, C. Starr's *Biology: Concepts and Applications* (Belmont, CA: Wadsworth), focuses on main concepts and unifying themes with chapters averaging ten pages.

Dr Beverly Krilowicz, Assistant Professor of Biology, has contributed the following information about Bio. 155 course enhancements. They include:

- providing students, at the beginning of each class, with lecture outlines that include sufficient space for students to add additional comments and diagrams
- careful definition of new terms, including the meaning of prefixes, roots, and suffixes so that students eventually will be able to deduce word meanings without memorization
- major revision of the laboratory to allow students to actually participate in scientific investigations for which there are no known 'correct' answers. Previously, the Bio. 155 laboratory had consisted of displays and demonstrations. This was changed for Project LEAP to small group inquiry-based exercises which allow students to perform simple experiments or a series of observations as a team and to then think through and to discuss several thought questions
- the writing of a formal journal style paper based on the students' biorhythms from data collected over a period of approximately two weeks using measurements of pulse, eye-hand coordination, and adding speed.

Evaluation is a very important part of Project LEAP. Although the number of LEAP students in Bio. 165 in the winter of 1992 was relatively small, comparisons have been made between LEAP (those taking the enhanced course plus the supplemental study group) and 'control' students (those taking only the enhanced course).

In the case of Bio. 165, 71% of the LEAP students were 'Special Admits' compared to 55% of the control students. The two groups were fairly similar in ethnicity except that Asian students made up 29% of the LEAP population and only 14% of the control students. English was the home language of 11% of the LEAP students and 27% of the control students. Although the English Placement Test (EPT) scores were essentially the same for the two groups, the reading test (Gates-Mac Ginitie) and verbal SAT scores were slightly lower for the LEAP students.

Nevertheless, the LEAP students faired well in Bio. 165. None received a grade of A (three students—4%—of the controls did), but 79% received grades of B and C (compared to 72% of the controls). Only one (7%) LEAP student received a grade of D, and none received an 'F'. Among the controls, 8 students (10%) received grades of D, and one (1%) received an F. Two LEAP students (14%) ended up with an 'unauthorized incomplete'. Eleven control students (13%) received 'no credit', 'unauthorized incomplete', 'withdrawal', or 'no grade'.

The overall Grade Point Averages (GPAs) of the LEAP students were consistently higher than those of the controls (2.58 versus. 2.18) even when factors such as differences in EPT (2.67 versus. 2.12) and verbal SAT scores (2.63 vs. 2.10) were controlled.

Although the outcomes for the two groups (control and LEAP students) were not statistically different, the results look promising. LEAP students may not be earning grades of 'A' in Bio. 165 (which is a difficult achievement for high risk freshman students). However, they are persisting and seem less likely to fail, withdraw or to take a grade of 'incomplete'. LEAP students were highly satisfied with their experience, and 100% reported that they would recommend LEAP courses to their friends.

Student outcomes data is not yet available for Bio. 155.

Finally, we hope that the exercises and activities developed specifically for targeted courses in Project LEAP will be adapted to other general education classes with the same academic language demands.

For additional information about Project LEAP at California State University, Los Angeles, contact:

Project LEAP
California State University, Los Angeles
5151 State University Drive, Library South 1062
Los Angeles, CA 90032-8305
Phone: 213-343-3968
Fax: 213-343-2670

Dr Marguerite Ann Snow
Associate Professor, School of Education
California State University, Los Angeles
5151 State University Drive
Los Angeles, CA 90032-8305
Phone 213-343-4373
Fax: 213-343-4318
email: ASNOW@ATSS.Calstatela.edu

Dr Beverly L. Krilowicz
Assistant Professor of Biology
California State University, Los Angeles
5151 State University Drive, BS262
Los Angeles, CA 90032-8305
Phone: 213–343-2064
Fax: 213–343-6451

Our Lady of the Lake University (San Antonio, Texas): Cooperative learning in math and science for Hispanic students

In the abstracts of the 1992 annual meeting of AAAS (American Association for the Advancement of Science), there is listed a poster presentation entitled 'Mathematics and Science for Hispanic College Students' by Professors Mary

Ellen Quinn and Isabel Ball of Our Lady of the Lake University (OLLU or 'The Lake') in San Antonio, Texas. It briefly describes how cooperative learning groups that draw upon reading, writing and discussion skills are being used as 'a means of developing the language needed for mathematics' for a predominantly bilingual undergraduate population.

This case study—based on information provided by Dr Quinn (Visiting Professor of Mathematics), with the help of Drs Ball (Dean, College of Arts and Sciences) and Benoist (Vice President and Dean of Academic Affairs)— describes how cooperative learning has been institutionalized at Our Lady of the Lake University:

Our Lady of the Lake University in San Antonio, Texas, is a private, Catholic institution offering the Doctorate as its highest degree. According to Dr Howard Benoist, Vice-President and Dean of Academic Affairs, 'The Lake' enrolls approximately 1,300 full-time equivalent undergraduates and 450 FTE graduate students. The undergraduate population is 75% Hispanic, 15% White, 5% African-American, and 5% Other. The ESL program at 'The Lake' serves a small number of undergraduate and graduate students (about 20 per semester). Approximately 50% of the ESL students are native speakers of Spanish. The rest speak languages such as Japanese, Korean, Chinese and Turkish. There are three levels of ESL instruction, and students are admitted to the ESL program even if they do not know any English. No academic credit is granted for successful completion of the ESL courses.

As reported by Dr Quinn,

There are a variety of programs that operate simultaneously to improve science instruction at OLLU for undergraduates of limited English proficiency. Grouped together under the title of 'Science and Mathematics Programs', they serve approximately 650 students per year and are supported by grants from the US Department of Education, the National Science Foundation, and the Office of Naval Research. The overarching objectives of these Programs are to recruit and retain minority students in the sciences, to provide minority students with modern technical equipment and learning experiences, and to support and encourage instructors in using modern equipment and teaching practices.

One of the programs at The Lake has made cooperative learning study teams an integral part of both math and science instruction. This move away from the traditional lecture mode of instruction resulted from a project carried out under the auspices of CASET (The Center for the Advancement of Science, Engineering, and Technology of Huston-Tillotson College). Twenty different programs throughout the United States were designed to recruit and retain minority students in the sciences; each involved intervention and control groups. At OLLU the intervention that was selected was cooperative learning (CL) study teams.

Numerous studies have shown that Hispanic students—the largest of the minority groups served by OLLU—prefer cooperation to competition. In addition, CL provides language minority students with many more opportunities than lecture classes to do that which causes language to develop: to speak and interact with other speakers of the target language. Since both mathematics and science have their own highly specialized 'registers', students in CL science and math classes have multiple chances to 'talk' science and math. ('Register' refers to variation in language usage depending on the circumstances. For example, our everyday, informal use of language to talk to friends and family is different from what we use when presenting a paper at a conference. Similarly, the language of science is different from the language of religion or the language of sports.) The implementation of cooperative learning seemed culturally appropriate for our institution.

Our program was designed for the mathematics courses which all potential science and mathematics majors must take, precalculus (Math 1411, four credits) and calculus (Math 2412, four credits).

For a period of five semesters beginning in the fall of 1988, approximately 400 students participated in our study. The control group consisted of those students who attended the traditional four class hours of precalculus and/or calculus lectures per week. The intervention group students attended three regular lecture sessions and one CL session per week. What we found at the end of the five semester study was that the differences between the intervention and control groups all favored the students who had participated in the cooperative learning study groups. For example, 38% of the intervention students were currently science, engineering, and technology (SET) majors in comparison to 22% of the controls. Our data also show that CL in their required math courses apparently helped students to persist in SET majors even if they failed and had to repeat a math course.

Because of the success of cooperative learning in the CASET study, The Lake is in the process of institutionalizing CL in as many math and science courses as possible. In order to do this, the faculty had to be trained in cooperative learning techniques. The Administration of OLLU has been particularly supportive of this endeavor. Two workshops were held on campus by Dr Karl Smith (who along with Drs David and Roger Johnson co-authored *Cooperative Learning: Increasing College Faculty Instructional Productivity*, 1991) and books about cooperative learning were made available to the faculty. As a result, faculty who were going to include cooperative learning groups in their courses have been able to use many of the techniques recommended by Smith, Johnson, & Johnson.

While a formal study of the academic outcomes of cooperative learning groups in science classes at The Lake is currently in progress, there are anecdotal findings that indicate that students are responding well to this pedagogical change. For example, *General Chemistry* now includes group activities in both the lecture and laboratory components of the course. These tasks are highly structured, and each student has an assigned role within the group. As one student in *General Chemistry* wrote, 'I thought the group work was pretty good. I think that compared to lectures every day (no offense), group work is less monotonous. I find myself drifting off—not just in this class—during lectures. But when we do group work I have to be on my toes, pay attention, and get the work done.' The same student also expressed concern about the limitations of what could be achieved within the cooperative learning group: 'The only thing I don't like about group work is that I feel really bad when some group members don't understand. I try to explain and get everyone involved, but there is only so much I can do. However, I do think that they learned more from our group discussion than they might have done alone.'

Other student comments include:

'I think the people in my group helped me as much as they could and they didn't get impatient with me no matter how much I needed help. When they explained I could understand better.'

'… having to explain the work to others made me understand what we were doing even more.'

'Group work is great. I feel that studying what I learn with the group helps a great deal.'

Commenting on the impact of cooperative learning in *General Chemistry*, one of the instructors observed, 'When students are so involved in what they are doing that you have to tell them it is time to go, then you know they are really interested, motivated to learn.'

As Dr Quinn sums up the situation, 'We are proud to say that the mathematics and science faculty are exercising leadership among the total faculty by moving into a student-centered pedagogy with cooperative learning.'

For additional information about the use of cooperative learning in math and science at Our Lady of the Lake University contact:

Dr Mary Ellen Quinn
Visiting Professor of Mathematics
Our Lady of the Lake University
411 SW 24th Street
San Antonio, Texas 78207
Phone: 210-690-4190
Fax: 210-690-4414

Dr Howard Benoist
Vice President and Dean of Academic Affairs
Our Lady of the Lake University
411 SW 24th Street
San Antonio, Texas 78207
Phone: 210-434-6711 (ext. 233)
Fax: 210-436-0824
email: benoist@ollac.ollusa.edu

Dr Isabel Ball
Dean, College of Arts and Sciences
Our Lady of the Lake University
411 SW 24th Street
San Antonio, Texas 78207
Phone: 210-434-6711 (ext. 240)
Fax: 210-436-0824
email: BALL@OLLAC.OLLUSA.EDU

Glendale Community College (Glendale, California): Supplemental instruction for language minority students taking science courses

Glendale Community College (GCC) in Glendale, California, is a two-year public college offering an Associate's degree and other certified programs. In the fall of 1993 the college enrolled almost 14,300 students. Located nine miles north of Los Angeles, GCC attracts an extraordinarily diverse student population, the largest group (29%) being Armenian immigrants. As for the remaining students, approximately 25% are Euro-Caucasian; 10% Mexican-American; 5% Filipino; 4% Chinese; 4% Korean; 4% Central American; 7% Cuban, South American, and other Hispanic; 2% Japanese; 2% Vietnamese; 1% African-American; 1% American-Indian; and 6% other Asian/Pacific or mid-Eastern.

In order to provide appropriate academic support for its students, GCC has both a large ESL program as well as Supplemental Instruction. (For background information about supplemental instruction see Box 5.1 beginning on page 102). Ms Jan Freemyer, GCC's SI Specialist and Faculty Coordinator, contributed the following description of Glendale's ESL and Supplemental Instruction Programs.

In Ms Freemyer's words:

The English as a Second Language Program at Glendale Community College serves approximately 2,000 students per semester, and there is always a waiting list of others trying to enroll. The program admits GCC students as well as adults from the community at large. Some of the students do not know any English at all, and others are illiterate in their native language. There are essentially five levels of ESL instruction for which students are awarded academic credit. The primary language groups of the students are Korean, Armenian, and Spanish. There is a signficant Japanese population as well. Other groups include Chinese, Thai, Brazilian, Filipino, Hungarian, Bulgarian, French, Russian, Lebanese, Indian, and Palestinian.

In the Spring of 1990, GCC piloted a program in Supplemental Instruction (SI). The Program is currently funded by a five year Title III Grant, but the costs of SI will be picked up by the College at the end of the grant. The goals of SI are to improve students' grades and, as a result, their grade point averages (GPA's), and to increase retention and persistence—both in specific courses and in college in general.

SI provides out-of-class student-led workshops directly related to the content of high risk courses. At GCC, high risk courses are defined as those in which:

- 30-50% of the students have traditionally received grades *other* than A, B, or C,
- enrollment is generally large (60-100 students), and/or
- both the students and faculty consider the content to be difficult for students to master.

In other words, high risk courses pose a particular academic hurdle for many students. The academic departments work closely with the SI personnel to determine which courses would be best served by inclusion in the workshop program.

Approximately 40-50 sections per semester at GCC have SI attached in disciplines as diverse as history, accounting, psychology, math and statistics. The SI Program also includes several science courses: *Human Biology, General Chemistry I* and *II, Organic Chemistry, General Physics I and II,* and *Engineering Physics.*

SI workshops meet 1-4 times per week for one to two hours. Attendance by students enrolled in targeted courses is usually voluntary; as a result, participation rates vary from a small percentage of the class to 100%. Workshop activities include discussion of content; problem solving techniques; the use of worksheets (graduated in difficulty) in small, collaborative study groups; content review and synthesis; practice tests and essays, and hands-on activities (such as reviewing models of bones or skeletons for a biology course). What goes on in each workshop reflects the course content, and in the case of the sciences and math, is generally planned by the instructor.

The SI workshop leaders are students who have already taken (and passed with a grade of 'A' or 'B') the course to which they are assigned. These students are recommended by their instructors and are prepared to be SI leaders by enrolling in *Student Development 155.* This one-credit, pass/fail course provides new SI leaders with the opportunity to network with the SI Coordinator and other SI leaders, to discuss the various communication and interpersonal skills necessary to be an effective facilitator, and to address topics such as small group processing, study skills, and problem-solving techniques. The SI student leaders for the science workshops are encouraged to meet weekly with the course instructors to help plan workshop activities.

Large numbers of students have had the opportunity to participate in GCC's SI program. For example:

- In the fall of 1992, approximately 850 students were enrolled in courses that offered SI workshops; 49% attended at least one workshop while 29% attended half or more.
- In the spring of 1993, there were about 1450 students taking courses with SI workshops; 58% attended at least one workshop, and 25% attended half or more.
- In the fall of 1993, just over 1,400 students took courses offering SI workshops; 39% attended at least one workshop, and 31%, half or more.

At the end of each course, a questionnaire is distributed to evaluate students' reaction to the SI program. As a result we have learned that students who do attend SI workshops report that SI has helped them to achieve success in the course, that they plan to attend the SI workshops of other classes if available, and that they would recommend SI workshops to their peers. Those who do not attend most frequently cite conflicts (with other courses, with jobs, in terms of obtaining child care, etc.) as the reason for lack of participation in the SI workshops. Since we began tracking our students in the spring of 1990, we have observed that attending half or more SI workshops per course improves both students' passing rates in the SI supported courses as well as semester grade-point-averages.

The rate of student participation in SI is consistently higher in math and science courses and in business, technical education, and nursing than in the social sciences. In the fall of 1992, 315 students had SI workshops attached to their science courses; 74% of these students attended at least one workshop while 43% attended more than half. In the spring of 1993, with 404 eligible science students, 77% attended at least one SI workshop, and 52%, half or more. For the fall of 1993, there were 338 students with 85% attending at least one, and 53% attending half or more of the SI workshops.

Although we have no specific breakdown of the data according to ethnicity or limited English proficiency, it can be assumed from the demographics of the College's student body that many non-native English speaking students are benefiting from SI workshops in the sciences as well as in other disciplines.

For additional information about Glendale Community College's Supplemental Instruction Program contact:

Ms Jan Freemyer
SI Specialist and Coordinator
Glendale Community College
1500 North Verdugo Road
Glendale, CA 91208-2894
Phone: 818-240-1000 ext. 5497
Fax: 818-549-9436

8 The Theoretical Basis for Linguistically Modified Science Instruction

Some US colleges and universities enrolling relatively large numbers of non-native English speaking undergraduates have begun to take into consideration the specific linguistic needs of these students in content-area courses. In this chapter the two major strategies that are being used are described: content-based ESL instruction and introductory content-area instruction using the students' native language. In Chapter 9, case studies are presented illustrating how these approaches actually have been put into practice in the college science classroom.

With content-based ESL instruction students are actively developing their proficiency in English while studying subject matter other than English. There are three models: sheltered, adjunct, and sheltered-adjunct. Descriptions of each are provided below along with discussion of their advantages and disadvantages.

Some colleges have chosen a completely different route to meeting the linguistic needs of language minority students. In addition to providing traditional ESL instruction, they offer introductory coursework taught in the students' native language. Depending on the specifics of the program, such courses may be taught partially or fully in the native language. Either way, students can begin working toward their college degree (in their native language) while they are still in the process of learning English as a second language.

Clearly, there are significant differences in the rationales behind and the methods used in content-based ESL instruction and academic coursework in the students' native language. Nonetheless, no matter how dissimilar, both approaches recognize that:

- the acquisition of English as a second language by adults is a lengthy and difficult process,
- lack of proficiency in English should not prevent qualified students from moving forward in obtaining a college education,
- for LEP students to learn a new subject area, both the language of instruction as well as the course content must be comprehensible.

In Chapters 5 and 7 instructional modifications and support programs to assist LEP students enrolled in traditional content-area courses (taught in English) were described. In this chapter and in the case studies presented in Chapter 9, the focus shifts to instruction that explicitly addresses the linguistic needs of non-native speakers of English, particularly as it relates to science instruction.

Content-based ESL Instruction

Recently, there has been a trend to integrate ESL and content-area instruction for intermediate and advanced ESL students. Among the many reasons for doing this are the following:

- Some students get bored in traditional ESL courses; yet in many cases, they cannot begin their 'mainstream' coursework until the ESL program is completed.
- Other students become frustrated when they are paying tuition for non-credit ESL courses that do not count toward their degree requirements nor teach them anything related to their major.
- Second language learning is most meaningful when it takes into consideration 'the eventual uses the learner will make of the target language' (Brinton, Snow & Wesche, 1989: 3). For the ESL college student, learning English in order to successfully complete coursework that will count toward a degree and which will enhance employment opportunities provides more motivation than studying English for its own sake (Benesch, 1988; Brinton, Snow & Wesche, 1989; Krashen, 1991; Mohan, 1986; Reilly, 1988).
- Traditional ESL instruction does not adequately prepare most students for mainstream, content-area coursework taught in English. Both the ESL students themselves and their content-area instructors agree on this point (Ostler, 1980; Russikoff, 1994; Smoke, 1988; Snow & Kinsella, 1994; Swartley, 1994). Often, the aspects of English learned in an ESL class are quite different from the kinds of language skills needed to cope with learning chemistry, economics, or history when English is the medium of instruction and of assessment. Content-based ESL instruction helps students to overcome some of these difficulties.

Sheltered instruction

With sheltered instruction (Brinton, Snow & Wesche, 1989; Freeman & Freeman, 1988; Krashen, 1991; Sasser & Winningham, 1991), intermediate and advanced ESL students (who are often speakers of many different native languages) are grouped together in a content-area course. The content matter is taught in English which is the language shared by the students, professor and text.

The instructor is a content-area specialist who prior to teaching a sheltered course receives training in ESL methodologies. The focus of a sheltered course is on mastery of the subject matter, not the study of English. Nevertheless, students cannot help but improve their L2 proficiency in a sheltered classroom.

There are several advantages to grouping together ESL students in a sheltered classroom. The professor can use specific teaching methods that will increase the students' comprehension by more closely meeting their linguistic needs. The students experience less anxiety since they are not forced to compete with classmates who are native English speakers. The comfortable and supportive environment which is characteristic of a sheltered classroom promotes content learning as well as L2 acquisition.

The kinds of strategies used by instructors to make the content more comprehensible in a sheltered classroom include:

*   using numerous visual aids (such as charts, models and demonstrations) which provide extra-linguistic clues to what is being discussed,
*   the selection of appropriate reading materials, ones that the students will actually use and can comprehend,
*   writing major terms and definitions on the chalkboard,
*   periodically summarizing the topic under discussion, and
*   monitoring their own use of the English language to make sure that they repeat important concepts, use lots of synonyms for words that students might not understand, and keep their sentences relatively short and simple.

In a sheltered classroom, the instructor frequently checks to make sure that the students are understanding what is being taught. There is a lot of teacher/student and student/student interaction as well as small group work. During class, students do not just listen to the teacher; they speak, read and write in order to learn the subject matter. Activities and their pace are varied in order to tap into all the students' senses: aural, visual, kinesthetic and tactile.

Testing in the course evaluates knowledge of the content-material, not development of L2 skills. Therefore, assessing subject matter knowledge needs to take into consideration the level of English proficiency of the students (Fichtner, Peitzman & Sasser, 1991). Teachers of sheltered classes need to be as flexible and creative with their testing as they are with their teaching. For example,

*   Sufficient time must be allotted so that students will be able to read and respond to the questions.
*   When writing short essays, students might be asked to include labeled diagrams or illustrations to help explain their answers.
*   If there are true/false questions, students are asked to write down why they think certain answers are false.

- Multiple choice tests are straightforward with students looking for the one correct answer choice. The 'stems' and the answer choices are not 'tricky' linguistically or conceptually. This means the instructor intentionally writes test questions that do not include double negatives, 'if' statements, nor very subtle differences between answer choices.
- For fill in the blank items, students are given the list of words to study before the test and/or the words they can choose from are listed on the test paper.
- If a student's written answer seems totally incomprehensible, the teacher will talk to the student and find out if the student's verbal explanation makes sense. Only then will a decision be made as to how the written answer should be evaluated.

Many of the techniques used in a sheltered classroom also appear in the list of recommendations in Chapter 5.

The Adjunct Model

In the Adjunct Model, a content-area and an ESL support course are paired (Brinton, Snow & Wesche, 1989; Iancu, 1993; Snow & Brinton, 1988a, b). The students enrolled in the content-area course (which is taught in English) are a mixture of both native and non-native speakers of English. Only the ESL students must be co-registered in both the subject matter and the paired adjunct ESL course.

A specialist in the academic discipline (for example a biology or chemistry professor) teaches the content-area course, and an ESL instructor, the adjunct ESL course. Content-area specialists may choose to modify how they teach in order to make their presentations more comprehensible for the non-native speakers enrolled in the course. Sometimes, it is the ESL co-instructor who 'coaches' the content-area teacher.

The instructor of the adjunct course attends the content-area classes both to learn the material and to determine what the ESL students need to know. The lectures, labs and text of the subject matter course are the basis for most of the activities in the adjunct ESL course. Here, writing, reading, listening and speaking activities as well as cooperative learning groups are used so that the ESL students can work with and manipulate the subject matter of the content-area course. The end result is that students not only learn the subject matter but also increase their proficiency in English.

Evaluation of the two courses is carried out separately. The focus in the content-area course is on mastery of the subject matter while the emphasis in the paired ESL course is on the development of L2 skills. Academic credit is usually earned in the subject matter course while credit may or may not be granted for the adjunct class.

For the Adjunct Model to be successful, the two instructors must work together closely. The content-area instructor may need to help the ESL teacher learn the subject; in addition, the content-area teacher should be willing to adopt ESL strategies into his or her way of teaching. The adjunct course instructor must not only master the content-area material but also develop creative activities and supplementary materials which the ESL students can use to learn the subject-matter.

The Sheltered-Adjunct Model

Some colleges have designed sheltered-adjunct courses which are particularly useful when the students are both non-native speakers of English and academically underprepared (Snow & Brinton, 1988a, b). In this model, only non-native speakers of English can enroll in a specific content-area course (which is taught in English by a subject-matter specialist); this is the sheltered component. The same students also must register for a study skills or language development course taught by an ESL instructor; this is the adjunct component. Here, ESL techniques are used to promote the learning of the subject matter of the content-area course, and students work on developing the kinds of skills that they will need to function successfully in mainstream courses. As its name implies, the sheltered-adjunct model incorporates the main features of the adjunct and sheltered forms of content-based ESL instruction. Academic credit may or may not be granted for sheltered-adjunct courses.

Science Instruction in the Students' Native Language

Several colleges that enroll large numbers of Hispanic students offer introductory coursework, including science courses, taught totally or partially in Spanish. For example, at Kean College of New Jersey (Union, NJ), as part of its Spanish-speaking Program (see the Prologue for a description of this Program), students can take principles of biology or chemistry (including the laboratories) in Spanish for academic credit. At Hostos Community College (Bronx, NY), 80% of the student body is Hispanic; many courses are taught in Spanish including general biology, environmental science, and a developmental chemistry course.

Depending on the college, its program design, and its educational philosophy, the lectures may be solely in Spanish or partly in Spanish and partly in English; the textbook may be in Spanish or English, and the course may or may not be offered for academic credit.

Lest the reader be given the wrong impression, the students who take academic coursework in Spanish are also enrolled in a program of study of ESL. As their proficiency in English increases, the amount of coursework taken in the native language decreases until students are only enrolled in mainstream courses taught in English.

Most of the college courses taught in Spanish are in the humanities and social and behavioral sciences. The reason for this is that it is very difficult to find qualified *science* faculty who are also Spanish speaking. According to the National Center for Education Statistics (US Department of Education), Hispanics earned 101 Master's degrees and 66 Doctorates in the life sciences in 1990-91; in the physical sciences the numbers were 86 Master's and 67 Doctorates. As shown in Table 1.2 (Chapter 1, page 20), the number of Hispanics attending college increased by more than 60% between 1980 and 1990. Nevertheless, very few of these students are studying science so that the potential pool of native Spanish speaking science faculty remains very small. (See Box 8.1 for the autobiography of an Hispanic physicist.)

What are the advantages of providing content-area instruction in the native language of the students?

- As already described in Chapter 2, it allows students to gain knowledge and skills which will transfer from their native to their second language (Cummins, 1980; Cummins & Swain, 1986).
- It keeps students from getting bored and/or frustrated which can occur if they are only allowed to take English courses. Such students are much more likely to drop out of college than those who are allowed to begin working toward their degree.
- Instruction in the native language helps students retain their mother tongue even as they are learning English. Balanced bilingualism has been associated with greater cognitive flexibility and enhanced creative thinking (Baker, 1993: 117–120) which are qualities that should be nurtured in students.
- Academic coursework offered in the students' native language recognizes that immigrants and refugees may be intellectually and academically ready for college even if they are not proficient in English.

Conclusion

Clearly, there is no one 'right' way, no one correct 'solution', for dealing with the needs of non-native English speaking undergraduates enrolled in content-area courses. How a specific college or university addresses this situation depends on a variety of factors. These include the total number of non-native English speaking students; if they mostly speak one 'foreign' language or many different languages; how many LEP undergraduates are enrolled in a specific course; the desire and ability of ESL and content-area faculty to work together; the funds available to provide academic support services and faculty training; the willingness of the faculty and the administration to implement non-traditional kinds of instruction; the educational philosophy of the institution; and the level of commitment of the academic departments, administration, and the institution to the recruitment and retention of ESL students.

Content-based ESL instruction and content-area instruction in the students' native language are not just 'educational theories'. They are practical ways of addressing the linguistic needs of college students who are non-native speakers of English. The case studies that follow in Chapter 9 illustrate both types of instruction and show how they are being used to teach science on campuses across the nation.

Box 8.1 A Border Physicist

In 1986, at the age of 31, Jorge Alberto Lopez Gallardo received his doctorate in nuclear physics from Texas A & M University in College Station, Texas. Born in Mexico, he began his college studies on a student visa at the University of Texas at El Paso.

Jorge's 'success' story is unusual; few Hispanic undergraduates study science, especially the physical sciences (see Tables 1.6, 1.7 and 1.8). Even fewer continue on to obtain graduate degrees. For example, in 1986 a total of 606 Doctorates were awarded in physics to US citizens; only ten were Hispanic. Combining US citizens and permanent visa holders, a total of 643 PhDs were awarded in physics in 1986, with 13 going to Hispanics (National Research Council, Survey of Earned Doctorates).

Now an Associate Professor at the University of Texas at El Paso, teaching and providing research opportunities to both undergraduate and graduate students, Dr Lopez shares his 'story' with us.

In Dr Lopez's words:

I was born in 1955 in Monterrey, Mexico, and was the seventh of nine children. My father was a truck driver and my mother a housewife. We were poor and lived in rented houses. Although we had no car or telephone, we did have gas, electricity and running water. My parents only finished elementary school; nonetheless, my mother was particularly aware of the benefits of education, and she pushed her children to go as far as possible academically. My family originally had planned that I would be educated in Mexico, becoming a physician. Instead, I fell in love with physics and attended college in the United States.

In 1957 when I was two years old, my mother's family (my grandmother, four aunts, and three uncles) moved to the US-Mexico border looking for better work opportunities. My brother Francisco (who was a year and a half older than me) and I were 'loaned' to our grandmother. She was used to caring for small children. We settled in Juárez, Mexico, which lies directly across the Rio Grande River from El Paso, Texas, in the United States. My uncles quickly moved away, two to Los Angeles, California, and one to serve in the United States Army. My aunts began sewing jeans in a Levi's factory in El Paso, Texas. Francisco became homesick, missing our parents and brothers and sisters, so he returned to Monterrey. As the only child in a four-salary home, I considered myself very lucky!

In Juárez, at home, and at work in El Paso, my aunts spoke Spanish. My grandmother knew English but rarely used it. One of my aunts had to learn English when she became a supervisor at the Levi's factory. In other words, at home and in school I only spoke Spanish. It wasn't until the fifth grade that I began studying English in school, and this continued until I graduated from high school.

The border was not a strange place to my family. My great-grandfather was born in Arizona, my grandmother was educated in in Laredo, Texas, and she had lived in San Antonio, Texas, where one of my aunts was born. Nevertheless, Mexico was our country, and the decision was made to live in Juárez and to cross the border into the United States to work every day.

In Juárez, I attended a private Mexican elementary school where my love affair with science began. My earliest recollections about science are from when I was in the fourth grade and about nine years old. I was introduced to simple 'hands-on' experiments and by the age of ten was generating electricity from chemical reactions. Science was never scary for me.

Next, I attended a public middle school in Juárez. It is there that I had my first formal science courses including biology, chemistry and physics. By the age of 14, I had already been introduced to the basic concepts of physics. My physics teacher was a sophomore industrial engineering student (studying at the Instituto Technológico Regional de Ciudad Juárez). It is ironic that while he was encouraging my interest in physics, my middle-school counselor was advising me to forget physics and to be more realistic, studying engineering instead. However, by the age of 15, I knew that physics was for me.

In Juárez, I then attended a public high school which had a strong orientation toward science and engineering. As in my previous schools, the language of instruction was Spanish. However, I do remember that one of my textbooks was in English; I think it was a math book. By the time I graduated from high school, I knew how to do double integrals, a little bit of differential equations, and had finished two years of calculus-based physics. My calculus and physics teachers were graduate students at the University of Texas at El Paso (UTEP). As did my physics teacher from middle-school, they mentored me: telling me about topics not covered in my regular classes (such as special relativity, time travel, and tachions), and introducing me to UTEP.

I enrolled at UTEP in September of 1974 through the Inter-American Science and Humanities Program (see the UTEP Case Study which describes this Program in Chapter 9). Thanks to this Program, I had a smooth transition from Spanish to English, taking general courses taught in Spanish (including political science, history, and math) while studying English as a Second Language. Although I had studied English from the fifth grade until graduation from high school, I tested at the intermediate level and needed three semesters of ESL coursework. Even after completing the ESL program, I still encountered some difficulties in the courses for which English was the language of instruction. For example, I used to, literally, translate my textbooks; my Spanish notes on Eisberg & Resnick's modern physics textbook later became famous among many Spanish-speaking students.

I soon learned that my situation at UTEP was not unique. Literally hundreds of Spanish speaking students were benefiting from the services of the Inter-American Science and Humanities Program (IASHP). IASHP allowed us to enroll in an American university in spite of our deficiencies in English and then provided us with the opportunity to develop the knowledge and skills that we needed to succeed in college. I met other students who were also the children of

Levi's factory workers in Juárez. Some of the graduates from the IASHP have gone on to achieve extraordinary success in science. For example, Enrique Gomez (who earned his BS and MS in math at UTEP) directed the development of the software for the National Aeronautic and Space Administration's (NASA) space shuttle program. Victor de la Peña is now an Associate Professor of Mathematics at Columbia University; he received his BS (Bachelor of Science) in math from UTEP and his doctorate in statistics from the University of California, Berkeley. Both Gomez and de la Peña grew up in Juárez in the same neighborhood that I did.

At UTEP I earned both my BS and MS (Master of Science) degrees in Physics. My graduate supervisor in physics at UTEP strongly recommended that I continue with my studies. I applied to several doctoral programs (including the University of California at Berkeley, the Massachusetts Institute of Technology in Cambridge, the California Institute of Technology in Pasadena, and Texas A & M University in College Station). The only program that accepted me was Texas A & M, so in 1979 I began my doctoral studies there and in 1986 received my Doctorate in nuclear physics.

I actually left Texas A & M in 1985 and finished my graduate work in absentia so that I could begin a two-year post-doctoral fellowship funded by the government of Denmark at the Niels Bohr Institute (Copenhagen, Denmark). Here, I worked with researchers from all over the world including Danes, Germans, South Americans, Italians and Spaniards. I learned that physics has no nationality, and that one can do physics in any language.

After Copenhagen, I went to the Lawrence Berkeley Laboratory (Berkeley, California) for two more years of post-doctoral work, and from there moved on in 1989 to California Polytechnic State University in San Luis Obispo, California, as an Assistant Professor of Physics. Nevertheless, my eyes were in a different place; for a variety of reasons—such as family, life style and language — I very much wanted to return home to El Paso.

Fortunately, I was able to return to UTEP in 1990 and am now an Associate Professor of Physics. I teach both undergraduate and graduate courses in physics, supervise the research of several Master's candidates (UTEP does not offer the Doctorate in physics) as well as some undergraduate research projects. I also am the local adviser of the Society of Physics Students as well as the Chair of the Committee on Minorities of the American Physical Society. The latter with 43,000 members is the largest association of physicists in the world. In addition to this, I have educational and outreach programs funded by a variety of sources including NASA to increase the number of local high school students who choose physics as a career. About 80% of the participants are Mexican-American.

I feel that I have been particularly lucky with the educational opportunities that have come my way. Of my seven surviving brothers and sisters, all finished elementary school. One completed eighth grade, another technical school, another secretarial school, another secondary and technical schools, another holds a BA in education from the Universidad Autónoma de Ciudad Juárez, and the youngest received a degree in Computer Science from UTEP. Of my extended family, I have noticed that many more of my cousins who grew up in Mexico obtained university degrees than those living in the United States. In addition, drugs have been a problem for several of my relatives in the United States while this has not occurred on the Mexican side of the family.

I know first hand—both as a student and as a faculty member —the educational problems faced by Mexican-American students. From my own experience, I am aware of the importance of mentoring as well as just how helpful it was for me to be able to begin my college coursework in Spanish while I was still learning English.

I also am aware that the issue of language of classroom instruction is very controversial. Nonetheless, what is definitely needed is good communication between instructors and students. Although I teach my physics courses in English, students often ask questions in Spanish. In class my answers are in English. During office hours, however, I speak whatever language the students use. My undergraduate research assistants (who are from El Paso) speak to me and to each other in 'Spanglish' (about 80% Spanish and 20% English), switching back and forth between the two languages and often mixing the two together. My graduate students are usually non-Hispanic, and for them, English is the preferred language.

For many years, Spanish was considered a second-class language in El Paso. However, nowadays, it is 'politically correct' to speak Spanish. Of course, the language has not changed, just the public's attitude toward the language.

I strongly feel that one should try to avoid mixing a political argument with what could be a recipe for better education. Many people argue that English is needed in order to function properly in the United States. This is correct, but I am living proof that bilingualism exists and that it is not in conflict with high productivity even in the sciences. Hispanic students are fully capable of learning and doing science, but it may mean offering introductory science courses taught in Spanish. Different ethnic groups which share common problems may need to find individual solutions. After all, teaching students science in the language they use at home sounds like a good idea to me.

Dr Lopez can be reached at the following address:

Dr Jorge Lopez
Physics Department
University of Texas at El Paso
500 W. University Avenue
El Paso, Texas 79968-0515
Phone: 915–747-7538
Fax: 915–747-5447
email:Bitnet: GC00@utep.bitnet
    Internet: LOPEZ@PANCHOVILLA.UTEP.EDU

For more information about Mexican-American students in higher education see Flores (1994).

9 Case Studies II: Linguistically Modified Ways of Teaching Science to Undergraduates of Limited English Proficiency

The case studies that are presented in this chapter exemplify the linguistically modified forms of science instruction which were described in general terms in Chapter 8. These include content-based forms of ESL instruction (adjunct, sheltered, and sheltered-adjunct models) as well as science instruction involving the use of the native language of the students (Spanish). While most of the case studies focus on the needs of immigrant and refugee students, the methods are equally as applicable to international students. Therefore, two case studies include courses specifically designed for international students.

Each case study includes the characteristics of the institution and its students and a description of the linguistically modified science course or program. The names and addresses of individuals who can be contacted for additional information are also listed at the end of each case study. All the information that appears here was contributed by faculty, staff, and/or members of the administration at each college or university. Both public and private, two-year and four-year, as well as graduate degree granting institutions of higher education are included.

Case Studies: Content-based ESL Instruction

Sheltered instruction: The Bridge Program at the Community College of Philadelphia (Philadelphia, PA)

The Community College of Philadelphia (CCP) is located in downtown Philadelphia, PA. It is a two-year, public institution offering the Associate's degree. There are approximately 25,000 students enrolled at the College, and they are racially and ethnically diverse: 40% Black, 38% White, 5% Oriental, 5% Spanish-American, less than 1% American Indian, and 11.5% Other/Unknown. Because of its large enrollment of non-native English speaking students, CCP established a 'Bridge Program' which provides credit-bearing academic coursework in sheltered classes. The information that appears in this case study—including the demographics of CCP's students, the material about the College's ESL and Bridge Programs, and the descriptions of the sheltered science courses—was contributed by Ms Sheila Pearl (Coordinator of English as a Second Language/Bilingual Programs and Services) and by Professors Jose Cruz (Biology), John Braxton (Biology), and Jerold Price (Chemistry).

The ESL Program at CCP provides five levels of non-credit English instruction to more than a thousand students per semester. The students in the Program vary considerably in terms of their prior English language instruction, ranging from not at all to a great deal. CCP does admit students who do not know any English. However, the latter must take an integrated group of cultural and communicative skills courses which include speaking, listening, reading, writing, and American culture before entering regular ESL classes. There are about 50 language groups represented at the College, with the largest number of ESL students speaking Vietnamese, Cambodian, Russian and Spanish.

At one time, CCP offered a variety of courses taught in Spanish. However, with the exception of introductory Sociology, they have been phased out and replaced by the Bridge Program. The Bridge Program is financially supported by the College and better meets the needs of an increasingly linguistically diverse student body. It allows high intermediate ESL students to take certain courses taught in English for academic credit. Only ESL students can enroll in these sheltered sections. The Bridge courses are taught by regular, content-area faculty who cover the same material as the equivalent non-Bridge sections. Nevertheless, to provide a sheltered environment, the Bridge courses are characterized by smaller class size (about 24 students per section); sympathetic faculty who understand and assist students who are still improving their English skills, and a supportive classroom environment in which all students are 'in the same boat' linguistically. Among the Bridge offerings are Bio. 101 *General Biology* and Chem. 110 *Introductory Chemistry*. Successful completion of these courses fulfills a science requirement and/or begins to prepare students for careers in the health fields. (Another related Bridge course is HIT 105, *Medical Record Terminology*, for students interested in the health professions.)

The Bridge section of *General Biology* serves as an introduction to modern cellular and molecular biology. The text is *Biology—Parts 1, 2, and 3*, by Sylvia Mader (Dubuque, IA: W.C. Brown). The laboratory manual that accompanies the Mader text is also used. Two different instructors have taught the Bridge section of Bio. 101, Jose Cruz (a part-time instructor in the Biology Department) and John Braxton (a visiting lecturer). Each has made his own adaptations and instructional modifications to better meet the needs of the ESL students.

Professor Cruz speaks at a slower pace, repeats terms and their meanings, allows students to use dictionaries in class and during exams, holds frequent question/answer sessions following lectures, and gives students additional time during written quizzes and tests.

Professor Braxton began teaching the Bridge section of *General Biology* in the spring of 1994. In that class, the students were mostly Asian (primarily Vietnamese), but there were also Eastern Europeans, Hispanics, and one Ethiopian. As a result of teaching a class entirely composed of non-native speakers of English, Professor Braxton admits that he has become more 'thoughtful' about his choice of words, enunciation, and rate of speech. Although he frequently pauses to solicit questions, he has found that students will not necessarily tell him if there is material that they do not understand. He has prepared for distribution to his students a list of relevant biological terms and their definitions and also has developed an electronic matching game which allows students to self-test their understanding of the language of biology.

The Bridge section of *Introductory Chemistry* (both lecture and lab) is taught by Associate Professor Jerold Price of CCP's Chemistry Department. The course covers the fundamental theories and laws of chemistry including: the arrangement of electrons in atoms, electronegativity, metals, non-metals, oxidation-reduction, nomenclature of inorganic compounds, shapes of molecules, hybridization, symmetry, molecular orbital theory, moles, stoichiometry, thermodynamics, gas problems, and organic chemistry.

Dr Price teaches as if the students did not have a science or chemistry background (even though some do), and he assumes that most of the students are afraid of chemistry (which he says is often the case). In order to make the content in the course more comprehensible for the ESL students, he slows down his rate of speech, simplifies his language, spends more time explaining terms, uses handouts, draws more diagrams on the chalkboard, and de-emphasizes the text—essentially using it as a reference. The text, which is used in all the sections of *Introductory Chemistry* including the Bridge section, is *Essentials of Chemistry* by Ralph A. Burns (New York: MacMillan). There is a workbook/problem solving manual written by Dr Price which takes the students step-by-step through the topics of the course, contains solved mathematical problems, and prototypes of hourly tests. Almost every semester, there is a peer tutor assigned to the course who is available to provide additional assistance to the students.

All Bridge instructors are volunteers; they are coached in how to teach LEP students through consultation with ESL faculty. Students in the Bridge sections who need additional help can go to the Learning Lab where tutors are available to provide assistance to all CCP students. Some of the tutors are bilingual.

The students enrolled in the Bridge science courses do well in them and in additional science courses which they may take. For example, in Bio. 101 (fall 1991 and fall 1992, total enrollment for both semesters = 16), 69% of the students received grades of A, B, or C. Nine of the Bridge biology students continued on to take 13 other biology courses. In ten of these courses (77%) grades of A, B, or C were earned. As for Chem. 110, a total of 36 students took the course in the fall 1992 and spring 1993 semesters. Of these, 78% received grades of A, B, and C. Eleven students from the fall 1992 cohort subsequently took a total of 13 additional chemistry courses, with 85% of the courses being passed with grades of A, B, or C.

The Bridge Program helps students to simultaneously master English and academic content-area subject matter in a sheltered environment. Students like this because they are able to earn college credit for Bridge coursework and to more quickly begin working toward their goal of earning a college degree. Clearly, in the case of the sciences, the Bridge sections are successful in preparing LEP students for additional coursework in the field. The Bridge courses have become so popular that each is now offered every semester (instead of every other semester). In fact, it seems that the Bridge Program is attracting more non-native English speakers to CCP and as a consequence, enrollment in the ESL Program at the College has doubled since the fall of 1989.

For additional information about the Bridge Program at CCP and the sheltered science courses contact:

Ms Sheila Pearl
Coordinator of ESL/Bilingual Programs and Services
Community College of Philadelphia
1700 Spring Garden Street
Philadelphia, PA 19130
Phone: 215-751-8528
Fax: 215-751-8248

Sheltered-Adjunct Pre-Anatomy and Physiology at Union County College, Elizabeth, New Jersey

At the Elizabeth, New Jersey, campus of Union County College (UCC) the sheltered-adjunct model of content-based ESL instruction has been adopted to meet the needs of a rapidly growing immigrant/refugee population. The following information about the College, its students, and the sheltered-adjunct pre-anatomy and physiology course was provided by Associate Professor Deborah Pires.

UCC is a public, two-year institution offering an Associate's degree. In 1992, it enrolled more than 10,400 full-time and part-time students. Each semester, between 1,000 and 1,200 students take courses in UCC's Institute for

Intensive English. In the fall of 1992, the students at the Institute represented 60 different nationalities including 148 from Colombia, 130 from Haiti, 116 from Russia, 83 from Poland, and 62 from Peru. Students who do not know any English may enroll at the Institute if they are literate in their native language. Six levels of non-credit ESL instruction are offered.

Many UCC students, including those who are non-native English speakers, are interested in the allied health fields and nursing. Nevertheless, in the early 1980s it became apparent that ESL students had an exceptionally high failure rate in *Anatomy and Physiology* and other science courses. Many of the students lacked exposure to the language of biology, and they also needed help with study skills and learning strategies. With funding from a grant and the shared efforts of both ESL and Biology faculty, an innovative sheltered-adjunct (non-credit) course was launched.

In order to enroll in *Pre-Allied Health Anatomy and Physiology* (Bio. 091), the students must be at least a 'level 5' at the Institute for Intensive English; this means that they are 'high intermediates' in terms of English language proficiency. As explained by Associate Professor Deborah Pires, who teaches the ESL (adjunct) component of the course, 'By level 5, the students are getting tired of traditional ESL courses. If they are going into the health fields, Bio. 091 is excellent preparation for future courses. Students are eager to take it.'

Bio. 091 has been taught every spring semester since 1987. Enrollment is limited to about 20 students. The text is Thibodeau and Anthony's *Structure and Function of the Body* (St Louis, MO: Mosby), and it was selected not only for its readability but also for its clear diagrams, end of chapter summaries and review tests (with answer key), and for its organization.

Topics covered in the course include: cells and tissues, homeostasis, the skin, and the skeletal, muscular, nervous, sensory, circulatory, respiratory, endocrine, digestive, urinary, and reproductive systems. Among the various laboratory activities are dissection of a fetal pig, working with the microscope, a demonstration of a reflex arc in a frog, and the showing of several videos on the systems of the body. A videodisc created and developed for the course is used to simulate blood work and to demonstrate anatomical terms (superior, inferior, transverse, sagittal, frontal, etc.) and the location of body structures and regions.

Bio. 091 (the sheltered science component) is taught by Dr Hugh Potter (Associate Professor of Biology). The class meets once a week for three hours; this session includes lecture, lab work, and recitation. Some of the ways that Dr Potter has modified his science lectures for non-native English speakers include increasing the use of diagrams, simplifying his sentence structure, trying to be a bit cautious about the use of idioms and jokes, and reviewing new vocabulary. He moves from the concrete to the abstract. Although he tries to provide a friendly classroom atmosphere, Dr Potter is well aware that once these ESL students are 'mainstreamed', their experiences in science classes may not be so supportive.

The ESL adjunct course taught by Professor Pires meets twice a week for one and a half hours a session. In it, Professor Pires reviews the coursework of the week's biology class utilizing techniques which also help the students to learn how to study and to improve their study skills. She describes what goes on in the ESL class as follows:

> The students retell what they understood from the biology class; work in cooperative groups to study the material; carry out various activities including labelling, matching, dictations, reading from the text, card games, writing essays, doing crossword puzzles, and asking questions. In addition, the following study skills are reinforced: the taking of and studying from classroom notes, memorization techniques, test-taking skills, essay writing, skimming and scanning techniques, outlining, summarizing, finding the main idea, identifying signal words, making good use of the text, and using study groups to learn. Other activities in the ESL course include pronunciation practice and the study of the roots and affixes used in medical terminology.

Students are evaluated in both the Biology and ESL components by means of weekly quizzes and a mid-term and a final exam. However the final course grades are pass/fail.

Clearly, the ESL instructor for the adjunct course has to work especially hard. Professor Pires, for example, had to learn the biology and for many semesters sat in on Dr Potter's lectures. She also developed a variety of supplementary materials and dittos (such as crossword puzzles, diagrams, and vocabulary lists) that pertain to the anatomy and physiology lectures.

For any adjunct or sheltered-adjunct model to be successful, the content-area and ESL instructors must cooperate with each other. As Dr Potter and Professor Pires describe this, they work together 'down to the detail'. Their goal is not only to insure that the students do well in these particular courses (Bio. 091 and the adjunct class) but also to prepare the students to move into 'less friendly', mainstream, science courses that they make take in the future.

For further information about this sheltered-adjunct pre-anatomy and physiology course at Union County College contact:

Professor Deborah Pires
Union County College
12 West Jersey Street
Elizabeth, NJ 07202
Phone: 908-965-6040

Sheltered-Adjunct Biology Instruction at Cañada College, Redwood City, California

Cañada College, located in Redwood City, California, is a two-year public institution, offering the Associate's degree as well as vocational two-year certificates. About 6,000 students are enrolled at the College; approximately 63% are White, 20% Hispanic, 7% Asian or Pacific Islander, 5% African-American, 2% Filipino, 1% American Indian/Alaskan Native, and 2% Other.

In the fall of 1990, Cañada College began a program of content-based ESL instruction using the sheltered-adjunct model. The information that follows was provided by three individuals who have been directly involved with this Program: Ms Alicia C. Aguirre (English Institute Coordinator), Mr Mervin Giuntoli (Biology Instructor), and Mrs. Jennifer Castello (ESL instructor).

The English Institute at Cañada College serves about 400 students per semester, providing four levels of ESL instruction. Students who enroll at the English Institute must have a level of knowledge of basic English that is equivalent to at least one year of previous study in programs such as Adult Basic Education, a language school, or English language instruction in their native country. Students do not receive academic credit for ESL coursework. About 70% of the English Institute students are native Spanish speakers (mainly from Mexico and Central America) while most of the others are speakers of Vietnamese, Polish, Russian, Hungarian, Chinese, Japanese, Tongan, Pilipino, and Thai.

As a result of academic difficulties encountered by ESL students who exited the English Institute and who were directly mainstreamed into vocational or degree programs, a transitional program was initiated in the fall of 1990. It consists of a series of non-credit content-based ESL courses (using the sheltered-adjunct model) plus a study skills course. Originally funded by a grant, this program is now directly supported by the College.

Sheltered-adjunct non-credit introductory courses in social science, Western civilization, mathematics, and science were specially designed for high intermediate/advanced ESL students. These courses meet three times a week for 50 minutes. During two of the class meetings, the students receive content-area instruction from a faculty member who is a specialist in the particular academic discipline; this is the sheltered component. For the third session of the week, the students meet with an ESL instructor who, using ESL methodology, reinforces the vocabulary and content of the subject matter course and further develops the students' proficiency in English; this is the adjunct component. Students taking sheltered-adjunct courses are also required to enroll in English 880 which is a non-credit study skills course. During a given semester, students take a minimum of two sheltered content-area courses and at some point while participating in the content-based ESL program, must complete English 880.

Students are recruited into the content-based ESL program in a variety of ways: as a result of scores obtained on placement tests taken by entering students; by ESL instructors, and by other counselors and faculty members. The instructors of the sheltered content-area courses are mainstream faculty members who participated in an intensive two-day workshop (which was given just prior to the fall 1990 semester) to learn about L2 acquisition as well as a variety of ESL techniques to enhance their teaching.

The science course developed for this sheltered-adjunct program is Biology 880, *Introduction to the Sciences*. It enrolls about 20 ESL students per semester. They meet twice a week with Biology instructor Mervin Giuntoli for the sheltered science lectures/demonstrations and once a week with ESL Instructor Mrs Jennifer Castello who teachs the adjunct component of the course.

Bio. 880 is a survey of the natural and physical sciences and covers the following topics: characteristics of living things, inorganic and organic chemistry, cell and organelle structure and function, cell division (mitosis and meiosis), nucleic acids, enzymes, photosynthesis, and cellular respiration.

The purpose of Biology 880 is to prepare the students for further credit-bearing coursework in the sciences. All lectures, demonstrations, discussion and classwork are carried out in English, and there is no required text. Professor Giuntoli provides students with lecture topic outlines which they complete in class. Students watch various film loops and examine cells and tissues with the microscope. Unlike most science survey courses, Mr Giuntoli does not have 'to rush to complete the course.' Rather he is more concerned that the students master the most important concepts and develop the study skills and basic vocabulary that are essential for further coursework in the sciences. He has noted that the students often have had little or no background in science, particularly in biology.

Students receive letter grades in Bio. 880. There are four or five unit exams (multiple choice, matching, fill in the blanks, true/false, short answer, etc.). Although students may be assigned homework, they do not receive grades for this work.

Between the fall of 1990 and the spring of 1994, 75 students took Bio. 880; 24 students (32%) received final grades of A, 22 students (29.3%) received grades of B and another 22 (29.3%) grades of C. The remaining seven students (9.3%), withdrew from the course or received grades of D or F.

Mr Giuntoli credits much of the success of his students in Bio. 880 to the activities they carry out in the adjunct component of the course which meets once a week with Mrs Castello. In these sessions, she teaches vocabulary, grammar, and some study skills, focusing on the content of the biology course. (Study skills are not, however, emphasized here since the students are also enrolled in English 880, *College Study Skills*, which is a separate course.)

Some sample activities (often done in small groups of two or three students) that Mrs Castello uses in the adjunct course are:

- Analysis of prefixes, roots, and suffixes of scientific terms: what they mean and examples of their usage.
- Word forms: the noun, verb, adjective and/or adverb forms of frequently used scientific terms such as dehydration (noun), to dehydrate (verb), and dehydrated (adjective) or reaction (noun), to react (verb), reactive (adjective), and reactively (adverb). In activities of this type, the useful forms of the words are emphasized.
- Forming wh- (what, which, when, why, how) questions: students are given an answer and then write wh- questions. For example, if the answer is 'photosynthesis', the question might be, 'What is the process carried out in plants which produces oxygen?'

All students taking sheltered-adjunct classes also enroll in English 880, *College Study Skills*, which meets three times a week for 50 minutes. It is taught by Professor Castello. The text for *College Study Skills* is *The Confident Student* by Carol Kanar (Burlington, MA: Houghton-Mifflin).

The purpose of this study skills course is to help students develop the kinds of academic skills they will need in mainstream content-area classes. These include listening to lectures and taking notes, reading the textbook, using memory techniques, improving vocabulary and spelling, preparing for and taking exams, using the library, and time management. Students keep journals and must write summaries from the notes they take during lectures given in class. In addition, there are guest speakers from student support services and extra-credit earned by attending college events. However, students must submit written summaries of the speaker's presentation or what occurred at the special lecture, club meeting, or sporting event that they attended.

Students receive a letter grade in this course but may opt for pass/fail grading. Grades are based on journal writing, classwork assignments, unit tests, and a final exam.

Initial evaluation of the effectiveness of Cañada's content-based ESL program indicates that participating students are doing well in mainstream courses and that for the most part their grade-point-averages increase by at least one point.

Follow-up of the students ($n = 48$) who took Bio. 880 prior to the spring 1994 semester indicates that those who have taken additional science courses (biology and/or chemistry) have done very well. The distribution of the grades earned was 15% A, 38% B, 41% C, and 6% D.

For additional information about Cañada College's content-based ESL program and in particular, Biology 880, contact:

Ms Alicia C. Aguirre, English Institute Coordinator
Cañada College
4200 Farm Hill Boulevard
Redwood City, CA 94061
phone: 415-306-3222
FAX: 415-306-3457
email: messner@smcccd.cc.ca.us

Mr Mervin Giuntoli, Biology Instructor
Basic and Applied Sciences
Cañada College
4200 Farm Hill Boulevard
Redwood City, CA 94061
Phone: 415-306-3202
Fax: 415-306-3457

Mrs Jennifer Castello, ESL Instructor
English Institute
Cañada College
4200 Farm Hill Boulevard
Redwood City, CA 94061
Phone: 415-306-3472
Fax: 415-306-3457

Sheltered-Adjunct 'Human Environment' at Eastern Washington University, Cheney, Washington

Eastern Washington University (EWU) in Cheney, Washington, is a public institution granting both Bachelor's and Master's degrees. The following information about Eastern Washington University, its students, and the Asia University America Program was provided by Ms Evelyn Renshaw (Curriculum Director) and Ms Janine Goldstein Alden (ESL Instructor) of EWU's Asia University America Program.

Eastern Washington University's total enrollment is about 8,000, and the majority of students are White (88.8%). Of those remaining, 1.9% are African-American, 3.1% Hispanic, 2.1% Asian, and 2.1% American Indian. The highest degree offered is the Master's. The University's English Language Program provides four levels of ESL instruction to 150-200 undergraduate and graduate students per semester.

The University is one of five northwestern colleges that participate in the Asia University America Program (AUAP). The other members of this consortium are Oregon State University in Corvallis, OR; Western Washington University in Bellingham, WA; Central Washington University in Ellensburg, WA; and Boise State University in Boise, ID. Each year, since 1989, these consortium members have received some of the sophomore class of Asia University (Tokyo, Japan) as part of a study abroad program. The students live and study at the five US campuses, and Eastern Washington University receives from 70–80 students per semester through this arrangement.

At Eastern Washington, the Japanese students are enrolled in six courses. One is a science course called *Human Environment*, and the others are interrelated ESL courses. The students vary in their proficiency in English, but the majority range from low to high intermediates.

The coordination and instruction of *Human Environment* (which follows the sheltered-adjunct model) is described below by Professor Janine Goldstein Alden, one of the participating ESL instructors.

In Professor Goldstein Alden's words:

Human Environment is a sheltered science course specially designed for the Japanese students. There are two 30–40 minute lectures a week given in English by a faculty member from the Biology Department. The students also meet in smaller discussion groups (17–20 students per group) for three 50-minute sessions per week in what makes up the adjunct component. The discussion classes are divided according to students' reading ability so that homework expectations are equalized.

The text for *Human Environment* is *The World We Live In: An Introduction to Environmental Studies for ESL Students*. It was written by Thomas Nicholas and William Pech and published by Old Maine Press (Bellingham, WA: 1990). The authors are faculty members in the Intensive English Language Program at Western Washington University. The topics covered in the text and course are basic biological concepts, human uses of energy, water and water pollution, air and air pollution, soil and soil pollution, biological resources (such as forests, biological diversity, and wildlife conservation), and the human population and world food supply.

The Biology faculty member who teaches *Human Environment* receives coaching in how to make the lectures more accessible to the students. This includes, for example, using simple language, repetition, and clear discourse markers (such as 'there are three main points. The first is...'). The instructor frequently uses examples and ask for questions. At the end of each lecture, *all* students write questions, and 10–20 additional minutes are spent in a question-answer format. Any remaining questions are taken up in the small discussion groups.

In advance of each lecture, students are given a brief vocabulary list (5–15 words) as well as a reading assignment (2–6 pages). These assignments vary according to the students' level of English proficiency and give the students a chance to become familiar with and to think and learn about the content of the lecture before coming to class. During the adjunct classes that follow the lectures, students use cooperative groups and occasionally whole class discussion to practice using the new vocabulary and to increase their understanding of the concepts covered in the lecture.

The facilitators of the adjunct discussion courses are professional ESL instructors. They use a variety of techniques to stimulate discussion and vocabulary and concept acquisition. Note-taking skills and oral language proficiency are emphasized. These ESL group facilitators meet periodically with the instructor of *Human Environment*. Besides planning all homework and classwork activities and choosing the vocabulary to be taught, the facilitators must attend the *Human Environment* lectures. They also write the tests and assign grades; students are evaluated for both the *Human Environment* course content as well as improvement shown in English language proficiency. The tests include short and long answer essays, definitions, true/false, vocabulary matching, multiple choice items, etc.

The students receive academic credit from Asia University for participation in the science as well as the ESL courses. Their most notable achievement at the end of the program is growth in both their self-confidence and proficiency in using the English language.

For additional information about the Asia University America Program or the *Human Environment* course contact:

Ms Evelyn Renshaw, Curriculum Director
Asia University America Program
MS #9, Louise Anderson Hall
Cheney, Washington 99004
Phone: 509-359-6432
Fax: 509-359-7855

Ms Janine Goldstein Alden (ESL Instructor)
Asia University America Program
MS #9, Louise Anderson Hall
Cheney, Washington 99004
Phone: 509-359-7359
Fax: 509-359-7855

Adjunct model: Paired Science and ESL Courses at Saint Michael's College (Colchester, Vermont)

Saint Michael's College (SMC) in Colchester, VT, is a private institution offering both the Bachelor's and five different Master's degrees. It enrolls almost 1,700 undergraduate and 1,200 graduate students; approximately 93-95% of the students are White.

Besides providing a 4-5 level ESL program that serves about 50 undergraduate and graduate students per semester, SMC is well known for its 23 year old University Academic Program (UAP) for International Students. The following description of the UAP was made possible by information provided by Dr Kathleen Mahnke (Director of Graduate Programs in Teaching English as a Second Language), Dr Daniel Bean (Professor and Chairman of the Department of Biology) as well as by others at Saint Michael's.

The present day University Academic Program for International Students is considered within the field of ESL to be a model program for integrating international students into regular undergraduate academic coursework. Its curriculum is based on current research in L2 pedagogy and the developing field of English-for-Academic-Purposes, as well as careful assessment of past UAP courses and student performance.

The Program currently enrolls between 25 and 30 students, and they come from approximately 30 countries, representing areas as diverse as Latin America, Europe, the Middle East and Asia. The UAP provides a 'bridge' to help students with the transition from intensive ESL coursework to regular academic undergraduate courses over a two-semester period of study. Students who enter the program are at least at a high intermediate level of English language proficiency.

At Level One of the Program, the UAP students take a college writing course and a cooperative course (which will be described shortly) that has both an academic and an English component. In Level Two, students enroll in two regular undergraduate courses as well as two 'sheltered' courses, one in advanced college writing and the other in English literature. Students who complete the program are prepared to meet the academic and cultural expectations of institutions of higher learning in the United States. Some matriculate at St Michael's while others transfer to other colleges and universities.

The cooperative content courses are one of the special features of UAP. Each semester one three-credit, regular academic course at SMC is specially designated to enroll traditional undergraduates as well as UAP students. The course is taught by a regular St Michael's faculty member.

The UAP students enrolled in this designated content-area course also meet for three hours a week with a trained ESL teacher. During these English-for-Academic-Purposes sessions (the adjunct component of the cooperative course), a variety of activities are carried out to help the students to master the content area of the course, to further develop their proficiency in academic English, and to reinforce the skills already acquired in *College Writing*. In order to be knowledgeable about the subject matter taught in the content-area course, the ESL instructor attends the lectures along with the students.

Although the majority of cooperative courses are in the humanities and social and behavioral sciences, six cooperative science courses for non-science majors (such as nutrition, genetics and chemistry) have also been offered since 1985. For example, in 1986 Dr Daniel J. Bean, Professor and Chairman of Saint Michael's Department of Biology, taught Bio. 107 (*Biology: A Human Perspective*) as a cooperative course. Bio. 107 is a three-credit science course. Lectures are held three times a week for 50 minutes. The text used in 1986 was G.E. Nelson's *Biological Principles with Human Applications* (Somerset, NJ: John Wiley) along with its study guide. Total enrollment in the course was 30, including 18 ESL students. Many of the latter were from Japan, Europe, the Middle East, and Central and South America.

The purpose of the course was to provide the students with an awareness of and an appreciation for the scientific methodology used to investigate problems in the life sciences and the current state of knowledge relative to some of these problems. Students were required to keep a journal and were asked to read the assigned material in the text before coming to class. Although there were no regularly scheduled laboratories, some field work was included.

Dr Bean notes that:

> When I agreed to offer *Biology: A Human Perspective* as a cooperative course, Dr. Mahnke (who would be teaching the paired English-for-Academic-Purposes sessions) explained some of the cultural attributes she thought I should be aware of before meeting the non-native students. This was particularly useful since I try to use an interactive approach in the classroom. For example, she told me that Japanese students are not accustomed to being called upon in class while Central and South American students are.

> I made other adjustments in the course to better meet the needs of the ESL students. I spoke slower than usual in class (and have continued to do this in other courses since it benefits all students). I became more aware of the need to define *all* biological terms (and often other words) as they occurred, and I reused them frequently. Prior to each exam, I gave Dr Mahnke a copy of the test to screen for vocabulary problems. She also informed me of potential difficulties with the wording of test questions so that I could clarify a question or substitute a new one. All my classes were audiotaped, and a few were videotaped. The ESL students found the tapes to be especially useful in review sessions. The American students (native English-speaking) were invited to join the ESL students in Dr Mahnke's bi-weekly gatherings since all students would benefit from the study activities and review of the course material. None of the Americans took advantage of this opportunity.

> I noticed that interpersonal exchanges occurred primarily among the Latin American students. Few North American students went out of their way to get to know the others. The Japanese were also somewhat shy. Two of the Latin students got to know each other so well they married the next year!

In the paired English-for-Academic-Purposes sessions, the ESL students worked with Dr Mahnke on a wide variety of activities. These included learning strategies to effectively listen to lectures and to take notes, how to build vocabulary, how to keep a journal, strategies for carrying out the reading assignments and making notes and outlines, learning how to speak up in class, to participate in discussions and to ask questions, how to study for and how to take tests, how to make oral presentations, how to use a dictionary, and how to use the library for research. There also was a final exam on the material covered in this English-for-Academic-Purposes course. It included sections devoted to essay writing, vocabulary review, listening and note-taking skills, and academic reading.

All students in Dr Bean's Bio. 107 course took two hour exams and a final exam; these contained both multiple choice and short answer questions. The final class average was 76. For the native English speaking students the average was 70 (range of 65–88) and for the ESL students the average was 80 (range of 66–95)!

For additional information about Saint Michael's University Academic Program for International Students or about cooperative science instruction contact:

Professor Kathleen Mahnke
TESL Program Director
Center for International Programs
Saint Michael's College
Winooski Park
Colchester, VT 05439
Phone: 802-654-2646
Fax: 802-654-2595

Dr Daniel J. Bean
Professor and Chairman
Department of Biology
Saint Michael's College
Winooski Park
Colchester, VT 05439
Phone: 802-654-2622
Fax: 802-655-3680

Case Studies: Science Instruction in the Students' Native Language

Bilingual Science Instruction at Erie Community College, Buffalo, New York

Erie Community College (ECC) in upstate Buffalo, New York, offers a bilingual program that includes several science courses taught in Spanish. The

Director of the Bilingual Program is Dr Eleanor Paterson, and the instructor of the science courses taught in Spanish is Ms Yolanda Lugo, a full-time faculty member. They have provided the following information about the College, its students, the ESL and the bilingual programs, and the science courses taught in Spanish.

Erie Community College (ECC) is a public two-year college which offers an Associate's degree; it is part of the State University of New York. ECC serves approximately 14,000 part-time and full-time students who attend classes on three campuses (City Campus in Buffalo, NY; North Campus in Williamsville, NY, and South Campus in Orchard Park, NY).

The racial/ethnic distribution of ECC's students as a whole is not unusual (85% White, 10% Black, 3% Hispanic, 1% Asian/Pacific, 1% Native American, and 1% Foreign). However, the majority of LEP students are enrolled at one campus (the City Campus). Here, the College provides three levels of non-credit ESL instruction for 300 students a semester. In addition, during the 1987-88 academic year, Erie Community College established its Bilingual Program (BP) at the City Campus. This Program serves all ECC linguistic minority students, a population that speaks more than 30 different languages.

However, most (75%) of the students in the Bilingual Program are native speakers of Spanish (mainly from Puerto Rico plus the Dominican Republic, Mexico, Peru and Colombia). If they do not know any English, they may begin studying English taking classes in the ESL program and concurrently register for credit-bearing academic courses taught in Spanish.

The College also features a Bilingual Lab which houses tutors in English, math, computers, science, and other academic areas. Students make appointments or are helped on a walk-in basis when possible.

Three science courses are taught in Spanish by Professor Lugo. These include:

1. *Human Biology* (BI107-HB, three credits)—This is a science elective for non-science majors who have little background in science or math. The course satisfies the science requirement for all degrees except those in Liberal Arts Science Majors. Topics include nutrition, respiration, sexuality, birth defects, sense organs, chronic and degenerative diseases, drugs, the nervous system, and population growth, control, and pollution. The text is Mader's *Human Biology* (Dubuque, IA: William C. Brown).

2. *Environmental Science* (PH120-HB, three credits)—This course can be used toward the science requirement for all students except those in Liberal Arts Science Majors. Particular attention is paid to the concept of energy and its role in the environment, pollution, population growth and control, resource use, and the factors that affect and alter ecosystems. The text is Raven, Berg, and Johnson's *Environment* (Orlando, FL: Harcourt Brace).

3. *Introductory Chemistry* (CH100-HB)—This is a preparatory course for students who later will take CH200 (*Introductory College Chemistry I*), CH250 (*General Chemistry with Introductory Organic and Biochemistry*), or CH300 (*General Chemistry for Science Majors*). Although there are no prerequisites for CH100-HB, CH101 (*Chemistry Lab*) is a corequisite. Topics in *Introductory Chemistry* include the scientific method, states of matter, atoms, elements, compounds, the periodic table, formulas and nomenclature, equations, the metric system, dimensional analysis, and the concept of a 'mole'. The text is Seese & Daub's *In Preparation for College Chemistry* (Englewood Cliffs, NJ: Prentice Hall). CH100-HB is a non-credit course and cannot be applied toward the Associate's degree.

The sections of these three classes are small (averaging 15 students per course per semester), and the students who enroll in them must be fluent speakers of Spanish. The courses help familiarize the students with scientific concepts and terminology and with background information that will be needed in upper level courses. They also serve as a 'testing ground' to see if a particular field of science is one that a student should pursue.

The lectures, tests, and quizzes are given in Spanish. However, the texts, transparencies, films and videos are in English. Technical vocabulary is introduced in English. Handouts are usually in English, but are sometimes translated into Spanish. The students have numerous opportunities to improve their English skills even as they study science in Spanish because the text and audiovisual materials are in English and English vocabulary is emphasized. Although there are no 'formal' or regularly scheduled laboratories, Professor Lugo includes demonstrations and the use of authentic materials, microscopes and slides, to make the classes more interesting and understandable. There is no difference at ECC between the course descriptions for classes taught in English or Spanish.

The science departments at ECC have been supportive of the courses taught in Spanish, and the faculty have come to understand the value of instruction in the students' native language. The 'passing rate' of students in the bilingual science courses is approaching that for students in the standard courses, and some of the Spanish speaking students go on to take and successfully complete upper level science courses taught in English. An increasing number of bilingual students are completing programs such as Nursing and Allied Health which require upper level science courses. In fact, in December 1993, ECC had five Hispanic graduates of Nursing, four females and the Program's first male Hispanic.

For additional information about Erie Community College's Bilingual Program or science courses taught in Spanish contact:

Dr Eleanor Paterson
Director, Bilingual Program
Erie Community College
121 Ellicott Street
Buffalo, NY 14203
Phone: 716-851-1049 (or 1079)
Fax: 716-851-1129

Professor Yolanda Lugo
Biology Department
Erie Community College
121 Ellicott Street
Buffalo, NY 14203
Phone: 716-851-1064
Fax: 716-851-1129

Bilingual Science Courses at Miami-Dade Community College, Wolfson Campus, Miami, Florida

Miami-Dade Community College in Florida is a public, two-year college which grants the Associate's degree. It was founded in 1960 and in 1972 began offering a bilingual mode of instruction (described below). The following information about Miami-Dade's students, ESL programs, and the InterAmerican Center and its bilingual courses was provided by Professor Maria del Carmen Vazquez (Acting Associate Dean of Instruction, InterAmerican Center, Wolfson Campus), Dr Margarita M. Cuervo (Mathematics Professor, Kendall Campus), Dr Jose Vicente (Dean of the InterAmerican Center, Wolfson Campus), and by Instructor Nidia Romer (Department of Arts and Sciences, InterAmerican Center, Wolfson Campus).

There are almost 118,000 students enrolled at Miami-Dade's five campuses: North Campus near Hialeah with 41,600 students; Kendall Campus in Kendall with nearly 46,700 students; Wolfson Campus in downtown Miami with 20,270 students; the Medical Center in the Hospital District with almost 6,900 students, and the Homestead Campus in Homestead with 2,500 students.

College-wide, 57% of the students are Hispanic (born in Spanish speaking countries, mainly in the Caribbean or Central and South America, or born to Hispanic parents in the United States). Of the remaining students, 21% are Black, 20% White, 2% Asian, and less than 1% American Indian and Other. A significant number of Miami-Dade's faculty members are bilingual, and the instructors, staff and administration are especially sensitive to diversity and multicultural issues.

At Miami-Dade, the English as a Second Language Program is college-wide, but each campus has its own ESL course offerings. The programs are similar from campus to campus, with the same course levels and competency goals. Miami-Dade's ESL Program, unlike those at many other institutions of higher education, accepts students even if they know no English; such students must enroll in ESL. There are six levels of ESL coursework, and students can apply up to 12 academic credits earned in ESL toward the Associate's degree. Only when a student has reached the fifth or sixth levels of ESL can he or she begin taking 'mainstream' courses.

On the Kendall campus, there are 1,800 students enrolled in ESL per semester. They come from more than 80 countries and speak more than 60 languages including French, Italian, Spanish and Portuguese. At the Wolfson Campus's InterAmerican Center, the ESL program enrolls 2,000 students per semester; 95% are native Spanish speakers.

The Wolfson campus' InterAmerican Center, the largest outreach center of Miami-Dade Community College, not only provides ESL instruction but also offers to its many Hispanic students credit-bearing, content-area courses in the humanities, social sciences, mathematics, and the sciences (biology, chemistry and physics) taught in a bilingual modality. (The only exceptions to this bilingual mode of instruction are ESL which is taught strictly in English and foreign language instruction which is provided in the language being studied.) Bilingual modality means that the classes are conducted in English, the textbooks are in English (and are same as those used on other Miami-Dade campuses), and the tests are written in English. However, around 30% of the lecture is in Spanish. Students may ask questions and request clarification in Spanish; and instructors may use Spanish to answer questions as well as to highlight and emphasize concepts and problem solving techniques.

The aim of using both languages in the classroom is to assist students who are still developing proficiency in English while encouraging the maintenance and development of Spanish academic vocabulary and grammatical construction. However, the content and textbook are the same whether a course is taught monolingually in English or bilingually in English/Spanish.

The InterAmerican Center's Bilingual Program is coordinated by the Dean of the InterAmerican Center, Wolfson Campus. The program is open to all students; in other words, native English speaking students who want to improve their Spanish can also enroll in the bilingual courses. In fact, about 14% of students enrolled in bilingual sections are native English speakers.

Nidia Romer, an Instructor in the Department of Natural Sciences and Chemistry, has provided the following information about her experiences teaching a variety of science courses in the bilingual mode:

In Ms Romer's words:

During the five years that I have been teaching in this program, 99% of my students have been native speakers of Spanish. They are supposed to have passed all of their required ESL courses as well as the first two English courses required for all students (both native and non-native English speakers who are pursuing a college degree).

I give my lectures in English, only using Spanish to answer questions and sometimes to emphasize key concepts. I also may give examples or tell jokes or anecdotes in Spanish. Most students prefer having the entire lecture in English and resent when I speak Spanish, especially those who came here as children or young adolescents and who finished their high school education in the United States. The older students, who came to the U.S. as adults, are the ones who ask questions in Spanish when they want clarification. I encourage adult students (who tend to be shy) to ask me questions after class, or to come visit me during my office hours.

Often, when we are working with numbers or mathematical concepts, students switch from English to Spanish (especially the older students). During the laboratory sessions, many students ask questions or talk to me in Spanish. During my office hours, I respond to students in the language in which they ask their questions.

My tests—which are written in English—are mostly multiple choice and true/false. I have had a few students who complained about difficulties understanding some of the questions, but I then changed the wording to make it easier for them. I do not allow bilingual dictionaries in the class during tests; however, students can ask me questions or the meaning of words in Spanish, and I will provide the necessary clarification.

The science courses that I have taught in this bilingual mode include *General Chemistry* (which is a sequence of three courses required for science majors; each of these courses is worth three credits); *General Chemistry Laboratories* (a three course sequence for science majors totaling 4 credits); *General Biology Laboratories* (a two course sequence for science majors totaling 4 credits); *Energy in the Natural Environment* (a three-credit course for non-science majors), and *Human Nutrition* (a three-credit course for science and non-science majors). Depending on the particular course, enrollment is limited to about 20 or 30 students per semester.

The textbooks for these courses are in English; they are the same as those used in all other sections of the course.

- The *General Chemistry* text is Brady's *General Chemistry: Principles and Structure* (Somerset, NJ: Wiley). The students are required to buy this book and to use it for the three course sequence. Students are assigned entire chapters as well as questions and problems at the end of chapter. I recommend that they read the book before the lecture, but most of them only read it after the lecture.

- For the *General Chemistry Laboratories*, we use Beran & Brady's *Laboratory*

Manual for General Chemistry: Principles and Structures (Somerset, NJ: Wiley) and in the *General Biology Laboratories*, Eberhard's *General Biology Laboratory Manual* (Orlando, FL: Saunders). These manuals meet the objectives of the courses and include questions at all levels of Bloom's Taxonomy (Bloom, 1956). Students are asked to read assigned pages before coming to class.

- For *Energy and the Natural Environment*, the recommended textbook is Burrus & Yaffa's *Energy in the Natural Environment* (Needham Heights, MA: Ginn Press). Purchase of the book is optional, and as a result, only about a third of the students buy it. The book is easy to read and relatively inexpensive. I recommend that the students read the book both before and after the lecture.
- *Understanding Human Nutrition* by Whitney and Rolfes (St Paul, MN: West) is the text for *Human Nutrition*. Students are assigned chapters to read before lectures as well as end-of-chapter questions to answer.

Although most of my students are non-native speakers of English, none have complained about difficulties understanding the textbooks.

As for the bilingual mode of instruction, I think you have to accommodate your teaching to the preference of the majority of the students. Here at the InterAmerican Center, the students say they need to speak and hear as much English as possible since their job opportunities are better when they understand and speak good English. Since they use Spanish at home, they want to practice their English in school. I think the fact that I personalize the language which I speak to the students according to their preferences helps them to feel more comfortable using both languages and to prepare themselves for the job market.

The InterAmerican Center's Bilingual Program has been successful not only in providing access for Hispanic students to higher education but also in preparing students for the CLAST (College-Level Academic Skills Test) exam. In the state of Florida, all college students must pass the CLAST prior to being awarded the Associate in Arts (A.A.) or the Baccalaureate degree. This exam has four subtests which assess mathematics, English language, reading, and essay writing skills, and passing scores have been established by the State Board of Education. In a recent study, it was found that of the InterAmerican Center's students (academic years 1991-92 and 1992-93) who had successfully completed (with grades of A, B, or C) the math (MGF 1113) and English (ENC 2301) preparatory courses, an average of 70% passed the CLAST exam. Furthermore, there was no significant difference between the passing rates of InterAmerican students and those students attending Wolfson's main campus and taking courses taught monolingually in English.

For additional information about Miami-Dade Community College's InterAmerican Center or bilingual science courses contact:

Dr Jose A. Vicente
Dean, InterAmerican Center
Miami-Dade Community College
Wolfson Campus
627 S.W. 27th Avenue
Miami, Florida 33135-2966
Phone: 305-237-3800
Fax: 305-237-3859

Nidia Romer, Instructor
Department of Arts and Sciences
Miami-Dade Community College
Wolfson Campus/InterAmerican Center
627 S.W. 27th Avenue
Miami, Florida 33135-2966
Phone: 305-237-3810

Professor Maria del Carmen Vasquez
Interim Associate Dean of Instruction
Miami Dade Community College
Wolfson Campus/InterAmerican Center
627 S.W. 27th Avenue
Miami, Florida 33135-2966
Phone: 305-237-3825
Fax: 305-237-3859

Multiple Academic Support Programs Plus Academic Coursework in Spanish for Hispanic students at The University of Texas, El Paso

The University of Texas at El Paso (El Paso, Texas) is a public institution which grants Bachelor's, Master's and Doctoral degrees. The following information about its students, ESL, bilingual, and support programs was provided by Ms Debbie Agthe (Director of the Office of International Programs), Dr Jon Amastae (Professor of Linguistics), Dr Sally Andrade (Director, Center for Institutional Evaluation, Research, and Planning), Dr Jack Bristol (Dean, College of Science), Dr Rigoberto Delgado (Coordinator, Mexican Student Services), Ms Mary Lou Gibson (Coordinator of Math and Science Tutoring), Dr Philip Goodell (Associate Professor, Department of Geological Sciences), Ms Lynda Rushing (Coordinator of the English Language Institute), and Ms Gladys Shaw (Director of the Tutoring and Learning Center).

The University of Texas at El Paso (UTEP) enrolls approximately 14,700 undergraduate and 2,400 graduate students. It is located directly across the Río Grande from Ciudad Juárez (the city of Juárez in Chihuahua, Mexico), so it is not surprising to learn that its student body is predominantly Hispanic

(64.9% Hispanic; 24% White; 5.4% Mexican National; 2.9% Black; 1.3% Asian; 0.3% Native American; 1.2% Other).

There are nearly 1,000 students per semester who arrive daily from Juárez, Mexico. Many of these students, when first entering UTEP, are much in need of the services of the Inter-American Science and Humanities Program (IASHP). These include:

- a 2-day orientation program conducted in Spanish to introduce new students to the academic and cultural life of the college and to plan their program of study;
- placement testing in English and math;
- a sequence of ESL courses;
- a series of study skills courses. The first two are required and taught in a bilingual (Spanish/English) format; the last two are taught in English, assigned according to student need, and help prepare students for the TASP (Texas Academic Skills Program) test. TASP is a statewide exam in reading, writing and math. All three sections of the exam must be passed in order for students to proceed in college beyond 60 credit hours;
- a free, non-credit English conversation course which is given during the summer as well as during the fall and spring semesters;
- mandatory academic advisement every semester; and
- a series of credit-bearing, introductory courses taught in Spanish. (Content-area courses taught in Spanish are offered at UTEP both as part of and separate from the Inter-American Science and Humanities Program).

Although the IASHP was founded in 1968 as a modest mathematics tutorial course, it is evident from the above description that it has evolved over the years into a comprehensive program to increase the retention rate of Inter-American students. The number of students in the Program has been increasing steadily. For example, in the fall of 1993 there were 460 students in the Program while in the fall of 1994, there were 670.

Although the credit-bearing courses offered in Spanish through the IAHSP currently include psychology, linguistics, history and political science, many other subject areas such as math, science, accounting, philosophy, religious studies, sociology, marketing, and economics have been taught in Spanish since 1973. The science courses offered in Spanish (both in the IAHSP and separate from it) have included: *General Chemistry*; *Geology* (Physical; Historical; and some geology laboratories); and *Physics* (General; Optics, Sound and Heat; Electricity and Magnetism; Mechanics; Heat, Waves, Motion, and Optics; and some physics laboratories). In these courses the lectures are presented in Spanish, but the reading assignments, papers, exams and student presentations are in English.

There are two separate sources of ESL instruction at UTEP. The English

Language Institute is part of the Division of Professional and Continuing Education and provides intensive instruction to help students learn English in the shortest possible time. Students do not receive any academic credit for coursework completed at the Institute. TOEFL (Test of English as a Foreign Language) preparation is emphasized. Admission to the Institute does not imply or constitute admission to the regular academic program at UTEP. The Institute serves a small number (about 50) undergraduate and graduate students per semester: 65% are Hispanic, 20% Asian, 5% Arabic, 5% German, and 5% Other.

The majority of the Hispanic students who enroll at UTEP enter through the IASHP and do not study ESL at the English Language Institute. Rather, after taking the SLEP (Secondary Level English Program) placement exam, they enroll in a series of ESL courses offered through the Department of Languages and Linguistics. Students who know no English are accepted into this program. While the lower level ESL courses are non-credit, the upper level courses count toward the degree and fulfill the University's English composition requirements. Upon successful completion of their program of required ESL classes, the students in the IASHP can declare a major and be admitted to one of UTEP's colleges. Although officially mainstreamed, many of these students still utilize the various services provided by the Inter-American Program.

An important student-retention program to assist all UTEP students is the Tutoring and Learning Center which provides a wide range of services. These include:

- non-credit courses in study skills, reading, writing, math and computer usage; standardized test (TASP, GRE, GMAT, TOEFL) preparation; English conversation for foreign students; and foreign language conversation classes (French, Spanish, Russian, German);
- small group and one-on-one peer tutoring (often bilingual) in most academic areas; the tutors are UTEP students who have completed a training program for national certification;
- a Learning Assistance Laboratory to help individual students with study skills and standardized test preparation;
- special services for disabled students such as computers adapted for mobility and visually impaired students and wheelchair accessibility to all tutoring rooms; and
- a microcomputer laboratory facility for word processing and computer assisted instruction.

The Tutoring and Learning Center has been designated as one of 166 exemplary programs nationwide by the National Center for Developmental Education. More than 14,400 students used its services during the 1992-93 academic year, and more than 70% of these students represented ethnic minority groups (mainly Hispanics).

For additional information about UTEP's many programs, the following individuals may be contacted:

Ms Debbie Agthe
Director, Office of International Programs
211 Union West
The University of Texas at El Paso
El Paso, Texas 79968-0619
Phone: 915-747-5664
Fax: 915-747-5794

Dr Jack Bristol
Dean, College of Science—Bell Hall
The University of Texas at El Paso
El Paso, Texas 79968-0619
Phone: 915-747-5536
Fax: 915-747-6807

Dr Rigoberto Delgado
Coordinator, Mexican Student Services
Office of International Programs
211 Union West
The University of Texas at El Paso
El Paso, Texas 79968-0619
Phone: 915-747-5664
Fax: 915-747- 5797

Ms Gladys Shaw
Director, Tutoring and Learning Center
The University of Texas at El Paso
Library, 3rd Floor
El Paso, Texas 79968-0619
Phone: 915-747-5366
Fax: 915-747-5486

Epilogue

The recent wave of immigration has dramatically increased the number of language minority students enrolling in schools and colleges across the United States. As already described in Chapter 1, there are many reasons why the scientific community should be particularly interested in this population of students. Nonetheless, students of limited English proficiency—particularly undergraduates—are rarely mentioned in the literature about science education or science education reform. This book helps to fill that gap, providing the reader with information about:

- how college students learn English as a Second Language and the difficulties inherent in this process;
- the linguistic and cultural barriers encountered by non-native speakers when enrolled in mainstream content-area courses taught in English;
- what science faculty members can do in traditional lecture/laboratory courses to facilitate science learning by students who are still mastering the language of instruction i.e. English;
- the kinds of programs that can and are being used on various college and university campuses to provide academic support to limited English proficient students who are enrolled in traditional science courses;
- the theory behind and the actual practice of linguistically modified ways of teaching science, such as using the students' native language or content-based ESL instruction, and
- where to obtain additional information about science instruction and limited English proficient students.

Every effort has been made to stimulate dialogue by supplying names, addresses, and phone numbers (at the end of the case studies and 'Boxes') of colleagues who are already involved in activities in this area. There are abundant references to relevant articles and books, and the addresses of various organizations and resource centers that can provide assistance are listed in the Appendix (page 180).

Today's students are unquestionably more culturally and linguistically diverse than ever before. While some instructors consider this an asset, to others it is a liability. It might be 'easier' for the teacher if students were equally proficient in one language, if they all had the same learning styles, and if they shared a similar cultural background. However, just as we cannot select our parents (who determine our ethnicity and many of our physical characteristics), we also cannot choose our native language and culture. They are determined by where our parents live and where we grow up. Students are not to be blamed for their 'differences', and 'difference' does not mean inferiority.

Unfortunately, in the corridors of academe, faculty members too often can be overheard complaining about today's students: their deficiencies in many skills, and their historical, geographic, linguistic, and scientific ignorance (Bennett & Dreyer, 1994). Colleges are admitting all sorts of students: 'under-prepared', minority, students with disabilities, and students who are still in the process of learning English. Thus confronted, some instructors dig in their heels and refuse to consider changing how or what they teach for fear of 'lowering their standards.'

Today's students are different in many ways from those who attended college here in the United States twenty or thirty years ago. Since the 1960s, the number of college students has been growing steadily, from more than 3 million to almost 12 million. However, only 43% of today's undergraduates are 'traditional' college students, under the age of 25 and attending a four-year college on a full-time basis. Women now represent 55% of all matriculants, and more than one student in six is non-white. The majority of today's undergraduates are older than 25 years of age, attend school on a part-time basis, and/or are enrolled at a two-year college. With families to care for and part-time or full-time jobs, students may need eight or more years to complete their degree requirements (The Changing Faces of the American College Campus, 1993).

This 'snapshot' is, however, incomplete because it makes no reference to the cultural and linguistic diversity of today's students nor to the fact that for many undergraduates, English is a second language. Some of these students are just beginning to study English while others are at intermediate and advanced levels of proficiency.

Living in the United States, it is easy to forget that the majority of people in the world are bilingual (Padilla, 1990: 24). They speak more than one language, and students around the world receive their education in many languages other than English. In contrast, in the United States, schooling for the most part has promoted monolingualism. This is true even though English is not and never was the 'official' language of the land; this is true even though there is no evidence that the monolingual mind is superior to the bilingual mind. To the contrary, there are studies showing that bilingualism produces certain cognitive advantages (Baker, 1993).

Unquestionably a change is taking place in the United States, and it is not one that makes everyone comfortable or happy. As data gathered in the 1990 Census show (see Table 1.4), millions of Americans are non-native speakers of English. While many learn English as a second language, they often use their native language at home, in their local communities, and at social and religious events. In fact, to accomodate the needs and demands of these new Americans (and consumers), businesses are taking into consideration language diversity. For example, television programming is now available in languages such as Japanese, Spanish, Hindi, and Haitian Creole; at some banks and in car rental facilities, automated machines provide instructions in several languages; 'ethnic foods' are now readily available in supermarkets. Many aspects of American life—including business, politics, and education—are being affected by an increasingly multilingual population.

It is interesting to note that the influx of non-native English speaking students has occurred at the same time there has developed immense concern nation-wide about the quality of education that students are receiving and whether or not they will have the skills and knowledge that will be needed to function in a technologically based, global society. For example, the scientific community has become increasingly dismayed by the scientific illiteracy of the public, with the declining number of undergraduate science majors, and with the continuing under-representation of women and minorities in the sciences. These issues have spurred on efforts to reform and improve science education so that science (finally) can become accessible to all students.

This new position expressed by the scientific community as to who can learn and do science is a dramatic shift from the elitism that has prevailed for so long. It also highlights a major attitudinal difference between traditional science educators and those individuals working in the field of English as a second language. The literature on second language acquisition (SLA) may describe how some students learn a second language more quickly and easily than others; how motivation, affect, and personal characteristics of the learner as well as the methods of language instruction and the classroom atmosphere influence the rate of second language acquisition; how there are certain developmental stages through which all second language learners must pass; yet, each learner progresses according to his or her own internal timetable. What the SLA literature does not say nor even hint at is that only some small, uniquely qualified segment of any population is capable of becoming proficient in a second language nor that students who are struggling with a second language should stop trying. This is markedly different from traditional science education in which introductory courses have been used to weed out low achieving students, who in fact make up the majority of the students in the class. The notion of helping such students, nurturing their interest in science, encouraging them to continue studying the sciences, and improving the nature of science instruction has only recently begun to achieve some popularity.

Think of it this way: if novice ESL learners were cast aside for all the errors they made, none would remain in any ESL program. None would ever master the English language. Yet, this is essentially what we have always done in introductory science courses; there is a history of filtering out students—potential majors, students who are interested in science and capable of doing science—based on 'novice' errors and a mismatch between what faculty members offer and what students need in order to learn science. Then science educators worry about scientific illiteracy, a decrease in the number of students studying science, and the under-representation of minorities and women in the sciences.

One of the first lessons learned by all beginning science students is that observation is the basis of the scientific method. They are taught this by the same faculty members who use the methods of science to carry out research. Nevertheless, these same research scientists/educators do not necessarily apply their own observational skills nor the scientific method in the classroom to investigate who they are teaching, how successful are their instructional practices, and what is and is not working to recruit and retain students in the sciences. In most instances, the principles that guide scientific research are not applied to the practice of science teaching.

Few researchers would maintain the same protocol if experiment after experiment failed. They would reevaluate their hypotheses, reassess the literature, check for errors, develop new procedures, and redesign their experiments. Yet, when it comes to their teaching, some of the same individuals resist any form of change, any innovation, which might improve student interest and achievement in science.

It may seem a bit unusual to be comparing and contrasting attitudes that are inherent in two fields of study as different as science and second language acquisition. However, the two merge when we consider the educational needs of students of limited English proficiency who are studying science. There is no science without language, and effective science instruction depends on meaningful language.

The majority of the literature about teaching language minority students addresses students in kindergarten through grade twelve. However, the number of language minority students studying at the college-level—especially immigrants and refugees—is growing rapidly. While much of what has been learned from looking at LEP students in elementary and secondary schools can be applied to college students, there are some significant differences. First, science is not taught the same way in college as in grade school. Second, LEP college students are adult learners and bring to the classroom a wide range of previous educational experiences, skills, and knowledge. Third, language minority college students often have numerous responsibilities related to their families and jobs that may interfere with their studies.

Perhaps the most important point made in this book is that language minority college students are just as capable of learning and doing science as their traditional, native English speaking peers. However, innovative forms of instruction may be needed in order to overcome existing linguistic and cultural barriers.

If the scientific community is sincere in its desire to make science accessible to all students, then college science faculty, not just school teachers, must be willing to meet that challenge. This may mean collaborating with colleagues who are specialists in English as a Second Language, teaching science in the native language of the students, or modifying traditional classroom practices. As the case studies in Chapters 7 and 9 demonstrate, changes such as these are already being implemented on some college campuses across the United States.

To recruit and retain more students in the sciences means putting the needs of the students first. This book includes many recommendations which faculty, staff, and administrators can follow to improve the teaching of science to language minority college students. They range from what the individual instructor can do in his or her classroom to college-wide academic support programs. Given that we cannot bring back the past, and many of us would not want to, then the challenge is to work with today's students and to help them develop the skills and acquire the knowledge which they will need—and this country will need—as we enter into the twenty-first century.

Appendix

Center for Applied Linguistics
1118 22nd Street, N.W.
Washington, DC 20037
Phone: 202–429–9292

ERIC Clearinghouse on Languages and Linguistics (ERIC/CLL)
The George Washington University/Center for Applied Linguistics
1118 22nd Street, N.W.
Washington, DC 20037–0037
Phone: 202 429–9551
Fax: 202 429–9766

National Association for Bilingual Education (NABE)
1220 L Street, N.W., Suite 605
Washington, DC 20005
Phone: (202) 898–1829
Fax: (202) 789–2866

National Clearinghouse for Bilingual Education (NCBE)
The George Washington University/Center for Applied Linguistics
1118 22nd Street, N.W.
Washington, DC 20037–0037
Phone: (202) 467–0867 or 1–800–321–NCBE
Fax: (202) 429–9766

Teachers of English to Speakers of Other Languages (TESOL)
1600 Cameron Street, Suite 300
Alexandria, VA 22314–2751
Phone: (703) 836–0774
Fax: (703) 836–7864

References

ADAMS, M. 1992, Cultural inclusion in the American college classroom. In L.L.B. Border and N. Van Note Chism (eds) *Teaching for Diversity* (pp. 5-17). San Francisco: Jossey-Bass.

ADAMS, T.W. 1989, *Inside Textbooks: What Students Need to Know*. Reading, MA: Addison-Wesley.

ADAMSON, H.D. 1993, *Academic Competence*. White Plains, NY: Longman.

ALLIS, S. 1991, Kicking the nerd syndrome. *Time Magazine*, 25 March, 64 and 66.

AMBRON, J. 1987, Writing to improve learning in biology. *Journal of College Science Teaching* 16, 263-6.

AMERICAN ASSOCIATION FOR THE ADVANCEMENT OF SCIENCE, 1989, *Science for All Americans*. A Project 2061 Report on Literacy Goals in Science, Mathematics, and Technology. Washington, DC: American Association for the Advancement of Science.

—1990, *The Liberal Art of Science*. The Report of the Project on Liberal Education and the Sciences. Washington, DC: American Association for the Advancement of Science.

ANDERSEN, J.F. and POWELL, R. 1991, Intercultural communication and the classroom. In L.S. Samovar and R.E. Porter (eds) *Intercultural Communication* (pp. 208-14). Belmont, CA: Wadsworth.

ANDERSON, J.A. 1988, Cognitive styles and multicultural populations. *Journal of Teacher Education* 39, 2-9.

APPLE, M.W. 1992, The text and cultural politics. *Educational Researcher* 21, 4-11 and 19.

ATWATER, M.M. 1994, Research on cultural diversity in the classroom. In D.L. Gabel (ed.) *Handbook of Research on Science Teaching and Learning* (A Project of the National Science Teachers Association) (pp. 558-76). New York: Macmillan.

AXTELL, R.E. (ed) 1993, *Do's and Taboos Around The World*. White Plains, NY: The Benjamin Company.

BAKER, C. 1993, *Foundations of Bilingual Education and Bilingualism*. Clevedon, UK: Multilingual Matters.

BALLARD, B. and CLANCHY, J. 1991, Assessment by misconception: cultural influences and intellectual traditions. In L. Hamp-Lyons (ed.) *Assessing Second Language Writing in Academic Contexts* (pp. 19-35). Norwood, NJ: Ablex.

BANKS, J.A. 1993, The Canon debate, knowledge construction, and multicultural education. *Educational Researcher* 22, 4-14.

BENESCH, S. (ed.) 1988, *Ending Remediation: Linking ESL and Content in Higher Education*. Washington, DC: Teachers of English to Speakers of Other Languages.

BENNETT, C.I. 1990, *Comprehensive Multicultural Education*. Needham Heights, MA: Allyn and Bacon.

BENNETT, J.B. and DREYER, E.A. 1994, On complaining about students. *AAHE (American Assocation for Higher Education) Bulletin* 46, 7-8.

BILINGUAL EDUCATION OFFICE 1990, *Bilingual Education Handbook: Designing Instruction for LEP Students*. Sacramento, CA: California Department of Education.

BIRDWHISTELL, R.L. 1974, The language of the body: the natural environment of words. In A. Silverstein (ed.) *Human Communication: Theoretical Explorations* (pp. 203-220). Hillsdale, NJ: Lawrence Erlbaum.

BLOOM, B.S. (ed.) 1956, *Taxonomy of Educational Objectives. Handbook I: Cognitive Domain*. New York: McKay.

BORDER, L.L.B. and VAN NOTE CHISM, N. (eds) 1992, *Teaching for Diversity*. San Francisco, CA: Jossey-Bass.

BOWEN, E. 1988, Wanted: fresh, homegrown talent. *Time Magazine*, 11 January, 65.

BRADY, J.E. and HOLUM, J.R. 1993, *Chemistry*. New York: John Wiley.

BRINTON, D.M., SNOW, M.A. and WESCHE, M.B. 1989, *Content-Based Second Language Instruction*. New York: Newbury House.

BRITTON, B.K., GULGOZ, S., VAN DUSEN, L., GLYNN, S.M. and SHARP, L. 1991, Accuracy of learnability judgments for instructional texts. *Journal of Educational Psychology* 83, 43-7.

BRITTON, B.K., WOODWARD, A. and BINKLEY, M. (eds) 1993, *Learning from Textbooks: Theory and Practice*. Hillsdale, NJ: Lawrence Erlbaum.

BROWN, A.L., ARMBRUSTER, B.B., and BAKER, L. 1986, The role of metacognition in reading and studying. In J. Orasanu (ed.) *Reading Comprehension: From Research to Practice* (pp. 49-75). Hillsdale, NJ: Lawrence Earlbaum.

BUDNER, S. 1962, Intolerance of ambiguity as a personality variable. *Journal of Personality* 30, 29-50.

CALIFORNIA STATE DEPARTMENT OF EDUCATION 1986, *Handbook for Teaching Pilipino-Speaking Students*. Sacramento, CA: California State Department of Education.

— 1987, *Handbook for Teaching Japanese-Speaking Students*. Sacramento, CA: California State Department of Education.

— 1989, *A Handbook for Teaching Portuguese-Speaking Students*. Sacramento, CA: California State Department of Education.

— 1989, *A Handbook for Teaching Cantonese-Speaking Students*. Sacramento, CA: California State Department of Education.

— 1991, *The American Indian: Yesterday, Today, & Tomorrow*. Sacramento, CA: California Department of Education.

— 1992, *Handbook for Teaching Korean-American Students*. Sacramento, CA: California Department of Education.

CANTONI-HARVEY, G. 1987, *Content-Area Language Instruction*. Reading, MA: Addison-Wesley.

CARNEGIE COMMISSION ON SCIENCE, TECHNOLOGY, AND GOVERNMENT, 1991, *In the National Interest: The Federal Government in the Reform of K-12 Math and Science Education*. New York: Carnegie Commission on Science, Technology, and Government.

CARRANZA, M.A. 1982, Attitudinal research on Hispanic language varieties. In E.B. Ryan and H. Giles (eds) *Attitudes towards Language Variation* (pp. 63-83). London: Edward Arnold.

CASE, C. and LAU, G. 1991, Teaching strategies for the multicultural/multilingual classroom. *Strategies for Success in Anatomy & Physiology and Life Science*. Issue 6: 1–3. (Redwood City, CA: The Benjamin/Cummings Publishing Company, Inc.).

CASTAÑEDA, A. and GRAY, T. 1974, Bicognitive processes in multicultural education. *Educational Leadership* 32, 203-7.

CASTELLANOS, D. 1985, *The Best of Two Worlds*. Trenton, NJ: New Jersey State Department of Education.

CHALL, J.S. and CONARD, S.S. 1991, *Should Textbooks Challenge Students?* New York: Teachers College Press, Columbia University.

CHAMPAGNE, A.B. 1986, Children's ethno-science: an instructional perspective. In J.J. Gallagher and G. Dawson (eds) *Science Education & Cultural Environments in the Americas* (pp. 14-19). Arlington, VA: National Science Teachers Association

CHAPELLE, C. and ROBERTS, C. 1986, Ambiguity tolerance and field independence as predictors of proficiency in English as a second language. *Language Learning* 36, 27-45.

CHENG, L. 1993, Faculty challenges in the education of foreign-born students. In L.W. Clark (ed.) *Faculty and Student Challenges in Facing Cultural and Linguistic Diversity.* Springfield, IL: Charles C Thomas.

CLARKE, M.A. 1993 (May), Mainstreaming ESL students: disturbing changes. Paper presented at the City University of New York Faculty Development Colloquium, Baruch College, New York.

— 1994, Mainstreaming ESL students: disturbing changes. *College ESL* 4, 1-19.

CLAXTON, C.S. and MURRELL, P.H. 1987, *Learning Styles: Implications for Improving Educational Practices.* ASHE-ERIC Higher Education Report No. 4. Washington, DC: Association for the Study of Higher Education.

COCHRAN, E.P. (ed.) 1992, *Into the Academic Mainstream: Guidelines for Teaching Language Minority Students.* New York: The Instructional Resource Center of the City University of New York.

COLLIER, V.P. 1987, Age and rate of acquisition of second language for academic purposes. *TESOL Quarterly* 21, 617-41.

COLLIER, V.P. and THOMAS, W.P. 1989, How quickly can immigrants become proficient in school English? *The Journal of Educational Issues of Language Minority Students* 5, 26-38.

CONNOLLY, P. and VILARDI, T. (eds) 1989, *Writing to Learn Mathematics and Science.* New York: Teachers College Press, Columbia University.

CONNOR, U. and KAPLAN, R.B. 1987, *Writing Across Languages: Analysis of L2 Text.* Reading, MA: Addison-Wesley.

CORNETT, C.E. 1983, *What You Should Know About Teaching and Learning Styles.* Bloomington, IN: Phi Delta Kappa Educational Foundation.

CRANDALL, J. (ed.) 1987, *ESL Through Content-Area Instruction.* Englewood Cliffs, NJ: Prentice Hall.

CRAWFORD, J. 1989, *Bilingual Education: History Politics Theory and Practice.* Trenton, NJ: Crane.

— (ed.) 1992, *Language Loyalties.* Chicago, IL: University of Chicago Press.

CUMMINS, J. 1980, The cross-lingual dimensions of language proficiency: implications for bilingual education and the optimal age issue. *TESOL Quarterly* 14, 175-87.

— 1981, Age on arrival and immigrant second language learning in Canada: a reassessment. *Applied Linguistics* 11, 132-49.

CUMMINS, J. and SWAIN, M. 1986, *Bilingualism in Education.* New York: Longman.

CUTNELL, J.D. and JOHNSON, K.W. 1992, *Physics.* New York: John Wiley.

DAMEN, L. 1987, *Culture Learning: The Fifth Dimension in the Language Classroom.* Reading, MA: Addison-Wesley.

DE PALMA, A. 1990, Graduate schools fill with foreigners. *The New York Times* 29 November, 1 and A24.

DORNIC, S. 1980, Information processing and language dominance. *International Review of Applied Psychology* 29, 119-140.

DUBIN, F., ESKEY, D.E., and GRABE, W. (eds) 1986, *Teaching Second Language Reading for Academic Purposes.* Reading, MA: Addison-Wesley.

DULAY, H. and BURT, M. 1977, Remarks on creativity in language acquisition. In M. Burt, H. Dulay, and M. Finocchiaro (eds) *Viewpoints on English as a Second Language* (pp. 95-126). New York: Regents.

DULAY, H., BURT, M. and KRASHEN, S. 1982, *Language Two.* New York: Oxford University Press.

DUNN, D.J. 1988, People and the environment. In J.E. Penick, and J.A. Dunkhase (eds) *Innovations in College Science Teaching* (pp. 87-95). Washington, DC: Society for College Science Teachers.

DURAN, R., REVLIN, R. and M. SMITH 1992 (December), Draft of a paper entitled Verbal Comprehension and Reasoning Skills of Latino High School Students.

EBBING, D.D. 1993, *General Chemistry*. Boston, MA: Houghton Mifflin.

EDMONDSON, K.M. and NOVAK, J.D. 1993, The interplay of scientific epistemo-logical views, learning strategies, and attitudes of college students. *Journal of Research in Science Teaching* 30, 547-59.

EDMONSTON, B. and PASSEL, J.S. 1992, *The Future Immigrant Population of the United States*. Washington, DC: The Urban Institute.

EDWARDS, J.R. 1982, Language attitudes and their implications among English speakers. In E.B. Ryan and H. Giles (eds) *Attitudes towards Language Variation* (pp. 20-33). London: Edward Arnold.

ELLIS, R. 1986, *Understanding Second Language Acquisition*. Oxford: Oxford University Press.

EXTRA, G. and VERHOEVEN, L. 1993, *Immigrant Languages in Europe*. Clevedon, UK: Multilingual Matters.

FICHTNER, D., PEITZMAN, F. and SASSER, L. 1991, What's fair? Assessing subject matter knowledge of LEP students in sheltered classrooms. In F. Peitzman and G. Gadda (eds) *With Different Eyes* (pp. 143-159). Los Angeles, CA: California Academic Partnership Program.

FISHER, K.M., LIPSON, J.I., HILDEBRAND, A.C., MIGUEL, L., SCHOENBERG, N. and PORTER, N. 1986, Student misconceptions and teacher assumptions in college biology. *Journal of College Science Teaching* 15, 276-280.

FLORES, J. LE BLANC 1994 (September), Facilitating postsecondary outcomes for Mexican Americans. *ERIC Digest* (EDO-RC-94-4). Charleston, WV: Clearinghouse on Rural Education and Small Schools.

FORD, C.E. 1984, The influence of speech variety on teachers' evaluation of students with comparable academic ability. *TESOL Quarterly* 18, 25-40.

FREEMAN, D. and FREEMAN, Y. 1988 (October), Sheltered English Instruction. *ERIC Digest*. Washington, DC: Center for Applied Linguistics.

FRENKEL-BRUNSWIK, E. 1949, Intolerance of ambiguity as an emotional and percep-tual personality variable. *Journal of Personality* 18, 108-43.

FRY, E. 1977, Fry's readability graph: clarifications, validity, and extension to Level 17. *Journal of Reading* 21, 242-52.

GADDA, G. 1991, Writing and language socialization across cultures: some implica-tons for the classroom. In F. Peitzman, and G. Gadda (eds) *With Different Eyes* (pp. 55-74). Los Angeles, CA: California Academic Partnership Program.

GALLAGHER, J.J. and DAWSON, G. (eds) 1986, *Science Education & Cultural Environments in the Americas*. Arlington, VA: National Science Teachers Association.

GALLOIS, C. and V.J. CALLAN 1981, Personality impressions elicted by accented English speech. *Journal of Cross-Cultural Psychology* 12, 347-59.

GARNER, B. 1989, Southeast Asian culture and classroom culture. *College Teaching* 37, 127-130.

GILES, H. 1977, *Language, Ethnicity and Intergroup Relations*. New York: Academic Press.

— 1979, Ethnicity markers in speech. In K.R. Scherer and H. Giles (eds) *Social Markers in Speech* (pp. 251-89). Cambridge: Cambridge University Press.

GONZALES, P.C. 1981, Teaching science to ESL students. *The Science Teacher* 48, 19-21.

GOOD, T.L. 1987, Two decades of research on teacher expectations: findings and future directions. *Journal of Teacher Education* 38, 32-47.

GORDON, E.W., MILLER, F.Y. and ROLLOCK, D. 1990, Coping with communicentric bias in knowledge production in the social sciences. *Educational Researcher* 19, 14-19.

GREEN, K.C. 1989, A profile of undergraduates in the sciences. *American Scientist* 77, 475-80.

GREEN, M.F. (ed.) 1989, *Minorities on Campus: A Handbook for Enhancing Diversity.* Washington, DC: American Council on Education.

HALL, E.T. 1959, *The Silent Language.* Garden City, NY: Anchor Press/Doubleday.

— 1976, *Beyond Culture.* Garden City, NY: Anchor Press/Doubleday.

HARLEY, B. 1986, *Age in Second Language Acquisition.* San Diego: College-Hill Press.

HAUKOOS, G.D. and SATTERFIELD, R. 1986, Learning styles of minority students (Native Americans) and their application in developing a culturally sensitive science classroom. *Community/Junior College Quarterly* 10, 193-201.

HAYES, D.P. 1992, The growing inaccessibility of science. *Nature* 356, 739-40.

HEATH, S.B. 1992, Why no official tongue? In J. Crawford (ed.) *Language Loyalties*, (pp. 20-31). Chicago, IL: University of Chicago Press.

HELM, H. and J.D. NOVAK (eds) 1983, *Proceedings of the International Seminar on Misconceptions in Science and Mathematics.* Ithaca, NY: Cornell University.

HIEMENZ, P.C. and HUDSPETH, M.C. 1993, Academic excellence workshops for underrepresented students at Cal Poly, Pomona. *Journal of College Science Teaching* 23, 38-42.

HIGHER EDUCATION RESEARCH INSTITUTE, 1992, *Undergraduate Science Education: The Impact of Different College Environments on the Educational Pipeline in the Sciences.* Los Angeles, CA: Higher Education Research Institute, Graduate School of Education, University of California, Los Angeles.

HILL, N. 1991, AISES. *Change* 23, 24-6.

HILLIARD, A.G. 1989, Teachers and cultural styles in a pluralistic society. *NEA Today* January, 65-9.

HILTON, T.L. and LEE, V.E. 1988, Student interest and persistence in science. *Journal of Higher Education* 59, 510-26.

HIRSCH, L. 1988, Language across the curriculum: a model for ESL students in content courses. In S. Benesch (ed.) *Ending Remediation: Linking ESL and Content in Higher Education* (pp. 67-89). Washington, DC: Teachers of English to Speakers of Other Languages.

— 1991, Are principles of writing across the curriculum applicable to ESL students in content courses? Research Findings. ERIC Document Reproduction Service No. ED 319264.

HIRSCH, L., NADAL J., and SHOHET, L. 1991, Adapting language across the curriculum programs to meet the needs of diverse linguistic populations. In L. Stanley and J. Ambron (eds) *Writing Across the Curriculum in Community Colleges* (pp. 71-7). San Francisco: Jossey-Bass.

HODGKINSON, H.L. 1990, *The Demographics of American Indians.* Washington, DC: Center for Demographic Policy.

HOFSTEDE, G. 1986, Cultural differences in teaching and learning. *International Journal of Intercultural Relations* 10, 301-320.

HOLDEN, C. 1993, Foreign nationals change the face of US science. *Science* 261, 1769–71.

HOLLAND, R.P. 1989, Learner characteristics and learner performance: implications for instructional placement decisions. In B.J. Robinson Shade (ed.) *Culture, Style and the Educative Process* (pp. 167–183). Springfield, IL: Charles C Thomas.

HOOTS, R.A. 1992, An outsider's insights on neglected issues in science education. *Journal of College Science Teaching* 21, 300-4.

IANCU, M. 1993, Adapting the Adjunct Model: a case study. *TESOL Journal* 2, 20-4.

IGNASH, J.M. 1992a (November), Tracking the liberal arts over sixteen years. Paper presented at the Conference of the California Association for Institutional Research, Ontario, CA.

— 1992b (December). ESL population and program patterns in community colleges. *ERIC Digest* (EDO-JC-92-05). Los Angeles, CA: ERIC Clearinghouse for Junior

Colleges.

— 1992/1993, Study shows ESL is fastest growing area of study in US community colleges. *TESOL Matters* 2, 17.

Innovative Higher Education (whole issue), 1993, 17, 147-224.

JANES, J. and HAUER, D. 1988, *Now What?* Acton, MA: Copley Publishing Group.

JOHNS, A. 1991a, Faculty assessment of ESL student literacy skills: implications for writing assessment. In L. Hamp-Lyons (ed.) *Assessing Second Language Writing in Academic Contexts* (pp. 167-79). Norwood, NJ: Ablex.

— 1991b, Interpreting an English competency exam. *Written Communication* 8, 379-401.

JOHNSON, D.W., JOHNSON, R.T. and SMITH, K.A. 1991, *Cooperative Learning: Increasing College Faculty Instructional Productivity.* ASHE-ERIC Higher Education Report No. 4. Washington, DC: The George Washington University, School of Education and Human Development.

Journal of College Science Teaching, 1987, Writing in the Sciences. 16, 245–66.

KAGAN, J. 1966, Reflection-impulsivity: the generality and dynamics of conceptual tempo. *Journal of Abnormal Psychology* 71, 17-24.

KAPLAN, R.B. 1966, Cultural thought patterns in inter-cultural education. *Language Learning* 16, 1-20.

KEEFE, J.W. 1987, *Learning Style Theory and Practice.* Reston, VA: National Association of Secondary School Principals.

KELLY, G.J., CARLSEN, W.S. and CUNNINGHAM, C.M. 1993, Science education in sociocultural context: perspectives from the sociology of science. *Science Education* 77, 207-20.

KESSLER, C. and QUINN, M.E. 1987, ESL and science learning. In J. Crandall (ed.) *ESL Through Content-Area Instruction* (pp. 55-87). Englewood Cliffs, NJ: Prentice Hall.

KIRBY, J.R. (ed.) 1984, *Cognitive Strategies and Educational Performance.* Orlando, FL: Academic Press.

KOLB, D.A. 1981, Learning styles and disciplinary differences. In A.W. Chickering, and Associates (eds) *The Modern American College* (pp. 232-55). San Francisco, CA: Jossey-Bass.

KOTKIN, J. 1993, Enrolling foreign students will strengthen America's place in the global economy. *The Chronicle of Higher Education,* 24 February, B1-2.

KRASHEN, S.D. 1976, Formal and informal linguistic environments in language acquisition and language learning. *TESOL Quarterly* 10, 157-68.

— 1981, *Second Language Acquisition and Second Language Learning.* Oxford, UK: Pergamon Institute of English.

— 1982, *Principles and Practice in Second Language Acquisition.* Oxford, UK: Pergamon Press.

— 1991, Sheltered subject matter teaching. *Cross Currents* 18, 183-9.

KRASHEN, S.D., LONG, M.A. and SCARCELLA, R.C. 1979, Age, rate and eventual attainment in second language acquisition. *TESOL Quarterly* 13, 573-82.

LAMBERT, L.M. and TICE, S.L. (eds) 1993, *Preparing Graduate Students to Teach.* Washington, DC: American Association for Higher Education.

LARSEN-FREEMAN, D. 1991, Second language acquisition research: staking out the territory. *TESOL Quarterly* 25, 315-350.

LARSEN-FREEMAN, D. and LONG, M.H. 1991, *An Introduction to Second Language Acquisition Research.* New York: Longman.

LEAP, W.L. 1992, American Indian English. In J. Reyhner (ed.) *Teaching American Indian Students* (pp. 143-53). Norman, OK: University of Oklahoma Press.

—1993, *American Indian English.* Salt Lake City, UT: University of Utah Press.

LEKI, I. 1992, *Understanding ESL Writers.* Portsmith, NH: Boynton/Cook.

LEMKE, J.L. 1990, *Talking Science.* Norwood, NJ: Ablex.

LEVY, D. 1992, Bridging tribal, technological worlds. *Science* 258, 1231.

LICHTENBERG, J., 1994, Publishers, professors, and the importance of textbooks. *The Chronicle of Higher Education*, 18 May, A48.

LIEBMAN, J.D. 1992, Toward a new contrastive rhetoric: differences between Arabic and Japanese rhetorical instruction. *Journal of Second Language Writing* 1, 141-61.

LIPSON, A. 1992, The confused student in introductory science. *College Teaching* 40, 91-5.

LIPSON, A. and TOBIAS, S. 1991, Why do (some of our best) college students leave science? *Journal of College Science Teaching* 21, 92-5.

LOCKE, D. 1992, *Science as Writing*. New Haven, CT: Yale University Press.

LOCUST, C. 1988, Wounding the spirit: discrimination and traditional American Indian belief systems. *Harvard Educational Review* 58, 315-30.

LUMSDEN, A.S. 1992/1993, The rewards of institutional commitment: Florida State University's strategy for large-course science instruction. *Journal of College Science Teaching* 22, 192-4.

MACNAMARA, J. 1973, Attitudes and learning a second language. In R.W. Shuy and R.W. Fasold (eds) *Language Attitudes: Current Trends and Prospects* (pp. 36-40). Washington, DC: Georgetown University Press.

MADDOCK, M. 1986, Developing better science education programs: culture, alienation, and attitudes. In J.J. Gallagher and G. Dawson (eds) *Science Education & Cultural Environments in the Americas* (pp. 40-7). Arlington, VA: National Science Teachers Association.

MADER, S.S. 1990, *Biology*. Dubuque, IA: Wm. C. Brown.

MADIGAN, C. 1987a, Writing as a means, not an end. *Journal of College Science Teaching* 16, 245-9.

— 1987b, Writing across the curriculum resources in science and mathematics. *Journal of College Science Teaching* 16, 250-3.

MAGNER, D.K. 1993a, Colleges faulted for not considering differences in Asian-American groups. *The Chronicle of Higher Education*, 10 February, A32 and A34.

— 1993b, College's Asian enrollment defies stereotype. *The Chronicle of Higher Education*, 10 February, A34.

MARTIN, D.C., ARENDALE, D.R. and Associates 1992, *Supplemental Instruction: Improving First-Year Student Success in High-Risk Courses*. Columbia, SC: National Resource Center for The Freshman Year Experience, University of South Carolina.

MARTIN, K.H. 1989, Writing 'microthemes' to learn human biology. In P. Connolly and T. Vilardi (eds) *Writing to Learn Mathematics and Science* (pp. 113-21). New York: Teachers College Press, Columbia University.

MASON, C.L. and BARBA, R.H. 1992, Equal opportunity science. *The Science Teacher* 59, 22-6.

MASSEY, W.E. 1992, A success story amid decades of disappointment. *Science* 258, 1177-9.

MESSNER S.B. 1976, Reflection-impulsivity: a review. *Psychological Bulletin* 83, 1026-52.

MEYER, D.K. 1993, Recognizing and changing students' misconceptions. *College Teaching* 41, 104-8.

MIDDLECAMP, C.H. 1989 (November), But what about science courses...? Paper presented at the University of Wisconsin System Conference on The Challenge of Diversity: Curriculum Design for the 21st Century, Madison, WI.

— 1994 (January), Culturally-inclusive chemistry. Paper presented at the Winter Gordon Research Conference on Innovations in College Chemistry Teaching, Oxnard, CA.

— 1995, Culturally inclusive chemistry. In S.V. Rosser (ed.) *Teaching the Majority*. New York: Teachers College Press, Columbia University.

MIDDLECAMP, C.H. and MOORE, J.W. 1994, Race and ethnicity in the teaching of chemistry: a new graduate seminar. *Journal of Chemical Education* 71, 288–90.

MILLER, G.A. 1988, The challenge of universal literacy. *Science* 241, 1293-9.

MOHAN, B.A. 1986, *Language and Content*. Reading, MA: Addison-Wesley.

MORE, A.J. 1987, Native Indian learning styles: a review for researchers and teachers. *Journal of American Indian Education* 27, 17-29.

MULLIN, W.J. 1989, Qualitative thinking and writing in the hard sciences. In P. Connolly and T. Vilardi (eds) *Writing to Learn Mathematics and Science* (pp. 198-208). New York: Teachers College Press, Columbia University.

NATIONAL ASSOCIATION OF SECONDARY SCHOOL PRINCIPALS 1979, *Student Learning Styles*. Reston: VA: National Association of Secondary School Principals.

NATIONAL SCIENCE FOUNDATION, 1989, *Changing America: The New Face of Science and Engineering*. The Final Report on Women, Minorities, and the Handicapped in Science and Technology. Washington, DC: National Science Foundation.

— 1992, *Science and Engineering Degrees, by Race/Ethnicity of Recipients: 1977-90* (NSF 92-327, Detailed Statistical Tables). Washington, DC: National Science Foundation.

NYQUIST, J.D., ABBOTT, R.D., WULFF, D.H. and SPRAGUE, J. (eds) 1991, *Preparing the Professoriate of Tomorrow to Teach*. Dubuque, IA: Kendall/Hunt Publishing Company.

O'BRIEN, E.M. 1992, American Indians in Higher Education. *Research Briefs* 3, 1-16 (Washington, DC: American Council on Education).

OFFICE OF TECHNOLOGY ASSESSMENT, 1988, *Educating Scientists and Engineers: Grade School to Grad School*. Washington, DC: Office of Technology Assessment.

OSTLER, S.E. 1980, A survey of academic needs for advanced ESL. *TESOL Quarterly* 14, 489-502.

OVANDO, C.J. 1992, Science. In J. Reyhner (ed.) *Teaching American Indian Students* (pp. 223-40). Norman, OK: University of Oklahoma Press.

OXFORD, R. 1989, The role of styles and strategies in second language learning. *ERIC DIGEST*, December. Washington, DC: Eric Clearinghouse on Languages and Linguistics/Center for Applied Linguistics.

PADILLA, A.M. 1990, Bilingual education: issues and perspectives. In A.M. Padilla, H.H. Fairchild, and C.M. Valadez (eds) *Bilingual Education: Issues and Strategies* (pp. 15-26). Newbury Park, CA: Sage.

PEITZMAN, F. and GADDA, G. (eds) 1991, *With Different Eyes*. Los Angeles, CA: California Academic Partnership Program.

PENFIELD, J. 1987, ESL: the regular classroom teacher's perspective. *TESOL Quarterly* 21, 21-39.

PERSELL, R. 1993, Promoting active learning in a large introductory biology course through writing. *Annals of the New York Academy of Science* 701, 130-4.

PIPES, M.A., WESTBY, C.E. and INGLEBRET E. 1993, Profile of Native American students. In L.W. Clark (ed.) *Faculty and Student Challenges in Facing Cultural and Linguistic Diversity* (pp. 137-172). Springfield, IL: Charles C Thomas.

POPULATION REFERENCE BUREAU, 1992, *The Challenge of Change: What the 1990 Census Tells Us About Children*. A report prepared by the Population Reference Bureau for the Center for the Study of Social Policy. Washington, DC: Center for the Study of Social Policy.

PROJECT KALEIDOSCOPE, 1991, *What Works: Building Natural Science Communities— A Plan for Strengthening Undergraduate Science and Mathematics, Vol. 1.* Washington, DC: Project Kaleidoscope.

RAMIREZ, M. 1973, Cognitive styles and cultural democracy in education. *Social Science Quarterly* 53, 895-904.

REID, J.M. 1987, The learning style preferences of ESL students. *TESOL Quarterly* 21, 87-111.

— 1992, Helping students write for an academic audience. In P.A. Richard-Amato and

M.A. Snow (eds) *The Multicultural Classroom* (pp. 210-21). White Plains, NY: Longman.

REILLY, T. 1988, ESL through content-area instruction. *ERIC Digest*, May. Washington, DC: Center for Applied Linguistics.

RENDÓN, L.I. and TRIANA, E.M. 1989, *Making Mathematics and Science Work for Hispanics*. Washington, DC: American Association for the Advancement of Science.

REYES, M. DE LA LUZ 1992, Challenging venerable assumptions: literacy instruction for linguistically different students. *Harvard Educational Review* 62, 427-46.

REYHNER, J. (ed.) 1992, *Teaching American Indian Students*. Norman, OK: University of Oklahoma Press.

RICHARD-AMATO, P.A. and SNOW, M.A. 1992, *The Multicultural Classroom*. White Plains, NY: Longman.

ROBINSON SHADE, B.J. (ed.) 1989, *Culture, Style and the Educative Process*. Springfield, IL: Charles C Thomas.

ROSENTHAL, J.W. 1992/1993. The limited English proficient student in the college science classroom. *Journal of College Science Teaching* 22, 182-6.

— 1993a, Theory and practice: Science for undergraduates of limited English proficiency. *Journal of Science Education and Technology* 2, 435-43.

— 1993b, Science students who are still learning English. *The Chronicle of Higher Education*, 3 November, B1-B2.

— 1994, Some personal and professional comments about science education reform and the limited English proficient undergraduate. *College ESL* 4, 33-40.

ROSSER, S.V. 1990, *Female-Friendly Science*. Elmsford, NY: Pergamon Press.

ROWE, M.B. 1974a, Wait time and rewards as instructional variables, their influence on language, logic, and fate control: Part 1—Wait time. *Journal of Research in Science Teaching* 11, 81-94.

— 1974b, Relation of wait time and rewards to the development of language, logic, and fate control: Part II— Rewards. *Journal of Research in Science Teaching* 11, 291-308.

RUSSIKOFF, K. 1994, (March), Hidden expectations: faculty perceptions of SLA and writing competence. Paper presented at the Twenty-eighth annual convention of Teachers of English to Speakers of Other Languages, Baltimore, MD.

RYAN, E.B. and H. GILES (eds) 1982, *Attitudes towards Language Variation*. London: Edward Arnold.

SAMOVAR, L.A., PORTER, R.E. and JAIN, N.C. 1981, *Understanding Intercultural Communication*. Belmont, CA: Wadsworth.

SANTOS, T. 1988, Professors' reactions to the academic writing of nonnative-speaking students. *TESOL Quarterly* 22, 69-90.

SARACHO, O.N. 1989, Cultural differences in the cognitive style of Mexican-American students. In B.J. Robinson Shade (ed.) *Culture, Style and the Educative Process* (pp. 129-36). Springfield, IL: Charles C Thomas.

SASSER, L. and WINNINGHAM, B. 1991, Sheltered instruction across the disciplines: successful teachers at work. In F. Peitzman and G. Gadda (eds) *With Different Eyes* (pp. 27-54). Los Angeles, CA: California Academic Partnership Program.

SAVILLE-TROIKE, M. 1978, *A Guide to Culture in the Classroom*. Rosslyn, VA: National Clearinghouse for Bilingual Education.

— 1979, Culture, language, and education. In H.T. Trueba and C. Barnett-Mizhari (eds) *Bilingual Multicultural Education and the Professional* (pp. 139-8). Rowley, MA: Newbury House.

SCARCELLA, R.C. 1984, How writers orient their readers in expository essays: a comparative study of native and non-native English writers. *TESOL Quarterly* 18, 671-88.

— 1990, *Teaching Language Minority Students in the Multicultural Classroom*. Englewood Cliffs, NJ: Prentice Hall Regents.

SCHERER, K.R. and GILES, H. (eds) 1979, *Social Markers in Speech*. Cambridge: Cambridge University Press.

SCHROEDER, C.C. 1993, New students—new learning styles. *Change* 25, 21-6.

SECADA, W.G. 1991, Teaching mathematics and science to limited English proficient students. *NABE News* 14, 15-16.

SERWAY, R.A. and FAUGHN, J.S. 1992, *College Physics*. Orlando, FL: Saunders College Publishing.

SEYMOUR, E. 1992a, 'The Problem Iceberg' in Science, Mathematics, and Engineering Education: Student explanations for high attrition rates. *Journal of College Science Teaching* 21, 230-238.

— 1992b, Undergraduate problems with teaching and advising in SME majors— explaining gender differences in attrition rates. *Journal of College Science Teaching* 21, 284-92.

SHADE, B.J. 1989, The culture and style of Mexican-American society. In B.J. Robinson Shade (ed.), *Culture, Style and the Educative Process* (pp. 43-7). Springfield, IL: Charles C Thomas.

SHEA, C. 1994, Queens College and a measure of diversity. *The Chronicle of Higher Education*, 11 May, A37–9.

SHIH, F.H. 1988, Asian-American students: the myth of a model minority. *Journal of College Science Teaching* 17, 356-9.

SHEOREY, R. and MOKHTARI, K. 1993, Reading habits of university ESL students. *TESOL Matters* 3, 9.

SIMMS, R.B. and LEONARD, W.H. 1986, Accommodating underprepared students. *Journal of College Science Teaching* 16, 110-12.

SIMS, C. 1992, What went wrong: why programs failed. *Science* 258, 1185-7.

SINGLETON, D. 1989, *Language Acquisition: The Age Factor*. Clevedon, UK: Multilingual Matters.

SITARAM, K.S. and COGDELL, R.T. 1976, *Foundations of Intercultural Communication*. Columbus, OH: Charles E. Merrill.

SMITH, R.M., BYRD, P., NELSON, G.L., BARRETT, R.P. and CONSTANTINIDES, J.C. 1992, *Crossing Pedagogical Oceans: International Teaching Assistants in U.S. Undergraduate Education*. ASHE: ERIC Higher Education Report No. 8. Washington, DC: The George Washington University, School of Education and Human Development.

SMOKE, T. 1988, Using feedback from ESL students to enhance their success in college. In S. Benesch (ed.) *Ending Remediation: Linking ESL and Content in Higher Education* (pp. 7-19). Washington, DC: Teachers of English to Speakers of Other Languages.

SNOW, M.A. 1992, *Project LEAP Training Manual-Year One*. Los Angeles, CA: California State University, Los Angeles.

SNOW, M.A. and BRINTON, D.M. 1988a, The adjunct model of language instruction: an ideal EAP framework. In S. Benesch (ed.) *Ending Remediation: Linking ESL and Content in Higher Education* (pp. 33-52). Washington, DC: Teachers of English to Speakers of Other Languages.

— 1988b, Content-based language instruction: investigating the effectiveness of the adjunct model. *TESOL Quarterly* 22, 553-74.

SNOW, M.A. and KINSELLA, K. 1994 (March), ESL and content-area faculty: a call for collaboration. Paper presented at the twenty-eighth annual meeting of Teachers of English to Speakers of Other Languages, Baltimore, MD

SOYIBO, K. 1993 (August), Some sources of students' misconceptions in Biology: A review. Paper presented at the Third International Seminar on Misconceptions and Educational Strategies in Science and Mathematics, Cornell University, Ithaca, NY.

SPENCER, P.U. 1990 (Summer), A Native American worldview. *Noetic Sciences Review*, 15, 14-20.

SPENER, D. 1988, Transitional bilingual education and the socialization of immigrants. *Harvard Educational Review* 58, 133-53.

STANLEY, W.B. and BRICKHOUSE, N.W. 1994, Multiculturalism, universalism, and science education. *Science Education* 78, 387-98.

STARR, C. and TAGGART, R. 1992, *Biology*. Belmont, CA: Wadsworth.

STEIN, C.B. 1986, *Sink or Swim: The Politics of Bilingual Education*. New York: Praeger.

STEWART, D.W. 1991, Immigration and higher education: the crisis and the opportunities. *Educational Record* 72, 20-6.

— 1993, *Immigration and Education: The Crisis and the Opportunities*. New York: Lexington Books.

STEWART, E.C. 1972, *American Cultural Patterns*. Chicago, IL: Intercultural Press.

STRAUSS, M.J. and FULWILER, T. 1987, Interactive writing and learning chemistry. *Journal of College Science Teaching* 16, 256–62.

SUTMAN, F.X., ALLEN, V.F. and SHOEMAKER, F. 1986, *Learning English Through Science*. Washington, DC: National Science Teachers Association.

SUZUKI, B.H. 1989, Asian Americans as the 'model minority'. *Change* 21, 13-19.

SWAN, M. and SMITH, B. (eds) 1987, *Learner English*. Cambridge: Cambridge University Press.

SWARTLEY, E.C. 1994 (March), Communicative needs of freshman science students. Paper presented at the twenty-eighth annual convention of Teachers of English to Speakers of Other Languages, Baltimore, MD.

THARP, R.G. 1989, Psychocultural variables and constants. *American Psychologist* 44, 349-59.

TIERNEY, W.G. 1991, Native voices in academe. *Change* 23, 36-9.

— 1993, The college experience of native Americans: a critical analysis. In L. Weis and M. Fine (eds) *Beyond Silenced Voices: Class, Race, and Gender in United States Schools* (pp. 309-23). Albany, NY: State University of New York Press.

The Changing Faces of the American College Campus, 1993. *Change* 25, 57-60.

The Chronicle of Higher Education. Recipients of Doctorates From U.S. Universities, 1990. Oct. 16, 1991. A20.

The Chronicle of Higher Education Almanac. August 25, 1993, 13.

The Chronicle of Higher Education Almanac. College Enrollment by Racial and Ethnic Group, Selected Years. Aug. 26, 1992, 11.

The Chronicle of Higher Education Almanac. The States. Aug. 26, 1992, 39—112.

TOBIAS, S. 1989, Writing to learn science and mathematics. In P. Connolly and T. Vilardi (eds) *Writing to Learn Mathematics and Science* (pp. 48-55). New York: Teachers College Press, Columbia University.

— 1990, *They're Not Dumb, They're Different*. Tucson, AZ: Research Corporation.

— 1992a, *Revitalizing Undergraduate Science*. Tucson, AZ: Research Corporation.

— 1992b, Science education reform: what's wrong with the process? *Change* 24, 13-19.

TOBIN, K., TIPPINS, D.J., and GALLARD, A.J. 1994, Research on instructional strategies for teaching science. In D.L. Gabel (ed.) *Handbook of Research on Science Teaching and Learning* (A Project of the National Science Teachers Association) (pp. 45-93). New York: Macmillan.

UNITED STATES BUREAU OF THE CENSUS 1990, *Statistical Abstracts of the United States: 1990* (110th edn). Washington, DC: United States Bureau of the Census.

UNITED STATES DEPARTMENT OF EDUCATION 1992, *The Condition of Bilingual Education in the Nation: A Report to the Congress and the President*. Washington, DC: United States Department of Education.

UNITED STATES GENERAL ACCOUNTING OFFICE 1994, *Limited English Proficiency, A Growing and Costly Educational Challenge Facing Many School Districts: Report to the Chairman, Committee on Labor and Human Resources U.S. Senate* (GAO/HEHS-94-38). Washington, DC: United States General Accounting Office.

VANN, R.J., LORENZ, F.O. and MEYER, D.M. 1991, Error gravity: faculty response to errors in the written discourse of nonnative speakers of English. In L. Hamp-Lyons (ed.) *Assessing Second Language Writing in Academic Contexts*. Norwood, NJ: Ablex.

VANN, R.J., MEYER, D.C. and LORENZ, F.O. 1984, Error gravity: a study of faculty opinion of ESL errors. *TESOL Quarterly* 18, 427-440.

WANDERSEE, J.H. 1985, Can the history of science help science educators anticipate students' misconceptions? *Journal of Research in Science Teaching* 23, 581-97.

WANDERSEE, J.H., MINTZES, J.J. and NOVAK, J.D. 1994, Research on alternative conceptions in science. In D.L. Gabel (ed.) *Handbook of Research on Science Teaching and Learning* (A Project of the National Science Teachers Association) (pp. 177-210). New York: Macmillan.

WESTBY, C.E. and ROUSE, G.R. 1993, Facilitating text comprehension in college students: the professor's role. In L.W. Clark (ed.) *Faculty and Student Challenges in Facing Cultural and Linguistic Diversity*. Springfield, IL: Charles C Thomas.

WINK, J. 1992/1993, To LEP or not to LEP, that is the question. *TESOL Matters* 2, 10.

WITKIN, H.A., MOORE, C.A., GOODENOUGH, D.R. and COX, P.W. 1977, Field-dependent and field-independent cognitive styles and their educational implications. *Review of Educational Research* 47, 1-64.

WRIGHT, L. 1994, One drop of blood. *The New Yorker* 25 July, pp. 46-50 and 52-5.

ZAKALUK, B.L. and SAMUELS, S.J. (eds) 1988, *Readability*. Newark, DE: International Reading Association.

Index

Academic language proficiency, 46-50;
  Also see Cummins, J.
Accents, 40, 58-59
Accessibility
— of higher education, 15, 17, 24-25
— of science education, 5, 32, 179
Acculturation, ix, 16
Adjunct model, ix, 9, 143-144; *Also see*
  Content-based ESL instruction
— at Saint Michael's College (Colchester,
  VT), 161-164
Adult learners, 30, 178
— of a second language, 55, 58
Affective filter, ix, 60-61; *Also see*
  Krashen, S.
African American(s)/Black(s), ix; *Also see*
  Under-represented minorities
— undergraduate enrollment, 1980 and
  1990, 20
— college enrollment at public, private,
  4-year, and 2-year institutions, 1980
  and 1990, 21
— enrollment in public elementary and
  secondary schools, selected years, Fall
  1976-1990, 23
— learning style(s), 89
— number of earned bachelor's degrees
  in the physical and biological sciences
  (1977 and 1990), 28
— number of earned bachelor's degrees
  in the physical and biological sciences
  for male recipients: 1977 and 1990, 29
— number of earned bachelor's degrees
  in the physical and biological sciences
  for female recipients: 1977 and 1990, 30
— US Population, 1990-2090, 76
Age
— and ability to learn/acquire a second
  language, 54-55
— and pronunciation of L2, 54-55
Alaskan Native(s), *See* American Indian(s)
Ambiguity tolerance, *See* Learning
  style(s)
American, ix, 10

American Indian(s) and/or Alaskan
  Native(s), ix
— and the study of science, 68-70
— college enrollment at public, private,
  4-year, and 2-year institutions, 1980
  and 1990, 21
— enrollment in public elementary and
  secondary schools, selected years, Fall
  1976-1990, 23
— in higher education, 68-70
— learning style(s), 69, 81, 89-90
— limited English proficiency, 12
— nonverbal communication, 66, 69
— number of earned bachelor's degrees
  in the physical and biological sciences
  (1977 and 1990), 28
— number of earned bachelor's degrees
  in the physical and biological sciences
  for male recipients: 1977 and 1990, 29
— number of earned bachelor's degrees
  in the physical and biological sciences
  for female recipients: 1977 and 1990, 30
— undergraduate enrollment, 1980 and
  1990, 20, 70
— US Population, 1990-2090, 76
Aptitude for language learning/acquisi-
  tion, *See* Gift for language learning/
  acquisition
Asian(s) and/or Pacific Islander(s), ix
— aptitude for science, 28-29
— college enrollment at public, private,
  4-year, and 2-year institutions, 1980
  and 1990, 21
— enrollment in public elementary and
  secondary schools, selected years, Fall
  1976-1990, 23
— model minority myth, 29
— nonverbal communication, 66
— number of earned bachelor's degrees
  in the physical and biological sciences
  (1977 and 1990), 28
— number of earned bachelor's degrees
  in the physical and biological sciences
  for male recipients: 1977 and 1990, 29

— number of earned bachelor's degrees
in the physical and biological sciences
for female recipients: 1977 and 1990, 30
— undergraduate enrollment, 1980 and
1990, 20
— US Population, 1990-2090, 76
Assimilation, ix, 16
Auditory learner, *See* Learning style(s)
Autobiography of an Hispanic physicist,
146-149

Bachelor's Degrees earned in the sciences
— number of earned bachelor's degrees
in the physical and biological sciences
(1977 and 1990): by race/ethnicity, 28
— number of earned bachelor's degrees
in the physical and biological sciences
for male recipients by race/ethnicity:
1977 and 1990, 29
— number of earned bachelor's degrees
in the physical and biological sciences
for female recipients by race/ethnic-
ity:1977 and 1990, 30
Basic Interpersonal Communicative Skills
(BICS), ix, 46-50; *Also see* Cummins, J.
BEA, *See* Bilingual Education Act
BICS (Basic Interpersonal Communicative
Skills), ix, 46-50; *Also see* Cummins, J.
Bilingual, x, 12-13
Bilingual education: its history in the US,
14-16
Bilingual Education Act (BEA), x, 12, 14, 33
Bilingual higher education in the US, 15,
140, 144-145, 147, 151, 172; *Also see*
Bilingual science instruction
Bilingual science instruction, 9
— at Erie Community College, State Uni-
versity of New York (Buffalo, NY), 15,
164-167
— at Hostos Community College, City
University of New York (Bronx, NY),
15, 144
— at Kean College of New Jersey (Union,
NJ), 2-3, 15, 144
— at Lehman College, City University of
New York (Bronx, NY), 15
— at Miami-Dade Community College
(Miami, FL), 167-171
— at the University of Texas at El Paso
(El Paso, TX), 15, 152
Bilingual students, 12-13; *See* Limited
English proficient students
Bilingualism, 41, 176
— and cognitive flexibility, 145
— and reading, 115-118

— as a handicap, 25
— in Europe, 26, 40
— in the United States, 14-15, 40, 149, 176-177
Biology instruction
— at California State University, Los Angeles (Los Angeles, CA), 130-131
— at the Community College of Philadelphia (Philadelphia, PA), 151-153
— at Erie Community College, State University of New York (Buffalo, NY),
165-166
— at Florida State University (Tallahassee, FL), 35-37
— at Hunter College, City University of
New York (NY, NY), 35-37
— at Kean College of New Jersey (Union,
NJ), 2-3, 15, 144
— at Miami-Dade Community College
(Miami, FL), 168-170
— at National-Louis University (Chicago,
IL), 124-126
— at Saint Michael's College (Colchester,
VT), 163-164
— at Union County College (Elizabeth,
NJ), 153-155
Biological science(s), bachelor's degrees
earned
— number of earned bachelor's degrees
in the physical and biological sciences
(1977 and 1990): by race/ethnicity, 28
— number of earned bachelor's degrees
in the physical and biological sciences
for male recipients by race/ethnicity:
1977 and 1990, 29
— number of earned bachelor's degrees
in the physical and biological sciences
for female recipients by race/ethnic-
ity: 1977 and 1990, 30
Black(s), see African American(s)
Bridge, x
Brooklyn College, City University of New
York (Brooklyn, NY), 121-123
Brown University (Providence, RI), 15

California State Polytechnic University
(Pomona, CA), 35-37
California State University, Los Angeles
(Los Angeles CA), 128-132
CALP (Cognitive Academic Language
Proficiency), x, 46-50; *See* Cummins, J.
Cañada College (Redwood City, CA), 156-
159
Caretaker Speech (Motherese), x, 44-45
Center for Applied Linguistics, 33, 101,
180

Characteristics of L2 acquisition, 62-63
Chemistry instruction
— at California State Polytechnic University (Pomona, CA), 35-37
— at the Community College of Philadelphia (Philadelphia, PA), 151-153
— at Erie Community College, State University of New York (Buffalo, NY), 166
— at Miami-Dade Community College (Miami, FL), 168-170
— at Our Lady of the Lake University (San Antonio, TX), 135
Classroom language skills, 34
Cognitive Academic Language Proficiency (CALP), x, 46-50; *See* Cummins, J.
College, x
Common underlying proficiency (CUP), x, 46-50; *See* Cummins, J. *and see* Linguistic interdependence
Community colleges: growing number of ESL students, 24
Community College of Philadelphia (Philadelphia, PA), 150-153
Comprehensible input, x, 44-46, 60; *See* Krashen, S.
Content-area, x
Content-area instruction in the native language of LEP students, 5, 9, 15, 140, 144-145, 147-149
— at Erie Community College, State University of New York (Buffalo, NY), 15, 164-167
— at Hostos Community College, City University of New York (Bronx, NY), 15, 144
— at Kean College of New Jersey (Union, NJ), 2-3, 15, 144
— at Lehman College, City University of New York (Bronx, NY), 15
— at Miami-Dade Community College (Miami, FL), 167-171
— at the University of Texas at El Paso (El Paso, TX), 10, 15, 147-149, 171-174
Content-based ESL instruction, 8-9, 32, 140, 141-144
— adjunct model, ix, 143-144
    at Saint Michael's College (Colchester, VT), 161-164
— sheltered instruction, xiii, 141-143
— — at the Community College of Philadelphia (Philadelphia, PA), 150-153
— Sheltered-Adjunct Model, 144
— — at Cañada College (Redwood City, CA), 156-159

— at Eastern Washington University (Cheney, WA), 159-161
— at Union County College (Elizabeth, NJ), 153-155
Context embedded, x, 47, 49, 56
Context reduced, x, 47, 49
Contrastive analysis, 58
Cooperative learning, 61
— as a learning style, *See* Learning styles
— at Our Lady of the Lake University (San Antonio, TX), 132-136
Cultural misunderstandings, 65-67, 73
Culture
— and ethnicity, 64-65
— and how things are classified, 78-79
— and language, 104-107
— and learning style(s), *See* Learning style(s)
— and prior knowledge of science, 71-72
— and rhetoric, 105-107
— and science education reform, *See* Science education reform
— definition, xi, 64-65
— disparity between faculty and students, 75-77
— non-Western, 68
— of the classroom, 64, 72-74
— of science, 67-68, 77
— of the science classroom, 64, 71, 78
— Western, 68, 79
Cummins, J., xi, 6, 41-42, 46-52
— Basic Interpersonal Communicative Skills (BICS) ix, 46-50
— Cognitive Academic Language Proficiency (CALP) x, 46-50
— Common Underlying Proficiency (CUP), x, 50-52
— conversational v. academic language proficiency, 46-50
— linguistic interdependence, xii, 50-52
CUP (Common Underlying Proficiency), x, 50-52; *Also see* Cummins, J.

Decoding, 45, 57, 115
Decontextualized language (*See* Context reduced language)
Demographics, *See* United States
Developmental errors, *See* Errors
Discourse variations, 105-107

EAP (English-for-Academic-Purposes), *Also see* Learning English-for-Academic-Purposes
— at Saint Michael's College (Colchester, VT), 162

Eastern Washington University (Cheney, WA), 159-161
Elitism in science, 74, 177
English language, 55-58, 104-105
— grammar, 57-59
— how rapidly it can be learned, 19, 29-30, 62
— idioms, colloquialisms, slang, 42, 57, 105
— noun/adjective agreement, 57
— pronoun agreement, 57
— pronunciation, 56
— real life English, 56-57
— rhetoric, 105-107
— sounds of spoken English, 56
— spelling, 56
— verb endings, 57-58
— word order, 57
— writing, 105-107
English as a second language (ESL), xi, 12-15
— as remediation, 40, 41, 67
— compared with foreign language study, 39-41
— content-based, *See* Content-based ESL instruction
— history in the US, 15
— increased enrollments in, 24
— students, 13: *See* Limited English proficient (LEP) students
— typical program of study, 18-19,
— what it can accomplish, 18-19, 43-44, 49, 116
English-for-Academic-Purposes (EAP), xi; *See* Learning English-for-Academic-Purposes
— at Saint Michael's College (Colchester, VT), 162
Enrollment
— college enrollment by racial and ethnic groups at public, private, 4-year, and 2-year institutions, 1980 and 1990, 21
— in public elementary and secondary schools, by race or ethnicity, selected years, Fall 1976-1990, 23
— undergraduate enrollment by racial and ethnic group, 1980 and 1990, 20
Environmental science instruction
— at California State University, Los Angeles (Los Angeles, California), 130
— at Eastern Washington University (Cheney, WA), 159-161
— at Erie Community College, State University of New York (Buffalo, NY), 165
— at Hostos Community College, The City University of New York, (Bronx, NY), 127-128

— at Miami-Dade Community College (Miami, FL), 169-170
ERIC Clearinghouse on Languages and Linguistics, 33, 101, 180
ERIC/CLL, *See* ERIC Clearinghouse on Languages and Linguistics
Erie Community College, State University of New York (Buffalo, NY), 15, 164-167
Error correction, *See* Errors
Errors
— correction, 52-54, 61, 63
— developmental, xi, 43, 52
— interference, xi, 55-58
— significance of, 52
— unavoidability of, 43, 52
ESL, *See* English as a second language
ESL student(s), xi, 12-13; *See* Limited English proficient (LEP) students
Ethnic speech markers, 59; *Also see* Linguistic prejudice
Ethnicity
— and learning styles, 81, 89-90
— and science education, 82-91

Faculty reaction to LEP/ESL students, *See* Limited English proficient students
Females, bachelor's degrees earned in science
— number of earned bachelor's degrees in the physical and biological sciences (1977 and 1990): by race/ethnicity, 30
Florida State University (Tallahassee, FL), 35-37
Foreign language(s)
— ambivalence toward, 39-40
— as enrichment, 40, 67
— at Brown University (Providence, RI), 15
— at the University of Minnesota (Minneapolis, MN), 15
— compared with ESL, 39
— gift or aptitude for learning, 59-60; *Also see* Gift (or aptitude) for language acquisition/learning
— study of, 15, 38-40, 42
Foreign students, *See* International students
Foreigner talk, xi, 44-45
Fry readability test, 116-117

Geology instruction
— at Brooklyn College, City University of NY (Brooklyn, NY), 121-123
Gift (or aptitude) for language learning/acquisition, 40, 59-60

Glendale Community College (Glendale, CA), 136-139
Glossary, ix-xiv

Helping LEP students in mainstream classes, *See* Limited English students
High risk courses, xi, 102; *See* Supplemental instruction
Higher Education in the United States, *See* United States
Hispanic(s), xi
— college enrollment at public, private, 4-year, and 2-year institutions, 1980 and 1990, 21
— earned Doctorates in Physics (1986), 146
— earned Master's and Doctorates in the life and physical sciences (1990-1991), 145
— enrollment in public elementary and secondary schools, selected years, Fall 1976-1990, 23
— learning style(s), 8, 82, 89-90
— number of earned bachelor's degrees in the physical and biological sciences (1977 and 1990): 28
— number of earned bachelor's degrees in the physical and biological sciences for male recipients: 1977 and 1990, 29
— number of earned bachelor's degrees in the physical and biological sciences for female recipients: 1977 and 1990, 30
— undergraduate enrollment 1980 and 1990, 20
— US population, 1990-2090, 76
Hostos Community College, City University of New York (Bronx, NY) 15, 126-128, 144
How things are classified, *See* Culture
Hunter College, City University of New York (New York, NY), 35-37

Idioms, colloquialisms, slang, 42, 57, 105
Immigrant and/or refugee students, *See* Limited English proficient students
Immigration to the United States, *See* United States
Impulsive, *See* Learning style(s)
Interference errors, xi, 55-58; *See* Errors
International (foreign students), xi, 17-18, 33-34, 39
— as non-native English speakers, 58
— college enrollment at public, private, 4-year, and 2-year institutions, 1980 and 1990, 21
— Doctorates earned in the sciences and engineering, 33

— in graduate schools, 17-18, 33-34
— in the sciences, 17-18, 33-34
— undergraduate enrollment, 1980 and 1990, 20

Kean College of New Jersey (Union, NJ), 1-3, 15, 144
Kinesthetic learning style, *See* Learning styles
Korean speakers, 56-57
Krashen, S., xi-xii, 6, 41-46, 52-54
— affective filter, ix, 60-61
— comprehensible input, x, 44-46, 60
— error correction, 52-54, 61, 63
— language acquisition, xii, 42-44
— language learning, xii, 42-44
— Monitor Hypothesis, xiii, 42-44
— Natural Order Hypothesis, xiii, 43

L1
— definition, xii
— developing proficiency in, 38, 42, 104
L2
— definition, xii
— developing proficiency in, 38-39, 41-61
Language acquisition, xii, 42-44; *Also see* Krashen, S.
Language and culture, *See* Culture
Language aptitude, *See* Gift or aptitude for languages
Language of science, 30-31, 34
Language in the instructional process, 32, 34, 45, 61-62, 72, 104, 118
Language learning, xii, 42-44
Language minority (or Linguistic minority) student, xii, 12-13; *See* Limited English proficient student
Latino, *See* Hispanic
LEAP, *See* Learning English-for-Academic-Purposes
Learning English-for-Academic-Purposes (LEAP),
— at California State University, Los Angeles (Los Angeles, CA), 128-132
— definition, xii
Learning style(s)
— and choice of academic major, 83, 89-90
— and culture, 81, 89-90
— and ethnicity, 81, 89-90
— and science education, 82-91
— and science students, 82-91
— and student performance, 82-91
— classification of
— ambiguity tolerance, 85
— auditory, 87

— competition/cooperation, 84-85
— field independent/dependent, 83
— field insensitive/sensitive, 83
— global/analytic, 83-84
— impulsive/reflective, 87-88
— kinesthetic, 87
— need for structure, 86
— preferred perceptual modes, 86-87
— simultaneous/sequential, 83-84
— tactile, 87
— visual, 87
— definition, xii, 81
— general description, 80-82
— matching with teaching style(s), 89, 90
— origins of, 81
Lectures and lecturing, *See* Science instruction
Lehman College, City University of New York (Bronx, NY), 15
LEP, *See* Limited English proficient
Limited English proficiency, 12-13
Limited English proficient (LEP); *Also see* Limited English proficient students
— definition, xii, 12-13
— perjorative connotation, 13
Limited English Proficient (LEP) students
— academic needs 18-19, 61-62
— and the laboratory, 96
— and the lecture, 93-95
— and science education reform, 31-33, 75-77, 89-91
— and testing, 54, 98, 125, 142-143
— and the textbook, 31, 46, 95-96, 113-118
— and their science education, 4-5, 25-35, 44
— and written assignments, 97-98
— attitude of instructors toward, 17, 33, 40-41, 77
— definitions of, xii, 12-13
— difficulties in mainstream courses, 33, 37, 61-62
— educational backgrounds of, 18, 24, 26, 49-50
— how to teach, 7, 25, 26, 45-46, 50, 92-103
— how they learn English, 18-19, 62-63; *See* English as a second language (ESL)
— increasing number of, 11, 15, 19-24, 35-37
— immigrants, refugees, and their children, 17-18, 19-24
— international (foreign) students, *See* International students
— K-12, 21-23, 33

— learning styles of, 89-90; *Also see* Learning styles
— paragraph development in various language groups, 106
— preparing faculty members to teach, 26-27, 92-103, 127, 129, 134, 141-142, 143, 152, 157, 160
— pursuing advanced degrees, 17-18, 33-34
— reading ability of, 7, 26, 46, 61-62, 113-118
— undergraduate, 23-34
— writing ability of, 7, 26, 43, 53, 61-62, 105-107
Linguistic interdependence, xii, 50-52; *See* Cummins, J.
Linguistic minority student, *See* Language minority student
Linguistic prejudice, 40, 58-59

Mainstream, xiii
Mainstreaming, xiii
Males, bachelor's degrees earned in science
— number of earned bachelor's degrees in the physical and biological sciences for male recipients by race/ethnicity: 1977 and 1990, 29
Math instruction
— at Our Lady of the Lake University (San Antonio, Texas), 132-135
Melting Pot Theory, *See* Assimilation
Mexican American(s), *See* Hispanic(s)
Miami-Dade Community College (Miami, FL) 9, 167-171
Misconceptions about science, 71-72
Model minority, *See* Asian(s) and/or Pacific Islander(s)
Monitor hypothesis, xiii, 42-44; *See* Krashen, S.
Monolingualism in the United States, 14, 25-26, 176
Motherese, *See* Caretaker speech

NABE, *See* National Association for Bilingual Education
National Association for Bilingual Education (NABE), 33, 69, 101, 180
National Clearinghouse for Bilingual Education (NCBE), 33, 101, 180
National-Louis University (Chicago, IL), 124-126
Native American(s), *See* American Indian(s)
Native Language, *See* L1
Nature
— control of, 67-68

Natural Order Hypothesis, xiii, 43; *See* Krashen, S.

NCBE, *See* National Clearinghouse for Bilingual Education

Need for structure, *See* Learning style(s)

Non-native English speakers
— increasing number of, 15-16, 19-24, *Also see* Limited English proficient (LEP) students

Non-native English speaking students, *See* Limited English proficient (LEP) students

Non-resident aliens
— number of earned bachelor's degrees in the physical and biological sciences (1977 and 1990): 28
— number of earned bachelor's degrees in the physical and biological sciences for male recipients: 1977 and 1990, 29
— number of earned bachelor's degrees in the physical and biological sciences for female recipients: 1977 and 1990, 30

Nonverbal communication, xiii, 65-66
— and ethnicity, 65-66

Nutrition instruction
— at Miami-Dade Community College (Miami, FL), 169-170

Our Lady of the Lake University (San Antonio, TX), 132-136

Output, xiii, 42

Pacific Islander, xiii; *See* Asian(s)

Physical science(s), Bachelor's degrees earned
— number of earned bachelor's degrees in the physical and biological sciences (1977 and 1990): by race/ethnicity, 28
— number of earned bachelor's degrees in the physical and biological sciences for male recipients by race/ethnicity: 1977 and 1990, 29
— number of earned bachelor's degrees in the physical and biological sciences for female recipients by race/ethnicity: 1977 and 1990, 30

Physicist, Autobiography of an Hispanic, 146-149

Physics, doctorates earned in 1986, 146

Preferred perceptual mode, *See* Learning style(s)

Prior knowledge of science, 71-72

Productive skills, xiii, 31

Pronunciation, *See* English

Rate of language learning/acquisition, *See* Speed of language learning/acquisition

Reading, *See* Limited English proficient (LEP) students

Receptive skills, xiii, 31

Reflective learning style, *See* Learning style(s)

Reform, *See* Science education

Register, 134

Rhetoric, *See* Culture

Saint Michael's College (Colchester, VT), 161-164

Science education
— accessibility for all students, *See* Accessibility of science
— and limited English proficient students, *See* Limited English proficient students
— and learning styles of students, *See* Learning style(s)
— reform, 4, 5, 31-35, 75-78, 90-91, 177-179
— undergraduate environment of, 77-78
— why students drop out, 84-85

Science instruction for limited English proficient students
— case studies, 120-139, 150-174
— faculty interaction with, 99-100
— in their native language, *See* bilingual science instruction
— laboratories, 96
— lectures and lecturing, 93-95
— publications about, 32
— testing, 98
— textbooks, 31, 46, 95-96, 113-118
— tips for enhancing, 92-102
— written assignments, 97

Science is 'hard', 3-4, 61

Science majors: declining number of, 27, 28

Science students
— 'bad', 74-75 86
— learning styles, *See* Learning style(s)
— successful ('good'), 74-75, 86, 89

Science teachers (professors, faculty)
— attitudes toward error correction, 53-54
— attitudes toward students, 77
— attitudes toward students of limited English proficiency, *See* Limited English proficient (LEP) students
— characteristics of, 77
— how they can assist limited English proficient students, 92-101; *Also see* Limited English proficient (LEP) students
— interaction with students, 99-100

— preparation to teach 26-27
— taking advantage of resources on campus, 100
Science textbooks, *See* Textbooks, science
Scientific illiteracy, 4, 177, 178
Scientific writing, 105-107
Second language acquisition, 6, 19, 41-63
Sheltered instruction, xiii, 141-143; *See* Content-based ESL instruction
Sheltered-adjunct model, 144; *See* Content-based ESL instruction
SI, *See* Supplemental instruction
Speed of language learning/acquisition, 19, 29-30, 48-49, 62
Student centered pedagogy, 75, 77
Subject-area, *See* Content-area
Supplemental instruction (SI), xiii, 102-103
— and limited English proficient students, 102-103
— at California State University, Los Angeles (Los Angeles, CA), 129-130
— at Glendale Community College (Glendale, CA), 136-139

Tactile learning style, *See* Learning style(s)
Target language, xiii, 60
Teachers of English to Speakers of Other Languages (TESOL), 33, 101, 180
Teaching science, *See* limited English proficient (LEP) students
TESOL, *See* Teachers of English to Speakers of Other Languages
Test of English as a Foreign Language (TOEFL), xiv, 18, 173
Testing
— and limited English proficient students, 54, 98, 125, 142-143
— essay exams, 125, 142
— multiple choice exams, 125, 143
Textbooks, science, 31, 46, 95-96, 113-118
— and bilingual readers, 115-118
— comprehensibility, 31, 46, 95-96, 114-118
— readability, 31, 46, 95-96, 114-118
— selection of, 46, 95-96, 113-114, 118
— student usage of, 46, 95-96, 115
Title VII of the Elementary and Secondary Education Act, *See* Bilingual Education Act
TOEFL, *See* Test of English as a Foreign Language

Undergraduate demographics, 19-20, 35-37, 75-76, 176

Undergraduate enrollment by racial and ethnic group, 1980 and 1990, 20
Underprepared student(s), xiv, 17, 86, 176
Under-represented minorities
— in the sciences, 4, 27, 32, 74
— learning styles, 74, 89-90
— number of earned bachelor's degrees in the physical and biological sciences (1977 and 1990): 28
— number of earned bachelor's degrees in the physical and biological sciences for male recipients: 1977 and 1990, 29
— number of earned bachelor's degrees in the physical and biological sciences for female recipients: 1977 and 1990, 30
Union County College (Elizabeth, NJ), 153-155
United States
— changing demographics, 15-17, 20-24, 34, 75-76
— education of immigrants, 13-17
— growing population of non-native English speakers, 15-17, 20-24
— history of language usage, 13-14
— immigration to (1901-1910 and 1981-1990), 15-17
University, xiv
University of Minnesota (Minneapolis, MN), 15
University of Missouri-Kansas City (Kansas City, MO), 102-103
University of Texas at El Paso (El Paso, TX), 15, 146-149, 171-174
University of Wisconsin at Madison (Madison, WI), 78-79
Unknown object, *See* Writing to learn science
US Citizens and Permanent Residents
— number of earned bachelor's degrees in the physical and biological sciences (1977 and 1990): by race/ethnicity, 28
— number of earned bachelor's degrees in the physical and biological sciences for male recipients by race/ethnicity: 1977 and 1990, 29
— number of earned bachelor's degrees in the physical and biological sciences for female recipients by race/ethnicity: 1977 and 1990, 30;

Visual learner, *See* Learning style(s)
Vocabulary of science, 31

Wait-time, 88
White(s), xiv

— college enrollment at public, private, 4-year, and 2-year institutions, 1980 and 1990, 21

— enrollment in public elementary and secondary schools, selected years, Fall 1976-1990, 23

— number of earned bachelor's degrees in the physical and biological sciences (1977 and 1990): 28

— number of earned bachelor's degrees in the physical and biological sciences for male recipients: 1977 and 1990, 29

— number of earned bachelor's degrees in the physical and biological sciences for female recipients: 1977 and 1990, 30

— undergraduate enrollment, 1980 and 1990, 20

— US Population, 1990-2090, 76

Writing to learn science, 107-113

— description of, 107-108

— examples of, 108-113

— the unknown object, 110-113